KU-181-641

Prosperity and Parenthood

INTERNATIONAL LIBRARY OF SOCIOLOGY
AND SOCIAL RECONSTRUCTION

Founded by Karl Mannheim
Editor: W. J. H. Sprott

A catalogue of the books available in the INTERNATIONAL LIBRARY OF
SOCIOLOGY AND SOCIAL RECONSTRUCTION, and new books
in preparation for the Library, will be found at the end of this volume

PROSPERITY AND PARENTHOOD

*A Study of Family Planning
among the Victorian Middle Classes*

by

J. A. BANKS

ROUTLEDGE & KEGAN PAUL LIMITED
Broadway House, 68–74 Carter Lane
London

First published in 1954
by Routledge & Kegan Paul Ltd
Broadway House, 68–74 Carter Lane
London
Printed in Great Britain
By Latimer, Trend & Co Ltd
Plymouth

Contents

Acknowledgements

ACKNOWLEDGMENTS are due to the University of
London for permission to publish and to the London
School of Economics and Political Science for the
award of a Research Studentship which made the
work possible. I should also like to thank Professor
D. V. Glass whose generous advice and friendly interest were so unsparingly given.

J. A. BANKS

Leicester
December 1953

CHAPTER I

The Decline in Fertility

WHEN we look at the domestic history of England since the beginning of the nineteenth century we cannot fail to be impressed by the way in which the growth of the population over the past forty years has been much slower than it was during the previous hundred and ten. Whereas between 1801 and 1911 the rate of increase was uniformly high, fluctuating about the figure of 14 per cent per decade and at no time falling below that of 10 per cent, since 1911 it has fallen away to less than 6 per cent per decade and has been steadily diminishing all the while. The decrease moreover has every appearance of continuing further so that, as one authority has estimated it,[1] by another generation the growth of numbers will have come to an end altogether. Then, after a short period of stability around 1977, the population will enter upon a period of fairly rapid decline.

This gives the study of population trends an importance to the present generation which can hardly be exaggerated. Yet, strangely enough, apart from some excellent demographic work on the numerical features of change, very few substantial investigations have been made into the causal factors underlying variations in the growth or decline of numbers. Most writers on the subject seem to be content to make rather sweeping generalizations about the nature of the social fabric in Victorian England as compared with that of the post-Victorian world. Rarely do they appear to realize that although it is always possible to think of a number of likely explanations for any kind of phe-

[1] 'Report of the Royal Commission on Population, June, 1949' (*Parliamentary Papers*, 1948–9, Vol. XIX), Ch. 9.

nomenon, a real advance in knowledge begins only when a serious attempt is made to evaluate these claims. This does not mean that theoretical analysis of possible causes has no part to play in a systematic account of a particular social fact; on the contrary, it is an essential first step; but it is no more than a first step, and the explanation is not complete until the various possibilities opened up by analysis have been tested against the touchstone of empirical truth.

We may say that the size of the population at any given moment of time is the product of the forces making for migration, mortality, marriage, and the size of the family. A change in any one of these will necessarily affect the direction in which the balance of numbers is tending. For this reason an investigation into why twentieth-century England has experienced a decline in its rate of population growth may legitimately begin with a consideration of the relative influence of each of these forces; but the satisfactory conclusion of this analysis should not be taken as a sign that the study is nearing its completion. Rather should it be regarded as barely having begun; for although the field has been remarkably well explored by statisticians and demographers so that the issues involved are hardly beyond doubt, the causal factors are still uncertain. We shall not be justified merely to draw up a list of those we believe to be responsible. We should at least attempt to verify some of them in the light of the available evidence; and this should be done, not as is so often the case, in general terms, but in detail.

The influence of migration on the rate of population growth may be dispensed with very briefly. As the Royal Commission on Population pointed out, although for every decade between 1871 and 1911 the net balance of emigration over immigration represented a loss to Great Britain of some hundred thousands of people, it diminished the natural increase by no more than one-ninth over the whole period. Between 1911 and 1931 its effect was more serious since about one-third of the natural increase was lost in this way; but after 1931 the movement has been in the opposite direction, contributing more than one-eighth to the total increase between 1931 and 1951. The most important factor in the slackening off in the rate of growth

2

has undoubtedly been a decline in the excess of births over deaths.[1]

The influence of mortality, moreover, operated during this period to offset the decline in natural increase. Advances in sanitation, medical knowledge, and living standards combined to eliminate to a considerable extent the wastage of human life which formerly took place in adolescence and in middle age. Whereas in the 1870s the expectation of life at birth was about forty-three years, in the 1940s it was about sixty-five years, and it is remarkable that the number of deaths per decade after 1921 was actually less than in the 1870s in spite of the fact that the total population was some twenty millions greater.

What caused the fall in natural increase, therefore, was a decline in the number of births at a much faster rate than that in the number of deaths. Although the population in 1931–41 was about two-thirds as large again as that in the period 1871–81, there were nearly three million fewer births. This, in its turn, does not appear to have been the result of any important change in the proportion of people marrying before the age at which it was no longer possible for them to have children. In the years between 1871 and 1947, of those who lived to the ages of forty-five to fifty-four years, roughly 85 per cent to 88·5 per cent were, or had been married throughout the whole period, and the fluctuations between these extremes were relatively slight. The fall in the number of births was thus a direct feature of a decline in the number of children born per married couple. As opposed to an average size in family of 5·5 to 6 live children born to couples married in the mid-Victorian years, among the couples married in 1925–29 the figure has been estimated at 2·2. The families of five, six, and seven children which were formerly the most common had been replaced by one-

[1] Report of the Royal Commission on Population (*Parliamentary Papers*, 1948–9, Volume 19) Chapter 3. The figures in Table VII (p. 15) are for 1871–1941. For the period 1931–1951 as a whole, see Table 35 of *The Annual Abstract of Statistics*, No. 88, 1938–1950, Table 35, p. 36. The net gain in migration is given as 496,000 for Great Britain composed of 745,000 for England and Wales *minus* 249,000 (net loss) from Scotland.

For what follows in the text, see the *Report of the Royal Commission on Population*, Chapters 2–5, and Chapter 23, paragraphs 613–19.

and two-child families, while those of more than six had virtually disappeared.

It is, of course, theoretically possible that there has been some decline in the physical capacity of men and women to produce children since the mid-nineteenth century, but the Royal Commission on Population was unable to find any positive evidence to this effect. Indeed, all appearances are in favour of the opposite point of view. Because the people of the mid-twentieth century are on the average fitter and better fed than their parents and grandparents were, it is not inconceivable that reproductive potentialities may actually have improved. Certainly women suffer less from serious deformities of the pelvis, and this, so thought the Royal Commission, must to some extent have increased their average capacity to bear live children.

In fact the inquiry into family limitation and human fertility carried out for the Royal Commission by Dr. E. Lewis-Faning has demonstrated conclusively that present-day couples would not find it impossible to have families as large as those of Victorian times if they wanted to. The overwhelming weight of the evidence is in favour of the view that the rates of child-bearing in the twentieth century are being deliberately reduced by birth control and other methods of family limitation. The salient factor in the decline of population growth over the past eighty years or so has been a radical change in the attitude towards parenthood. People no longer wish to have the large families which were customary in the days of their grandparents.

At the same time, it is important to emphasize that the retreat from parenthood has not proceeded uniformly throughout the community. It began first and continued most rapidly amongst the highest socio-economic groups, as these have been defined by the Registrar-General. Unfortunately, it is not possible to be very precise in this kind of class analysis because of the paucity of reliable information and the real difficulty of classification. In the 'Fertility of Marrage' Report of the 1911 Census, which is the source of our present information on this topic, the composition of the social classes employed was rather in the nature of a compromise arrived at after other experiments

4

determine social status had failed.[1] It was based moreover upon a system of classification which was in part occupational and in part industrial, which resulted in farmers of ten acres and 1,000 acres being classified together, in shopkeepers being counted in with their assistants, in the heads of many industrial firms being added to the numbers of their employees, and in bankers being made indistinguishable from their clerks. Nevertheless, the differences in the fertility of certain groups was clearly marked by 1911, and it is no distortion of the truth to say that the earliest signs of the change in reproductive habits took place amongst the families of military and naval officers, clergymen, lawyers, doctors, authors, journalists and architects. Not far behind them came civil service officers and clerks, law clerks, dentists, school-masters, teachers, professors and lecturers, people employed in scientific pursuits, and accountants. Other groups of commer-cial men lagged some way behind, but all three classes were easily distinguishable in their fertility from textile workers, who of all the sections of the working class showed the earliest signs of family limitation.[2] In general, the decline in family size com-menced as an upper- and middle-class phenomenon at some time in the 1860's and 1870's. It was not until some time later that the new reproductive habits began to spread amongst the less privileged social groups.

About these facts there can be very little doubt. The demo-graphers have sifted the statistical material very carefully and their conclusions are reliable. When we turn, however, to con-sider the factors underlying this change in the attitude of mind towards the family, we find ourselves faced with problems of an entirely different character. The Royal Commission on Popula-tion, for its part, thought them insoluble. The inter-relationship of social and economic changes concerned, it stated, 'present a complex web, rather than a chain, of cause and effect and it would be exceedingly difficult to trace how they acted and re-

---

[1] See *The Census of England and Wales, 1911*, Vol. XIII, *Fertility and Marriage*, Part I (1917) and J. W. Innes: *Class Fertility Trends in England and Wales, 1876–1934* (1938), Ch. III, Sec. 1.

[2] See Innes, *op. cit.*, Ch. III, Secs. 2 and 4. The distinction is between Classes I, II and VI in his Table XIII (p. 42) and IA, IB, IIA and VI in his Table XVIII (p. 60). The reference is to completed fertility throughout.

acted on each other or to assess their relative importance'.[1] The Commission, therefore, was content to give a brief description of a number of them and to end up with a 'complex of causes' including the decay of the family handicraft system and the rise of large-scale industry and factory organization, the loss of security and the growth of competitive individualism, the relative decline in agriculture and the rise in importance of industry and commerce with their associated shift of population from rural to urban areas, the growing prestige of science and the slackening hold of traditional religious beliefs, the development of popular education and of higher standards of living, the growth of humanitarianism, and the emancipation of women. All these things and more made 'individual control over the size of the family seem desirable or necessary'. At the same time the invention of new and better methods of contraception provided the means whereby that control could become a practical possibility. 'The widespread adoption of family limitation in the 1870's, in our view,' the Report continued, 'was due to the cumulative affect of these circumstances and to the special jolts which the depression of 1875 onwards and the Bradlaugh-Besant trials of 1877–8 gave to public opinion.'[2]

This 'multiple-causes' approach to an historical problem seems to have developed in this field in opposition to an economic single-factor theory which predominated earlier. Thus Newsholme and Stevenson in their 'Decline of Human Fertility in the United Kingdom and other Countries as shown by Corrected Birth-Rates'[3] while rejecting poverty as the operative factor, nevertheless confined themselves to an economic explanation. The decline was associated, they said, 'with a general raising of the standard of comfort' and was an expression of the determination of the people to secure that greater comfort.

In this way they were in line with a tradition of linking vital statistics with economic phenomena which had descended from Malthus through William Farr to the statisticians of the turn of

[1] Report, *op. cit.*, para. 96.
[2] For a similar approach see *Population Policy in Great Britain: a Report by P.E.P.*, April 1948, Ch. III, and the quotation from N. E. Himes, below, p. 7.
[3] *Journal of the Royal Statistical Society*, March 1906, Vol. LXIX, Pt. 1.

the nineteenth century.[1] This tradition regarded the expansion of wealth as the factor of primary, if not sole, importance. With the development of large-scale industry and commerce men and women were presented with more and more objects of desire and greater opportunities for obtaining them. The levels of life once regarded as the prerogative of the few became the aspiration of the many. But financial resources are always limited in comparison with the possible wants that can be satisfied, and in the attempt to span the gap family limitation was called in to play the major role.

Himes, in his discussion of the 'immediate versus the long-run causes of the vital revolution'[2] rejected this approach. What he called 'democratized birth control' he regarded as the immediate causative factor, 'the catalytic agent, without which the whole reaction could not have taken place'. Yet we have to explain why it was that birth control, which was spurned in the 1820's, was taken up with enthusiasm in the 1870's, and he did not feel that to emphasize almost exclusively the rising standard of living to account for small families was anything other than an error.

'All the following social, economic, and intellectual changes', he wrote, 'have paved the way for widespread adoption of contraceptive practices; the growth of hedonism, utilitarianism, materialism; the declining hold of orthodox religion and the rise of rationalism and the scientific spirit; growing emancipation or independence of women and feminism, including careers for women outside the home and their industrial employment; urbanism, the automatic development of a controlled death rate consequent upon the progress of general and preventive medicine, a change necessitating socially a controlled birth rate; fear, in the early stages of the Industrial Revolution of over-population, a fear not totally unfounded before the opening of our agricultural West, and before the mechanization of agriculture and of ocean and land transport; a certain fear of land scarcity following the gradual settlement of the major inhabitable

---

[1] See Note A p. 218.
[2] *The Medical History of Contraception* (1936), Pt. Six, Ch. XIII, par. 6. 'A Methodological Note.'

vacant spaces of the globe as a consequence of one of the most phenomenal human migrations that the annals of history record —a migration caused basically by population pressure. To these should be added other social forces, a few newly accelerated: urbanism, making a large family costly and inconvenient, social mobility and social ambition likewise promoting family restriction; army instruction in sexual prophylaxis during the war; above all, improved means of communicating knowledge, especially the technical factors which have cheapened printing and brought people into closer contact or caused them to exchange ideas with greater facility and frankness. The widespread desire for self-advancement economically, which is such an outstanding characteristic of capitalistic civilization is no doubt fundamental. Most of the other forces mentioned have dovetailed well with personal ambition; hence the unique thoroughness and sweep of the Vital Revolution.'

This great web of forces is not unlike that drawn up by the Royal Commission on Population, and it is no doubt possible to think of further lists containing other likely factors omitted by these two. Yet, as we have already seen, there is no great advantage to be achieved in merely multiplying causal agencies if we have no intention of checking them against the facts. The lists may be made longer and longer, without adding anything of value to our knowledge. Indeed, there is an element of unsoundness in this multi-causal methodology, for an empirical investigation which tried to carry along every conceivable influence upon the fall in fertility would become tediously involved and complicated. If we are to make any progress at all, some kind of selection of the main influences is necessary. The real problem is: which factors shall we take as the most significant for our purpose?

In the study made by Lewis-Faning on the family limitation of more recent times, it is noticeable how frequently people were inclined to emphasize the importance of economic considerations when asked about their contraceptive practices.[1] Thirty-eight per cent of the 1,815 women known to be using

[1] 'Family Limitation and its Influence on Human Fertility during the past Fifty Years', *Papers of the Royal Commission on Population*, Vol. I (1949), Ch. XII, especially Tables 123 and 125.

birth control gave as their reason that they 'could not afford (more) children'. A further 25 per cent said that they wished to space pregnancies at appropriate intervals and although we do not know how far the cost of children was an influence in this spacing, Lewis-Faning himself thought that the two things were 'certainly bound together as motives for using contraception'. In addition, 27 per cent gave 'housing difficulties' and 'uncertainty due to the war' as their reasons, for the study was made between August 1946 and June 1947 when the impact of wartime conditions was still very great. It is likely that in more normal times these would give way to other urgent pressures, and certainly of those women married before 1935, no more than 10 per cent were recorded in these two categories. Again, when the women were subdivided according to the duration of their married life, it became apparent that the proportion motivated by financial reasons alone increased considerably with the lengthening of the period between the date of marriage and that of the inquiry, reaching as much as 60 per cent of those married before 1910. Similarly, a further subdivision according to the number of children already possessed in the family showed that the mothers of larger families were most influenced by considerations of cost. We do not know how far rationalization entered into the answers given to Lewis-Faning's questions, but even if its influence were great we should still be required to treat this rather widespread tendency of stressing the economic factor as an element of some importance.

Even Himes, it will have been noticed, listed the desire for economic self advancement as the most fundamental of his causes. We may use this as a clue to a rather important aspect of the matter which has, on the whole, been overlooked. When the economists have been criticized for making too much of the rising standard of living as the explanation for smaller families, it has not always been realized that one of the reasons for their over-emphasis has been the all-embracing nature of the concept used. In rejecting poverty as the operative factor by pointing out that the decline in fertility has proceeded most rapidly among the economically *favoured* groups, it has usually been implied that the falling birth-rate is associated with an expansion in wealth. But, as Newsholme and Stevenson pointed out, the association is not only with the general raising of the standard of comfort but 'with the determination of the people to secure this greater comfort'. What is just as important as the expansion in wealth, therefore, is the development in the attitude towards it. The level of life actually reached by one section of the community may well be no more than the aspiration of another.

Thus it is possible for the concept of the rising standard of living to entail two quite logically distinct ideas: (a) an increase in the actual material well-being of people; and (b) an expansion in the range of satisfactions considered appropriate for a civilized existence. If, therefore, we decide to concentrate upon the rising standard of living as a significant factor in the decline in fertility, we shall obtain a clearer view of our problem if we focus attention on these two aspects of the concept separately. How far was thought about the family affected by variations in the actual level of comfort? and how far by changes in aspirations? Here we have two important historical processes, the first the product of economic change, and the second involved in psychological states of mind, either of which by itself, or both acting together, may be the causal influence for which we are seeking. Before we may legitimately consider other possibilities, we ought fully to investigate, in the light of the available evidence, how far this double-sided concept will take us.

Our brief demographic analysis of the fall in family size showed that it began first and proceeded most rapidly amongst the professional and higher commercial sections of the community. To begin with, therefore, we need go no further than to their way of life for the solution to our problem. What kinds of change did they experience in their incomes and in their cost of living during the years about the 1870's? What norms of consumption and what standards of behaviour had been laid down for them to live up to in the generations before? In this study we shall concentrate upon the factual material which will help us to formulate an answer to these two questions. This must not be taken to imply that the way of living of other sections of the community did not in time become significant, nor must it be thought that other historical facts—the emancipation of middle-class women, for example, or the decline in conventional religious beliefs—had not also their parts to play. All we can do, and all we should do at any one time, is to eliminate the influence of a single manageable factor, what we may here call the middle-class standard of life. Once we know the precise nature of the part played by this in the fall in fertility, we shall be better able to consider the relative importance of other possible contributing influences.

CHAPTER II

The Population Controversy

THE 1870's are usually regarded as a period of rapid social and economic change. The tremendous expansion in private wealth which had gone on with only temporary interference from the early decades of the century, received its first serious setback in these years. Prices fell considerably, competition became very much fiercer, and a Great Depression spread throughout industry, bringing an atmosphere of uneasiness and insecurity into a world which had grown accustomed to thinking in terms of an ever-ascending march of Victorian progress and prosperity as an eternal, immutable law. The resulting confusion led to a general questioning of beliefs and to an anxious searching round for new ways of solving the difficult problems of this rather unfamiliar situation. More and more people were forced to face the fact that some kind of personal planning was necessary if their established levels of living were not to be drastically reduced. At the same time, the Bradlaugh-Besant trials, because they made birth-control propaganda less open to public prosecution, turned the limited percolation of contraceptive knowledge into a widespread flood of public opinion. Here at hand was provided a means whereby conscious control could be exercised to prevent a falling away from standards, at least in so far as it would be the result of bringing into the world further mouths to feed. It is not surprising that the impact of these two 'special jolts'—to use the language of the Royal Commission on Population—led to the unmistakable fall in the fertility rate after 1881.

This description, or one rather similar, which is the kind usually given nowadays of the crucial years for our problem,[1]

[1] See, for example, 'Victorian Climax', Ch. 6 of R. & K. Titmuss: *Parents Revolt, a study of the Declining Birth-Rate in Acquisitive Societies* (1942). For a rather different view of the 'Great Depression' see Ch. ix and the references given.

serves to emphasize the point that the *actual* pattern of well-being enjoyed did not become an operative factor in family limitation until it was seriously threatened. While their material standard of life remained more or less untouched by economic fluctuations, middle-class parents were not conscious of any need to reduce the size of their families, but once it became very difficult for them to continue living at the level to which they had grown accustomed, they were made increasingly aware of their children as an item of expense. This argument, however, is incomplete without reference to the building up of those customary standards in the years before. Presumably the impact of the Great Depression would not have been so startling had it not been preceded by a period in which there had been established a definite attitude as to what kinds of things were essential for middle-class family life. When to marry, and on how much to marry, had been discussed at great length and with some heat in the late fifties and early sixties, when a set of aspirations had been laid down which the members of the middle classes did not find it easy to give up. In order, therefore, to understand to the full how the Great Depression came to be regarded as a threat, it is necessary for us to obtain a clear idea not only of the factual content of the standard of living in those years, but also of those aspects of behaviour which formed the normative side of the concept as it was built up earlier.

At the same time, the discussions of the fifties and sixties were themselves the product of a long debate going back to the early years of the century. Out of the conflict of ideas between the supporters of Thomas Malthus and his opponents on the subject of working-class poverty, there had slowly emerged a growing awareness of the relevance of marriage and children to the middle-class standard of life. In focusing attention on their own aspirations as a model for the members of the working classes to copy, the writers from the middle classes became themselves self-conscious of the part these played in their own everyday behaviour. Hence we shall not go far wrong if we use the population controversy as a source of information on the growth of the middle-class attitude towards marriage and the family. By tracing this through from its beginning with the publication of Godwin's *Political Justice* in the spring of 1793, we should be able to see how it came about that the norms on these topics were developed, and we shall then have a clearer idea of what was involved at the time of the Great Depression.

It has been maintained that the Malthusian controversy really began with the appearance of Godwin's two quarto volumes in the early part of 1793. At that time the ferment caused by the French Revolution was at its height. 'Every day brought forth its bundles of pamphlets and broadsheets', wrote a contemporary biographer. 'Every man who had anything to say, or nothing to say, put it into print. The shops of Ridgway and Debrett were crowded every morning by politicians on tip-toe for the last rumour.' Almost any work dealing with the principles of politics was sure of a market. 'The booksellers' counters groaned under the weight of new views of the state of the representation, theories of reform, and philosophical treatises on the constitution.' Godwin's work was thus merely one of many nearly similar works appearing at the same time and the *New Annual Register* for 1793 discussed a dozen.[1] Godwin himself admits having rushed the work in order to profit from the ferment. If he could have done so, his preface records, he would have given more time to it 'but the state of the public mind and of the general interests of the species, operated as a strong inducement in favour of an early publication'.[2] The result was greater than he expected. 'Within a few weeks of the appearance of that work, his immediate object, the acquisition of fame and its consequent power in the application, was obtained. He was not merely made known to the public, but was ranked at once among men of the highest genius and attainments.'[3] In London he 'could not walk the streets without being gazed at as a wonder', and when he made a visit into the west of England in 1794, he found, his diary says, 'not a person almost in town or village who had any acquaintance with modern publications, that had not heard of the *Enquiry Concerning Political Justice*, or that was not acquainted in a great or small degree with the contents of that work'.[4]

---

[1] F. K. Brown: *The Life of William Godwin* (1926), Ch. 7.
[2] Quoted Brown, *op. cit.*, p. 43.
[3] 'Public Characters, 1799–1800', p. 370 in Brown, *op. cit.*, p. 43.
[4] Quoted in Brown, *op. cit.*, p. 59.

Godwin's actual aim in view was the perfectibility of man. The characters, actions and dispositions of men are not something they bring with them into the world but are moulded in them by external circumstances, by events and by the impressions they receive after birth. Hence the cause of misery and injustice is human institutions. Alter these; remove the fearful inequalities of society; give men a just and intelligent environment; teach them to use their reason; and right conduct will follow. Of course, man will never be made quite perfect, but he is at all times capable of continuous improvement. Given the will, all the rest follows as a matter of course.

It was this view of the possibility of continuous improvement that Malthus set out to refute in his *Essay on Population*, which is why Godwin's work has been taken here as the starting point for the development of the concepts with which we are concerned. In all his early life, his biographer tells us,[1] Malthus had been brought into close contact with the supporters of radical, even revolutionary views, for his father was a strong adherent of the Jacobin cause and it is likely that they discussed Godwin' *litical Justice*. Certainly with the publication of *The Inquirer: ctions on Education, Manners and Literature* by Godwin in 179?, they fell into disagreement over *Avarice and Profusion* when the son maintained that Godwin's equalitarian Utopia would not work because it would cause such an increase of population as to bring it toppling to the ground in ruins. His father pressed him to put his ideas into written form and the *Essay on Population* was born. The main idea, however, was not unknown. Godwin had himself discussed it in the seventh chapter of the eighth book of *Political Justice* entitled: 'Of the Objection to this System from the Principle of Population' where he displayed no misgivings whatsoever as to the increase of mankind beyond the means of subsistence. The whole question, he thought, was of no importance in the face of the omnipotence of reason, for the time would surely come when mind would control matter. In any case it was too remote a contingency to be considered.

Malthus reverted to this same point. 'The most important

[1] J. Bonar: 'Malthus' in Palgrave's *Dictionary of Political Economy*. See also J. Bonar: *Malthus and his Work* (1885), and J. M. Keynes: *Essays in Biography* (1933).

argument that I shall adduce', he wrote, 'is certainly not new. The principles on which it depends have been explained in part by Hume, and more at large by Dr. Adam Smith. It has been advanced and applied to the present subject, though not with its proper weight, or in the most forcible point of view, by Mr. Wallace.'[1] What he had in mind here was that Wallace, whose *Various Prospects of Mankind, Nature and Providence* had been the occasion of Godwin's seventh chapter, had regarded a perfect society as impossible only on a long-term view. 'An event at such a distance might fairly be left to providence', wrote Malthus, 'but the truth is, that if the view of the argument given in this essay be just, the difficulty, so far from being remote, would be imminent, and immediate.'[2]

This reference to Wallace raises a problem which occurs time and time again in a study of the development of opinion. Wallace's *Various Prospects* had appeared in 1761 but seems to have attracted very little attention.[3] Why then should Malthus's work which took an almost identical line have succeeded forty years later?

The answer to this question is usually given in terms of the political struggle: 'it appeared at a time when the upper classes, terrified by the French Revolution, found in it a much-needed justification for the existing order against the radical proposals of Godwin and Condorcet, whose theories Malthus attacked at great length.'[4] But we still have to find an answer to the further problem of why it was that Malthus's population argument succeeded in drawing attention upon itself whereas the other attacks on Godwin, considered important in their time, soon became forgotten.

Now it seems likely that the first edition of the *Essay* was a very small one and we know that it went out of print almost immediately. Nevertheless it did attract some notice and Bonar tells us that more than a score of pamphlets appeared in reply between 1797 and 1803.[5] Indeed, Godwin himself in his pamph-

---

[1] T. R. Malthus: *First Essay on Population, 1798*, reprinted for the Royal Economic Society with notes by J. Bonar (1926), p. 8.

[2] Malthus, *op. cit.*, p. 143.

[3] J. Bonar: *Theories of Population from Raleigh to Arthur Young* (1931), Ch. 6, especially p. 178.

[4] A. B. Wolfe: 'Population' in the *Encyclopaedia of the Social Sciences*. K. Marx: *Capital* (Everyman Edition, 1930), p. 680.

[5] J. Bonar: *Malthus and his Work* (1885), p. 2.

16

let of 1801 complained that it had converted 'friends of progress' by the hundred.[1] Yet it was published at a period of extensive warfare, combined from peculiar circumstances with a most prosperous commerce, and came, therefore, before the public at a time of an extraordinary demand for men and very little disposition to suppose the possibility of any evil arising from the redundancy of population.[2]

There was, however, a number of factors working in Malthus's favour. In the first place, the war with France had been running some four years and any attack on French theorists and Jacobin fellow-travellers was certain to obtain at least a sympathetic hearing in many quarters, not all of them necessarily upper class. Secondly, the expenses of the war, together with the difficulties of getting provisions from outside and the very bad harvests of 1794 and 1795 brought on an economic crisis, which although it passed off, was followed by another in 1799. This was partly the result of the depreciation of the Bank of England note on the foreign exchanges and partly the result of an extremely rigorous winter which had set in early and was followed by a cold summer and wet autumn in which all the crops were damaged and some destroyed.[3] It is not unlikely therefore that men's attention being turned towards the difficulties of providing food, they were in a mood to listen to a theory in which food held a prominent place. Certainly the poor rate at this time cost somewhere in the region of £4,000,000, a figure double that of seventeen years earlier, and the question of poverty and its cause was the topic of the day.[4] Finally, in 1801, there was taken the first census which confirmed what

[1] W. Godwin: *Thoughts occasioned by the perusal of Dr. Parr's Spital sermon . . . being a reply to the attacks of Dr. Parr, Mr. Mackintosh, the author of an essay on population, and others* (1801), p. 54.

[2] These are Malthus's own words in the Preface to the Fifth Edition of his Essay, 1817.

[3] The Eighth Annual Report of the Registrar-General (*Parliamentary Papers*, 1847–8, Vol. 25). Page xiii gives details of the effect of the weather. For the effect of the foreign exchanges see R. G. Hawtrey: *Currency and Credit* (3rd ed., 1927), Pt. 2, Ch. 8, especially p. 342.

[4] G. Nicholls: *A History of the English Poor Law* (1898), Vol. 2, p. 133, and K. Smith: *The Malthusian Controversy* (1951), Bk. 1, Ch. 2. For a list of the pamphlets and books produced see J. A. Banks and D. V. Glass: 'A List of Books, Pamphlets and Articles on the Population Question, published in Britain in the period 1793 to 1880' in D. V. Glass *et al.: Introduction to Malthus* (1953).

Malthus had said about the increase of population up to that time. His essay thus seemed to be borne out by the facts, and people who might not have accepted it on political, economic, or demographic grounds alone could not but have been impressed by what was for him a favourable conjunction of all three.

It is important here to consider exactly what it was that became accepted as the Malthusian argument. The experts, of course, read what Malthus himself wrote and agreed or disagreed with him according to their evaluation of his marshalling of the evidence. He is, however, reported as having complained that there were few books on political economy which had been more spoken of yet less read than his,[1] and it is abundantly clear that the popular notion of what his essay was about was not derived from a familiarity with his actual work. This fact raises an interesting methodological problem. When we consider any controversy, whether it be the Malthusian or any other, what criteria are we to use to assess the contributions of the various champions in the struggle? What weight are we to give to the numerous discussions which rage about the various nuances of meaning which are discovered in the terms employed? Malthus, for example, wrote of 'the constant tendency in all animated life to increase beyond the nourishment prepared for it';[2] and later writers, notably Senior and Archbishop Whately, spent much of their time in analysing what the word 'tendency' really meant. Should these arguments be included in a study of the Malthusian controversy? In one sense, of course, we can admit that they should be, if we are concerned to know every angle and facet of the development of an idea which may help us to appreciate the kind of pitfalls to avoid in using words like 'tendency' when discussing a similar kind of subject to-day. But in another sense, we cannot deny that they should be left out; for if we are concerned with what Whitehead has called the 'fundamental assumptions which adherents of all the various systems within an epoch unconsciously suppose';[3]

[1] M. A. Quetelet: *A Treatise on Man and the Development of his Faculties.* Preface to Knox's translation (1842), p. vii a.
[2] T. Malthus: *Essay on the Principle of Population* (2nd ed., 1803), Bk. I, Ch. 1.
[3] A. N. Whitehead: *Science and the Modern World* (1926). Ch. 3.

if we are concerned with those statements of opinion which give us some idea of the attitude of mind of the great mass of people, some idea of those currents of thought which influenced their outlook and their behaviour, we want to know not necessarily everything that was said by the main contributors in all its details and suggestiveness, but what it appeared to mean to the ordinary people of the day. This, however, is no easy task, for our sources must be not what the masses actually believed and thought, but the writings of the literate few about their own beliefs and thoughts and their impressions of those of other people living at their time. There is indeed a fruitful field for error here since the process of inferring from the known opinions of the few to the unknown opinions of the many is at best a hit-or-miss affair. The most that we can do if we would wish to avoid the kind of criticism Merton has made of the European school of sociologists of knowledge—that they do not set out the prosaic details of *how* their analysis was conducted—[1] is to document as fully as possible all statements that we make and to append a detailed list of sources to enable future investigators to cover the same ground and see if they arrive at the same conclusions. This is the nearest we can get to something approaching the experimental method in historical sociology.[2]

The Malthusian controversy, then, began as a protest against the perfectibility of man proclaimed by Godwin and the Jacobins. For the first decade it provoked 'refutation and bold acceptance'[3] and the issue hung in the balance; but during the second more and more people swung over to accept the Malthusian point of view. Even the *Quarterly Review*, which in 1812 had been definitely hostile,[4] had swung round by July 1817,

[1] R. K. Merton: *Social Theory and Social Structure* (1949). Introduction to Pt. 3.

[2] In the thesis which formed the basis of this present work the books and pamphlets used for this purpose were given in an appendix (see J. A. Banks: *The English Middle-class concept of the Standard of Living, and its relation to Marriage and Family Size*, 1850–1900. M.A. 1952. Senate House, University of London) Appendix A. This has now been incorporated into the larger list compiled by the author and Professor Glass. See D. V. Glass *et al.*: *Introduction to Malthus* (1953).

[3] J. Field: *Essays on Population and other Papers* (1931) I. *The Malthusian Controversy in England*, p. 79.

[4] R. Southey, review of P. Colquhoun's 'Propositions for ameliorating the Condition of the Poor' in the *Quarterly Review*, December 1812 (Vol. 8, No. 16, Art. 4. See p. 380.)

declaring it to be 'a much easier matter to disbelieve Mr. Malthus than to refute him'. Indeed it now went right over to utilizing the Malthusian argument for the support of the *status quo* and only regretted that Malthus himself would not do the same a little more stoutly.[1] Brougham, too, on 16th December 1819 was able to declare without contradiction in the House of Commons that the excess of population as one of the great causes of distress 'was the soundest principle of political economy'[2] and by July 1821, the *Edinburgh Review* expressed surprise at the reception of Godwin's last effort to oust his rival, confessing 'that we have, for many years, been in the habit of considering the question of the principle of population as set at rest by Mr. Malthus'.[3]

David Ricardo, it is true, was quite convinced that this review was the work of Malthus himself, but this did not detract from its value to his eyes.[4] 'The reviews of Godwin's work both in the *Quarterly* and the *Edinburgh* were I think very good' he wrote, '—surely in the minds of all reasonable men the principle for which Malthus contends is fully established.'[5] Godwin's assertion that the imperfectibility of mankind was merely the product of social institutions was gradually giving way before the onslaughts of the populationists. Indeed this last attempt of the philosophical anarchist to refute Malthus provides an interesting example of the dilemma into which many seem to have found themselves falling at this time. *Of Population* is a difficult book to read, wandering, full of invective, emotional, and displaying a great deal of misunderstanding of Malthus's position. Briefly Godwin appears to have wished to maintain, first, that

---

[1] J. B. Sumner, review of R. T. Malthus, 'An Essay on the Principle of Population', 5th ed. in the *Quarterly Review*, July 1817 (Vol. 17, No. 34, Art. 4) pp. 396 and 402–3.

[2] Speech on Sir W. De Crespign's notion that a Select Committee be appointed to inquire into Robert Owen's plan for ameliorating the condition of the poor. (*Hansard*, Vol. 41, pp. 1195–1200.) Compare also his speech before the Committee on the Distressed State of Agriculture, 9th April 1816, where he referred to 'Mr. Mahthus's excellent tracts'. (*Hansard*, Vol. 33, p. 1109.)

[3] T. R. Malthus (?) review of W. Godwin: 'Of Population' in the *Edinburgh Review*, July 1821 (Vol. 47, Art. 6), p. 363.

[4] Letter to Trower, 4th October 1821, reprinted in J. Bonar and J. H. Hollander eds.: *Letters of David Ricardo to Hutches Trower and others, 1811–1823* (1899), p. 166.

[5] Letter to Trower, 25th January 1822, reprinted in Bonar & Hollander, *op. cit.*, p. 173.

there is no power or tendency in the human species to increase faster than subsistence; secondly, that there is such a tendency, but it operates only fitfully and is constantly kept in check; thirdly, that substance can be made to increase faster than men; and fourthly that there *is* a danger from over-population, but it is far off![1]

His contemporaries, however, no longer shared his views and even those who opposed the social conclusions to be drawn from the Malthusian argument accepted as its main tenet an iron law of necessity, that even if productivity were increased to overcome poverty, such was the nature of men and women that they would now hasten into earlier marriages and so destroy their former well-being. As Senior wrote to Malthus in 1829:

'Your work effected a complete revulsion in public opinion. You proved that additional numbers, instead of wealth, may bring poverty. That in civilized countries the evil to be feared is not the diminution, but the undue increase of inhabitants. That population, instead of being a torpid agent, requiring to be goaded by artificial stimulants, is a power almost always stronger than could be desired, and producing, unless restrained by constant prudence and self-denial, the worst forms of misery and vice.

'These views are as just as they are important. But they have been caricatured by most of your followers. Because additional numbers *may* bring poverty, it has been supposed that they necessarily *will* do so. Because increased means of subsistence *may* be followed and neutralized by a proportionate increase in the number of the persons to be subsisted, it has been supposed that such *will* necessarily be the case.

'These were the doctrines which I found prevalent when I began my lectures.'[2]

---

[1] W. Godwin: *Of Population: an Enquiry concerning the Power of Increase in the Numbers of Mankind; being an Anwser to Mr. Malthus's Essay* (1821). For a guide through the tangled skein of argument see N. Himes: 'Introduction' to F. Place: *Illustrations and Proofs of the Principle of Population*, edited by N. Himes (1930) text to Notes 30–33, and K. Smith: *The Malthusian Controversy* (1951) Bk. 2, Ch. 3.

[2] Letter of 9th April 1829, reprinted in N.W. Senior: *Two Lectures on Population delivered before the University of Oxford, 1828—to which is added a correspondence between the author and the Rev. T. R. Malthus* (1829), pp. 88–89.

There was indeed much about the contemporary situation which seemed to bear out the extreme Malthusian view. The Census of 1821 gave a figure of 12,000,236 for the population of England and Wales, exclusive of the numbers in the Army, Royal Navy, and Merchant Service at home and abroad. This represented an increase of 1,835,980 persons over the Census of 1811, an average increase of 1·8 per cent per annum.[1] Godwin's supporters could hardly ignore such a definite and rapid growth in the population. At the same time the amount spent on poor relief had risen from £6,656,106 in 1813 to £7,870,801 in 1818,[2] an increase of over 3·6 per cent per annum. Eighteen-seventeen was something of a peak year, but by 1820 the total was down only to £7,330,254 and this was compared with the £4,267,965 spent in 1802–3,[3] when the population was about two-thirds its size in 1821. It is not surprising, therefore, to find the question being much discussed about this time, and Parliament was sufficiently moved to set up a number of committees which reported on the Poor Laws in 1817 and 1818.[4] No one could pretend to ignore the relevance of these facts to the Malthusian argument, for it was manifestly plain that the importance of the pressure of numbers on food as a factor in the perpetuation of poverty was supported rather than contradicted by everyday experience. Indeed for the perfectionists as for the Malthusians there was only one way of looking at the problem: the population should be restrained; and the question at issue now turned on the form the remedy should take.

In his first reply to Malthus, Godwin had suggested infanticide:

'What was called the exposing of children prevailed to a considerable degree in the ancient world. The same practice continues to this hour in China. . . . If the alternative were com-

---

[1] Census 1951, England and Wales. *Preliminary Report* (1951), Pt. 3, Tables, p. 1.
[2] G. Nicholls: *A History of the English Poor Law*, Vol. 2, 1714–1853 (New Edition, 1898), p. 165.
[3] *Ibid.*, p. 133.
[4] Report from the Lords Committee on the Poor Laws (1817); Report from the Select Committee of the House of Commons on the Poor Laws (1817) and the 1st and 2nd Reports from the Select Committee of the House of Commons on the Poor Laws (1818), see Nicholls, *op. cit.*, Ch. 13, pp. 171, *et seq.*

plete, I had rather such a child should perish in the first hour of its existence, than that a man should spend seventy years of life in a state of misery and vice. I know that the globe of earth affords room for only a certain number of human beings, to be trained to any degree of perfection; and I had rather witness the existence of a thousand such beings, than a million of millions of creatures, burthensome to themselves, and contemptible to each other.'[1]

This same remedy had been taken up by Charles Hall in 1805[2] and was repeated by 'Marcus' in 1838,[3] but apart from the Chartist agitation about the latter's *Book of Murder!* no one seems to have taken it seriously.

Malthus's own remedy was moral restraint by which he meant 'prudential restraint' from marriage; but at that time, as Francis Place pointed out, this was no remedy at all. It was 'no more likely to be adopted than infanticide, nor less likely to produce intense suffering, but equally inefficient, to prevent the evil complained of. No one need be under any apprehension lest those propositions should be adopted; we are not in a condition to adopt either.'[4] So Place and his friends, Bentham and James Mill, recommended birth control.

The history of the neo-Malthusian movement, the democratization of birth-control technique, as Himes preferred to call it, has become fairly well known in recent times, especially since Field, Stopes, and Himes published their researches into the

[1] W. Godwin: *Thoughts occasioned by the perusal of Dr. Parr's Spital sermon* (1801), p. 64.

[2] C. Hall: *The Effects of Civilization on the People in European States, with an appendix containing Observations on the Principle Conclusion in Mr. Malthus's Essay on Population* (1805), p. 335.

[3] Marcus: *On the possibility of limiting populousness.* There was also an undated work by the same author (?) called: *Suppressed Work! the right of the poor to live: on the possibility of limiting populousness; an essay on populousness, to which is added the proposed theory of painless extinction of the children of the poor.* See also the anonymous *The Book of Murder! a vade-mecum for the Commissioners and Guardians of the New Poor Law throughout Great Britain and Ireland, being an exact reprint of the infamous Essay on the possibility of limiting populousness by Marcus, One of the Three. With a refutation of the Malthusian doctrine.* (1839)

[4] F. Place: *Illustrations and Proofs of the Principle of Population; including an examination of the proposed remedies of Mr. Malthus and a reply to the objections of Mr. Godwin and others.* (1822), Ch. 6, Sec. 1, p. 142.

activities of Francis Place and his colleagues in the 1820s.[1]
There is, however, a danger here that we may over-emphasize
the importance of this movement before 1877 when the Bradlaugh-Besant trial changed 'this limited percolation downward
of contraceptive knowledge into something hardly less than an
inundation'.[2] Himes himself called this period 'one of quiet,
limited percolation' and Professor Glass has shown that although the publications and propaganda from 1834 to 1876–7
were not inconsiderable, the fact that the trend of fertility
showed no signs of falling off in the fifties and sixties can lead
us to conclude no more than that the ground was being prepared.[3] We can, of course, find references to the birth-control
proposals, both favourable and unfavourable, throughout the
period. Thus Sadler's Committee of 1832 referred to 'certain
books, the disgrace of the age' which one witness considered to
be the reason why there was less illegitimacy among factory
folk than their alleged promiscuity in sex matters would have
led one to expect; and another witness remarked: 'Where individuals are congregated as in factories, I conceive that means
preventive of impregnation are more likely to be generally
known and practised by young persons.'[4] This, however, was
denied, at least for Leeds, by the witness examined for the
Inquiry Commission of the following year. Books and pamphlets
had been offered for sale in that district, but a prominent medical practitioner, Dr. Hunter, was of the opinion that very few
of them indeed had fallen into the hands of the working classes,
and he added: 'I firmly believe they are never acted upon.'[5]

Here the emphasis was on birth-control practices *outside*
marriage; and it is an interesting fact that throughout the early

[1] J. A. Field: *Essays on Population and other Papers* (1931), Ch. 3. 'The Early Propa-
gandist Movement in English Population Theory' reprinted from the *American
Economic Association Bulletin*, 4th Series, No. 2 (April 1911). M. Stopes: *Early Days of
Birth Control* (1921). M. Stopes: *Contraception* (1923). N. Himes: *Medical History
of Contraception* (1936).
[2] Himes, *op. cit.*, p. 238.
[3] D. V. Glass: *Population Policies and Movements in Europe* (1940), pp. 31–32.
[4] 'Report from the Committee on the Bill to regulate the Labour of Children in
the Mills and Factories of the United Kingdom' (*Parliamentary Papers*, 1832, Vol. 15,
Questions 3468–70 and 10887).
[5] 'Second Report of the Factories Inquiry Commission' (*Parliamentary Papers*,
1833, Vol. 21), Dr. Loudon's Report, p. 15.

history of contraceptive ideas in modern times, birth-control techniques are referred to as being used by unmarried men and women, by prostitutes and Casanovas, long before it is suggested that they are used or even that they might be used within the marriage tie.[1] The whole idea that 'the passions might be gratified, and the natural consequences of the intercourse of the sexes prevented from taking place' was so revolting to most of the writers on the subject that even 'a formal refutation . . . would be an insult to morality'. These matters were '*inter Christianos non nominanda*' wrote Sir George Rickards in 1854,[2] and we may infer that for some people at any rate at this time to recommend birth-control was to recommend the kind of practices carried on by prostitutes and people of loose morals, people beyond the pale already and therefore 'deservedly scouted'. To Rickards, John Stuart Mill who in some measure carried on the work of his father and Francis Place—a man 'of some intellectual pretensions'—had been led by 'the fanaticism of the over-population theory' into extravagance; and he seemed to be 'under the influence of a morbid apprehension in all his reasonings on the subject'.[2] We must not, however, read too much into these attacks. In the main the activities of the neo-Malthusians appear to have been passed over in silence, especially during the forties and fifties.

So far, then, the development of opinion is clear. Before 1800 little attention had been paid to population questions, except by a small coterie of people interested in the new and developing science of political arithmetic.[3] After 1800, and certainly by 1820, the notion that increased numbers was a major cause of poverty had come to be accepted as one of the most certain principles of economic thought. But it is not to be assumed from this that the shift of emphasis in itself had had any influence on the middle-class outlook on life. Whatever they may have had to say on the burning issue of large families and poverty,

[1] See N. E. Himes: *Medical History of Contraception* (1936) *passim*, and R. R. Kuczynski: *The Measurement of Population Growth* (1936), p. 2.

[2] G. Rickards: *Population and Capital, being a course of lectures delivered before the University of Oxford in 1853–4* (1854), p. 195.

[3] J. Bonar: *Theories of Population from Raleigh to Arthur Young* (1931), p. 36. See also G. E. Stangeland: *Pre-Malthusian Doctrines of Population* (1904), especially Chs. 4, 5, 8 and 9.

middle-class writers did not regard it as in any way a matter affecting their own way of behaving. It was solely a working-class problem and remedies proposed were put forward to be acted upon by members of the working classes. Nevertheless, no middle-class author who was sensitive to the opinions of his class and who did not react negatively against them, would make suggestions which were repugnant to those among whom he lived and moved and had his being. A consideration of the reaction to the birth-control proposals, therefore, reveals to a considerable extent the milieu from which it came. In the next stage of the population controversy a turn in the line of argument demonstrates how the middle classes became self-conscious of their own standard of life.

In 1822, Francis Place wrote: 'Mr. Malthus seems to shrink from discussing the propriety of preventing conception',[1] which indeed was very true of the middle class as a whole, as has been shown above. Instead, stress was laid on the need for prudential restraint from marrying. Place referred to this as 'no more likely to be adopted than infanticide', and went on in 1823 to recommend the use of the sponge as an effective remedy.[2] This period of the 'diabolic handbills', which lasted at least until February 1826, when Carlile reissued his contribution to the propaganda in the form of *Every Woman's Book; or What is Love?*,[3] was followed by a change in the line taken by the advocates of prudential restraint; and although it has not been possible to show a direct relationship between this birth-control propaganda and the new developments in the population controversy, it is highly suggestive that the change of line so closely follows upon the excitement over the handbills and precedes the period of doldrums for the neo-Malthusians.

In 1828 Nassau William Senior came forward with the view that Malthus had laid too much stress on fear as a motive for abstaining from marriage. Not only the fear of falling below the

---

[1] F. Place: *Illustrations and Proofs* (1822), Ch. 8, p. 173.

[2] See N. E. Himes: 'The Birth Control Handbills of 1823' in *The Lancet*, 6th August 1927. In all three of the handbills reprinted here, the sponge is recommended; although the first, 'To the Married of Both Sexes', also recommends *coitus interruptus*.

[3] N. E. Himes: 'Introduction' to Place's *Illustrations* (1930), pp. 44-47, and N. Himes: *Medical History of Contraception* (1936), pp. 220-2.

subsistence level, he maintained, but also the hope of rising in the social scale activates mankind:

'When an Englishman stands hesitating between love and prudence, a family actually starving is not among his terrors; against actual want he knows that he has the force of the poor-laws. But, however humble his desires, he cannot contemplate without anxiety a probability that the income which supported his social rank, while single, may be insufficient to maintain it when he is married; that he may be unable to give to his children the advantages of education which he enjoyed himself; in short, that he may lose his caste. Men of more enterprise are induced to postpone marriage, not merely by the fear of sinking but also by the hope that in an unencumbered state they may rise.'[1]

This view, of course, was not new. As early as 1803 Malthus himself had written: 'It is the hope of bettering our condition, and the fear of want, rather than want itself, that is the best stimulus to industry, and its most constant and best directed efforts will almost invariably be found among a class of people above the wretchedly poor.'[2] But, as we noted earlier in respect of Wallace's theory of population, what is significant in the history of ideas is not the fact that an idea is expressed but that it becomes part of the general consensus of opinion. Malthus had suggested that the notion of a standard of living to be achieved might motivate mankind, but in the course of the controversy over twenty-three years this was overshadowed by his emphasis on the fear of want as the necessary factor in stimulating prudential restraint. 'This constant pressure of population against food, which I have always considered as the essence of the principle which I endeavoured to explain in my work,' he wrote to Senior in 1829, 'appeared to me to be distinctly proved by the universally acknowledged fact, that whenever improvements in agriculture, or the effects of some

---

[1] N. W. Senior: *Two Lectures on Population* (2nd edition, 1831), p. 26. The lectures were originally given in the Easter Term of 1828.

[2] T. R. Malthus: *An Essay on the Principle of Population* (2nd edition, 1803), p. 475. A similar point of view was also expressed by J. Weyland in his *Principles of Population and Production* (1816), Bk. 1, Ch. 6, and W. Thompson in his *An Inquiry into the Principles of the Distribution of Wealth most conducive to Happiness* (1824), p. 545.

destructive plague, loosened the restraints which kept down the population, it made a start forward at a greater rate than usual.'[1] Senior's reply was to emphasize the nature of historical fact. 'If it be conceded that there exists in the human race a natural tendency to rise from barbarism to civilization, and that the means of subsistence are proportionately more abundant in a civilized than in a savage state, and neither of these propositions can be denied, it must follow that there is a natural tendency in subsistence to increase in a greater ratio than population.'[2] Thus, population which has the power to increase beyond subsistence actually increases more slowly than does production. Why? Because men are made prudent not merely through apprehension of a deficiency of necessaries, but by a desire for a greater share of luxuries. 'As wealth increases, what were the luxuries of one generation become the decencies of their successors. Not only a taste for additional comfort and convenience, but a feeling of degradation in their absence becomes more and more widely diffused. The increase, in many respects, of the productive powers of labour, must enable increased comforts to be enjoyed by increased numbers, and as it is the more beneficial, so it appears to me to be the more natural course of events, that increased comfort should not only accompany, but rather precede, increase of numbers.'[3] Thus, prudential restraint from marriage *is* possible. 'I consider the desire of bettering our condition as natural a wish as the desire for marriage.'[4]

What is important moreover is not only that Senior based the whole of his argument on this notion of levels of necessaries, decencies and luxuries, but that very rapidly his ideas took root. An interesting case of the swing in opinion may be seen in a comparison of the first three editions of McCulloch's *Principles of Political Economy*. In the 1825 edition he was a whole-hearted Malthusian: 'the population of all countries has been invariably

[1] Letter to N. W. Senior, Esq., 23rd March 1829, published in N. W. Senior's *Two Lectures on Population, op. cit.*, pp. 61–62.

[2] Senior, *op. cit.*, p. 49. This quotation is from the original lectures, but Senior's letter of 26th March to Malthus repeats the argument. See pp. 73, 76.

[3] Senior, *op. cit.*, p. 35.

[4] Letter to Malthus, 15th March 1829, reprinted in Senior's *Two Lectures, op. cit.*, p. 58.

proportioned to their means of subsistence.'[1] Moral restaint he noted but rarely. In the second edition (1830), it is admitted that prudential considerations operate 'in a greater or less degree' in civilized communities, and indeed there is a differ-ence between the social classes in this respect: 'the greater number of persons in the more elevated stations of life, as well as those who are peculiarly ambitious of rising in the world . . . regulate their passions for marriage': but since these people form but a minority of the population the Malthusian argu-ment can be said to hold generally.[2] By 1843 (3rd edition) he has completely rejected the Malthusian principle as being 'con-tradicted by the widest experience . . . a vast improvement has taken place in the condition of the people of almost every country, particularly of those in which population has increased with the greatest rapidity.'[3] 'The good sense of the people, and their laudable desire to preserve their place in society, have made them control the violence of their passions.'[4]

We may say, therefore, that from about 1830 onwards the population controversy took a new turn. In order to thrust home to the poor the moral of postponing marriage as a way of avoiding pauperism, the advocates of prudential restraint turned the spotlight of attention upon the behaviour of the middle and upper classes. Rarely mentioning Francis Place and the birth-controllers by name, they nevertheless appear to have been carrying on an argument against them. These people tell you, they seem to imply, that self-restraint is impossible, but see how the people who are better off control *their* passions! The poor should 'look to the conduct of the classes immediately above them. . . . Instead of yielding to the impulse of feeling, and making the entrance into matrimony contemporaneous with the approach to manhood, they prudently defer the

[1] J. R. McCulloch: *Principles of Political Economy* (1825), Pt. 2, Sec. 5, p. 195.
[2] J. R. McCulloch: *The Principles of Political Economy*. Second ed., correction and greatly enlarged (1830), Pt. 1, Ch. 8, pp. 212–13.
[3] J. R. McCulloch: *The Principles of Political Economy*. Third ed., enlarged and corrected throughout (1843). Preface, p. xiv. In this preface he refers to the influence of Senior.
[4] McCulloch, *op. cit.* (1843), p. 228. This general line was taken by the Census of 1851. See *Population Tables II*, Vol. 1, p. lxv. Subsequent censuses took their point of departure from this.

solemnization of such an engagement till they have obtained the means of maintaining a family.'[1]

Hence when the middle classes said to the working class: 'do not marry *until* you can afford it!' they were making imperative what they themselves already practised. There was no doubt in their minds that, in time, they would be able to afford it. For the young middle-class man and woman marriage implied a family, even perhaps a large family. It was therefore sensible to postpone it until the optimum income was actually achieved. Thus the concept of the standard of living which developed in the first part of the nineteenth century was fundamentally no different in its objective aspects from the kinds of standard of living operating in the late eighteenth, being merely the level at which the *established* member of the middle classes supported his wife and family on his income. What does appear to be new in the concept now was a subjective factor, an element of forward-lookingness which, if it had existed before, was confined to but a few. If we are to take notice of the material provided by the population controversy, we cannot avoid the conclusion that during the first thirty years or so of the nineteenth century, the middle class, as a class, became quite definitely conscious of the standard of living as something at which one aimed. People had married for money before, of course, but this was rather different. It had now become a moral issue, a part of the code of life, to consider the standard of living. As Wade put it in 1842, marriage had now become 'laudable or not, according to the state of society and the circumstances of individuals', and, he added, 'the *immorality* of marrying without the means of supporting a family is a doctrine of recent promulgation, and can hardly yet be considered generally impressed on the understanding and feelings of the community. Only a few years have elapsed since our most eminent statesmen and writers taught that to marry, and *marry young*, was meritorious.'[2]

Thus the population controversy by focusing attention on

[1] From the anonymous pamphlet: *General Remarks on the State of the Poor, and Poor Laws, and the Circumstances affecting their Condition* (1832), p. 16.

[2] J. Wade: *History and Political Philosophy of the Middle and Working Classes* (4th edition, 1842), p. 106. The italics are Wade's own. In this particular section of the book he develops the argument in some detail.

what the middle classes were doing, made into a definite ex-
plicit ethos with a favourable moral flavour, what had merely
been practised by them for some time without any moral
connotation whatsoever. In setting up their own behaviour as
a model for the working class to follow, they made it an imperative upon themselves: and it was from this notion of the *immorality* of imprudent marriages that the later developments of
the birth-control movement made their start.

CHAPTER III

The 'Proper' Time to Marry

THE last chapter ended at a turning point in the population controversy when attention was being drawn towards the marriage habits of the middle and upper classes. It was implied there that a change of mind on the subject of marriage was taking place around the 1830s. The evidence for this lies in the works produced as contributions to the population controversy, and it would make the account complete if it could be shown that books written for other purposes also gave indications of the same trend. Unfortunately, the number of works written during the period specifically on marriage was extremely small and it does not appear that any discussion was provoked. None of the books was reviewed in any of the important magazines of the day, and all without exception passed unnoticed from the scene. They are referred to here, therefore, merely as supplementary to the works of the population controversy and are not to be regarded as of themselves contributing significantly to our knowledge of the period. Like Wallace's *Various Prospects,* we should have had to discount them as having been the products of minds not in accord with the general outlook of their time, were it not for the fact that the books on population carry the same story in a different form.

The fiction of the period, too, is of little assistance to us here in this connection. This may seem surprising in the light of the fact that from 1824 to 1840 or thereabouts the novel of fashionable life flourished in England as it had never flourished before —and as it has never flourished since. Matrimony was, of course, as in most novels of the nineteenth century, the central theme; but the writings of Mrs. Gore, Thomas Lister, Edward Bulwer, and Benjamin Disraeli, to mention the most likely sources,[1] are less descriptive of the aristocracy as of the 'Dandia-cal Body' as Carlyle called it. There is indeed a great deal in the claim that their chief significance in literary history is for the ridicule they provoked, which received its finest form in Thackeray's subtle impaling of snobs. *Vanity Fair*, described by one critic as 'a fashionable novel to end fashionable novels', may in a sense be regarded as 'the flowering of what began as . . . a response to the curiosity of post-war new rich, concerning the manners of the aristocracy which they aspired to acquire'.[2] Such writings as these give only a distorted glimpse of the contemporary attitude we are trying to unveil.[3]

Marriage, from his point of view, would appear to have been regarded always as a business proposition, summed up in the maxim: 'I wouldn't marry the handsomest man under the sun, unless he was at least an independent gentleman, with a fortune large enough to allow me to have my carriage, and my opera box to myself.'[4] Yet, in spite of the distortion, it cannot be denied that affection and love as a basis for marriage did not come into fashion at least until the end of the eighteenth century, although admittedly there were poets who wrote of it before. In the main, marriage for the middle and upper classes had been the concern of the parents whose one great responsibility was the choice of a suitable partner for a son or daughter. The aim here was to settle the child well in life and to enhance the wealth and dignity of the family. 'Finance and the proper disposal of property were the chief considerations', we are told, 'if the betrothed couple were fond of each other, that was an added advantage, but it was not a matter of primary importance. . . . Amongst the poor a greater freedom of choice was

[1] See Note B, p. 218.

[2] E. Neff: 'Social Background and Social Thought' in J. E. Baker ed.: *The Reinterpretation of Victorian Literature* (1950).

[3] For a contemporary view of *Vanity Fair's* unrepresentativeness see N. W. Senior in the *Edinburgh Review*, January 1854, reprinted in his *Essays on Fiction* (1864), p. 389.

[4] This is the view of a work which is admittedly written in a satirical vein: 'When to Marry and How to get Married! or the Adventures of a Lady in Search of a Good Husband', ed. by the Brothers Mayhew (1854), p. 49. There was a certain amount of anti-feminism of this kind written about this time; see, for example, 'Hints on Husband-Catching; or, a Manual for Marriageable Misses' by the 'Hon. —— author of *Hints on the Nature and Management of Duns* (1846). Subscription: 'Man-traps set here.'

possible for there was no property to be considered.'[1] In the eighteenth century, however, we find so many examples of elopements and clandestine weddings 'most of which ended in the erring pair being forgiven by their parents', that this is an added testimony to the argument that the purely mercenary marriage 'was much less common than it had been, and even girls were allowed to follow their own hearts provided that the men they chose were suitable in other ways'.[2] Nevertheless, although a change of heart had clearly come about it cannot be denied that marriage for money continued to exist and that the fashionable novels merely exaggerate what was undoubtedly the case.

The middle- and upper-class spinster without money of her own was in an unenviable position. As Jane Austen pointed out in one of her letters: 'Single women have a dreadful propensity for being poor—which is one very strong argument in favour of matrimony.'[3] Yet it must be admitted that Austen herself never allowed any of *her* heroines to marry for any other reason than affection. 'Everybody should marry as soon as they can do it to advantage' is the maxim of the Mary Crawfords of her tales, not of the Anne Elliots: and even if Fanny Price (her favourite heroine?) is scolded as being ungrateful to her uncle when she refuses the opulent hand of Henry Crawford, true love triumphs in the end and she marries her childhood sweetheart.[4] Nevertheless, despite all this, it still cannot be denied that even for Jane Austen:

> *Love in a hut, with water and a crust*
> *Is—Lord forgive us!—cinders, ashes, dust.*[5]

Thus what does appear as new in this period—although the novelists do not really begin to show it until later—is the argument that people should give up 'the long-cherished idea that it is the first duty of a young woman deliberating about marriage

[1] C. Hole: *English Home Life, 1500 to 1800* (1947), Ch. 5, p. 55.
[2] *Ibid.*, Ch. 10, p. 127.
[3] Letter of 13th March 1817 to Fanny Knight, published in R. W. Chapman ed. *Jane Austen's Letters* (1932), Vol. 2, p. 483.
[4] The reference is to *Mansfield Park* (1814). Anne Elliot is, of course, the heroine of *Persuasion*, Austen's last novel, written about 1816, published posthumously.
[5] Quoted in the novel *Confidential Agent* by James Payn (1880).

to choose a man who has saved up a little money'.[1] His income?
Yes, that should be considered; but his capital? No!

There had, of course, been earlier attacks on marriage for
money, especially from a Christian point of view:

'To ask whether poverty or riches may ensue, or what sort
of figure you are to make in life, is a matter about which you
are not to be concerned. It is your business to cast all your cares
upon God, who careth for you. The ordering and success of all
future events belong to Him, and must be left entirely to His
disposal.'[2]

In tracts of this kind the Christian virtues of humility and
meekness, and above all piety, were the criteria to be used in
looking for a partner; but in the thirties, forties and fifties, even
the religiously minded tracts, like *Prudent Marriages and their
Effects on Posterity* (3rd edition, 1858) were emphasizing prudence in monetary terms. Compare for example:

A good house
Is no uncovertable thing: large rooms,
Servants, gay drapery, new furniture,
Nor undesired, nor undesirable.
But first take counsel of thy income; wait,
Till prudence speak in the affirmative.
Too dear thou purchasest these luxuries
If peace and independence be their price.
Such things to other men perchance may be
A credit, a necessity; to thee,
If thou canst not afford them, but a shame.[3]

Fearingly,
Shun not th'expenses of a wedded life,
Although they be not small. They rouse the man
To new exertion and fresh energy,
And oft develop capabilities

[1] *Prudent Marraiges and the Effects on Posterity* (1858), p. 28.
[2] *The Sure Guide to Domestic Happiness* by the author of *The Refuge* (new ed., 1825),
p. 45. The British Museum catalogue dates the first edition of this work as 1777.
[3] S. W. Partridge: *Upward and Onward: a Thought Book for the Threshold of Active
Life* (1857). Poem entitled, 'Within the Means'. Its theme was 'Oh, beware of debt'.

> *The owner never dreamed of. Children too,*
> *If they make lean th'estate, are yet themselves*
> *Riches, yea, riches most enjoyable.*
> *And He who giveth life will not deny*
> *The food that must sustain it. Yet with care,*
> *Prudence and forethought, first prepare thy home.*
> *For 'tis not manly to allure a girl*
> *From peace, and comfort, and sufficiency,*
> *To a sad cheerless hearth and stinted board.*[1]

In essence the theme of this faltering verse is no different from that of the purely secular Ward and Lock fourpenny pamphlets whose message can be neatly summed up in a single sentence taken from one of them: 'Worldly circumstances need not be very excellent, or sufficient for superfluity, let it suffice if they be enough for competence; but at the time of marriage they should present a reasonable probability of increase, or, at the least, of a firm certainty';[2] or hint No. 3 for those with £100 a year in *Economy for the Single and Married*, which advises: 'Steel yourself against the tender passion—for marry you cannot, with any propriety, or hope of providing for a family. If, however, you *must* fall in love, use every effort to better your situation; and having chosen, as Cowper says, "a proper mate", await prudently "a proper time to marry".'[3]

A 'proper' time to marry!—more and more as the century wore on, this became the theme of the middle classes, until the words 'prudence' and 'postponement' became the two most hackneyed in their vocabulary. 'Miss Osborne does not expect to be married for a year or perhaps two,' wrote a certain Captain Knox to his son, Tom, on 16th September 1839. 'The little man's talents may be great, but the trade is over-stocked, and he is too prudent to espouse the fair lady without bread to put into her mouth'[4]—thus a contemporary letter shows how

[1] *Ibid.* Poem: 'A Home'. See also *Hints towards the Formation of Character with reference chiefly to Social Duties* by a Plainspoken Englishwoman (1843) *passim.*
[2] *How to Woo, when, and to whom* (1855), p. 6.
[3] *Economy for the Single and Married* by One Who Makes Ends Meet (1845), p. 26. The italics were in the original. See also Note C, p. 219.
[4] W. Blake (ed.) *Memoirs of a Vanished Generation, 1813–1835* (1909), p. 81. The 'little man' was J. C. Chappell, a London doctor.

well the lesson had been learned; and a future Archbishop of Canterbury wrote to his friend on 11th January 1858: 'I feel more and more *queer* about leaving Rugby and coming up; more and more anxious to do so, yet more and more afraid of its postponing my marriage perhaps for years. Martin says the most contrary things about the chance of livings, and bothers me dreadfully. Sometimes says there is a good chance of £400 a year being attainable in 2 or 3 years (the longest I wish to wait) and sometimes says there is no chance for 10 years or more.'[1] Hesitation, and a weighing-up of the consequences were the true virtues; to plunge into an ill-considered early marriage was the height of folly.

The population writers of this later period give a clear indication of this changed attitude towards matrimony. With the sole exception of George Drysdale, who felt that 'preventive intercourse . . . (by which he meant contraception) . . . is already far more generally practised than we have any idea of',[2] they accepted as a fact the prudential restraint of the middle and upper classes. Moreton, for example, wrote of the influence of wealth in making for late marriages or permanent celibacy, adding that 'the marriages that do take place among the wealthy are less prolific than those which take place among the labouring classes',[3] and Alison referred to the 'common observation, that the nobility of every country are on the decline. . . . Marriages in that rank are contracted with extreme circumspection, and seldom before one of the parties at least has attained the middle of life.'[4] He too reverted to the view that the marriages of the wealthy were less prolific and attempted to explain it on the basis of a physical law of nature, viz. that marriages contracted in middle age are less fertile than those of early youth, quoting the researches of Quetelet on Belgian

[1] A. C. Benson: *The Life of E. W. Benson* (1899). Letter to J. B. Lightfoot, quoted in Vol. I, p. 133. At this time Benson was a tutor at Rugby. He was 29.

[2] (G. Drysdale): *The Elements of Social Science* (2nd ed., by a Graduate of Medicine, 1859), p. 382. The first edition under the title of *Physical, sexual and natural religion* by a Student of Medicine, appeared in 1854.

[3] A. H. Moreton: *Civilization or a Brief Analysis of the Natural Laws that regulate the Numbers and Conditions of Mankind* (1836), p. 140.

[4] A. Alison: *The Principles of Population, and their Connection with Human Happiness* (1840), Vol. I, p. 111.

material to support his thesis.[1] This particular aspect of the matter, however, was rejected by Doubleday, who maintained that 'by a special provision of nature, all attempts to limit the number of children, by delaying to middle life the period of marriage, are vain and futile; inasmuch as the rapidity of conception, at all events, amongst those classes whose manner of living presents no bar to fertility, may be shown to *increase* in the proportion of the lateness of the time when marriage has taken place.'[2] A marriage at thirty still permitted of 'a family of a dozen.'[3] It is nevertheless significant that he did not deny the truth of the proposition that the middle and upper classes postponed marriage; all that he was concerned to do was to show the ineffectiveness of postponement as a factor in the limitation of family size. Moreover, since the *True Law of Population* became one of the most referred to works of the next twenty years, it may be safely said that the population controversy now turned on the question: 'Does postponement of marriage in fact reduce fertility?'—although in outward form the discussion centred around the attempt to discover the real cause of national and class differences in family size.

It is an interesting reflection of the general movement of intellectual interest during the middle years of the nineteenth century, that this next turn in the population controversy was dominated by an attitude of mind which cannot be considered anything other than mechanistic in its approach to the problems of sociology.[4] *The Origin of Species* did not appear until 1859, twenty-one years after Darwin had chanced to read Malthus and was struck by the possibilities of a theory of selection, but it would seem that biological thinking held the centre of the stage

[1] *Ibid.*, p. 138. The reference was to M. A. Quetelet: *Sur l'homme et le développement de ses facultés* (1835), translated by R. Knox *et al.* as *A Treatise on Man and the Development of his Faculties* (1842). Quetelet's law reads: 'the fecundity of marriages, all things being equal, diminishes in proportion to the increasing age.' Original Vol. 1, p. 39. Translation p. 13.

[2] T. Doubleday: *The True Law of Population shewn to be connected with the Food of the People* (3rd. ed., enlarged and with a postcript, 1853). His italics, p. 23. Tables to support the thesis are given in Chs. 3 and 4, and the preface, p. iv.

[3] *Ibid.* Preface to the Second edition (1842), p. vi.

[4] P. Sorokin: *Contemporary Sociological Theories* (1928). Ch. I, p. 2 names this approach the 'social physics' branch of the 'mechanistic school'. His reference is to H. C. Cary whose *Principles of Social Science* (1858) took its point of departure on population questions from Doubleday and Spencer.

during the whole of this time. At any rate the most heatedly debated attempts at dealing with the problems of differential fertility between these dates were made in terms of alternative views of the reasons for *sterility* in the biological organism. It was not by moral and prudential restraint alone that the ends of the providential order were held to be secured, but by a *physical* law—'woven into the very texture of the organs concerned in the process of reproduction'—which adjusted the balances, maintained the harmonies, and achieved the beneficial results desired.[1]

Two champions played the major roles in the debate: Thomas Doubleday, whose *Great General Law* turned on the food-consumption habits of the different classes, and Herbert Spencer who put forward an evolutionary theory of the development of nervous and mental organization making self-preservation more secure and large-scale reproduction less necessary. Doubleday, indeed, emphasized the constant increase in numbers going on amongst the poorer sections of the community over against the decline amongst the rich. The former were insufficiently supplied with nutriment; while the latter, because of their luxurious ways of life, consistently over-ate.[2] Spencer rejected the factual basis of this view: 'much of the evidence by which Mr. Doubleday seeks to show that among men, highly-fed classes are infertile classes, may be outbalanced by counter-evidence.'[3] In fact, he argued, a state of plethora actually enhances fertility. Where the better-off classes were infertile was with those members who followed occupations involving excessive mental labour. 'Though the regimen of upper-class girls is not what it should be, yet, considering that their feeding is better than that of girls belonging to the poorer classes, while, in most respects, their physical treatment is not worse, the deficiency of repro-

---

[1] H. C. Cary: *Principles of Social Science* (1858), Vol. 3, Ch. 46, Sec. 8, p. 301. Cary was an American whose influence in England was probably very slight. He is quoted here for putting most clearly what was undoubtedly the view of most writers in the period.

[2] T. Doubleday, *op. cit.*, Chs. 1, 5 and 6.

[3] H. Spencer: *The Principles of Biology* (1864–7), Ch. 12. Spencer's theory was first put forward in an anonymous article written by him for the *Westminster Review* in April 1852. This was called 'A Theory of Population, deduced from the General Law of Animal Fertility'.

ductive power among them may be reasonably attributed to the overtaxing of their brains—an overtaxing which produces a serious reaction on the physique.' It was a matter of common remark too how frequently 'men of unusual mental activity leave no offspring'.[1]

Contemporary with this purely biological controversy, and largely overshadowed by it, a sociological approach *sui generis* was being followed up. Alison, in his attempt to deal with differential fertility, had fallen back on 'the progressive development of human reason' and 'the desire of bettering one's condition' as the factors most likely to account for the phenomenon. Since imprudent marriages were everywhere seen to be a cause of misery and ruin, there was every incentive for parents to keep down the numbers of their children. Important therefore in this respect was the 'continuous extension of *artificial wants* concomitant upon the extension of the division of labour'. Each offspring was bred up into habits of indulgence to which its parents had attained only after many years of exertion. Thus, the desire of every succeeding generation 'becomes to preserve the advantages which their predecessors had gained, and to raise itself above the level to which it was destined by its birth; and a fall from these advantages is felt as the severest penalty of imprudence or guilt.'[2]

To this Thornton added the importance of social pressure. Even if a couple considering marriage had sufficient means for procuring in abundance 'every necessary and substantive comfort' they might, nevertheless, hesitate for fear of not being able to keep up 'the outward appearance required in the circle in which they were accustomed to move'.[3] The role of the concept of the standard of living in the postponement of marriage, earlier sketched out by Senior in his treatment of necessaries, decencies and luxuries,[4] had become clearly recognized as integral to the question.

It is pertinent to ask at this point how far the population

---

[1] *Op. cit.* (3rd ed., 1880), p. 486.
[2] A. Alison: *Principles of Population* (1840), Vol. 1, Ch. 3. The italics were Alison's own.
[3] W. T. Thornton: *Over-Population and its Remedy* (1846), p. 119.
[4] See especially his *Political Economy* (1836) reprinted in 1850, pp. 36–38.

writers may be taken as an indication of popular middle-class opinion during this later period. Fortunately, we have an independent check in a series of letters written to *The Times* in the early months of 1858. A leader on 8th January of that year, roused by an attempt of 'many clergymen and gentlemen' to form an association to combat prostitution, declared that the preposterous amount of income which was considered necessary if a young man did not want to sink in the social scale, was no doubt a fruitful cause of the deplorable evil of which they were speaking. This provoked 'A Happy Man' to expatiate on the delights and responsibilities of married life. But, he exclaimed, agreeing with *The Times*, 'Fancy the derisive outburst you would excite at the club by asserting that "young Jones, with his £300 a year, might marry and be happy!" Why, that magnificent income hardly suffices now to keep him going.'[1]

The correspondence which followed turned on the question of whether it was, or was not, possible to marry on £300 a year. 'Caution' wrote to say that in his view it was not, at least, for certain members of the community. 'By no means do I contend that £300 a year, and much less than £300 a year, will not suffice to mtaintain a young couple in respectability and comfort, provided always that their antecedent social position has not been incompatible with that which they must be content to assume on such an income when married. . . . I deny that a young man belonging to a rank in society which renders him eligible for admission to a West-end club can maintain a wife of similar rank (to say nothing of a family) on an income of £300 a year without practically abdicating that position.' After all, £300 a year was only 16s. 6d. a day.[2]

On the other hand, those who thought that £300 sufficed, sought to clinch the matter by sending sample budgets of their own expenditure to show how it could be done. Thus, 'Another Happy Man' gave the following 'actual items of my wife's expenditure for housekeeping during the past year, extracted from our account books':

[1] *The Times*, 9th January 1858.
[2] *The Times*, 12th January 1858.

'Expenditure for housekeeping of self, and wife, and one child, one woman-servant, and one nursery-girl, from 1st January to 31st December 1857:

	£	s.	d.
Baker	8	0	5
Butcher	22	8	1
Beer	5	17	7
Cheesemonger	5	4	7
Coals and Wood	8	18	8
Fish	1	6	2
Greengrocer	8	1	4
Grocer	13	11	11
Milk	2	7	7
Rent	25	0	0
Taxes	3	12	7
Railway Ticket	8	0	0
Tallowchandler	6	3	7
Wages	12	6	0
Washing	3	7	2
Wines	2	0	4
	£136	6	0

Add to this an estimated outlay for

Clothes for self, wife and child	40	0	0
Insurance, life & fire	12	0	0
Medical attendance and monthly nurse	12	0	0
Travelling expenses, cabs, books and newspapers	10	0	0
Church and charity	20	0	0
Would amount to a total of	£230	6	0

Leaving a balance on the £300 a year of Jones and Smith   £69 14 0'[1]

This budget was examined item by item by the next writer in the series, who, on the basis of the rent paid and the railway ticket, hazarded the opinion that 'Another Happy Man' was a clerk in a respectable London office, 'earning £250 a year and living about six miles out in the suburbs in a small house with a drawing-room 14 feet by 10, a dining-room 10 feet by 8, three small bedrooms and a servant's room'. In making this income do, spending must be on the most economical and careful scale, seeing that the household was of four persons, (at

[1] *The Times*, 15th January 1858.

those wages one servant must be only occasional) and yet did not consume more than 9s. worth of meat, 3s. worth of bread, 2s. worth of coals and wood, 3s. worth of vegetables, and 5s. worth of every kind of grocery, each week. Luxuries were few, three pints of beer a day and one bottle of wine every five weeks, which suggested that the dinner beverage was beer and not wine. All in all, the budget was a miracle of economy, industry and self-denial, plus first-rate housekeeping on the part of the wife. 'Five years hence, if his family continues to increase, a reduction of even these comforts may be necessary.'[1] Clearly, for people of a different social position, as, for example, college fellows,[2] these standards of expenditure were regarded as being far too meagre.

Indeed the importance of the pressure to live up to what was required by one's status and to what one had been used to, came out time and time again. 'Caution', for example, explicitly remarked that 'social position is the touchstone of this matter', and a third leader of 22nd January took occasion to attack the whole conception:

'We do not think much of what are called the claims of society in connection with this question, the "duty"—oh, how conscientious we are!—of a man not marrying, except he can live in the style to which he has been accustomed, and can continue all the luxuries of which he was the uncharged enjoyer in a paternal establishment.'

Marriage was a law of nature, and a man ought, within limits, to consider only his happiness.[3] But happiness itself might depend upon other things. A person in quite a different position might legitimately regard 'Another Happy Man's' wife as 'a head nurse or head housemaid only without wages'.[4]

A long quotation from an article in the High Church paper, *The Guardian*, will perhaps give the best summing-up of the position as it was seen by contemporaries:

'People in these days have an acute sense of the duty of not

---

[1] *The Times*, 19th January 1858.
[2] See the letter from 'St. Boniface' in *The Times*, 13th January 1858.
[3] *The Times*, 22nd January 1858.
[4] Letter from 'A Bad Housekeeper' in *The Times*, 28th January 1858.

marrying without a competent support; but instead of tempering the idea of competency by habits of frugality and self-denial, so as to render marriage compatible with the means within their reach, they are daily adding expensive appliances for show or comfort to the list of necessaries, and so the upper surface of society rises higher and higher in the scale of luxury, while its base sinks deeper in corruption. It is not generally so much the mere taste for personal enjoyment which leads to this, as the opinion that a certain class of luxuries and scale of expenditure are necessary to the maintenance of a due social position. Considerable discussion has lately been carried on by letters in *The Times* as to the minimum amount on which it may be possible to marry with due regard to prudence and social considerations; and though the tone of the controversy verges on the burlesque, it is impossible not to perceive that it involves a social problem of the very highest importance. We shall not be guilty of the temerity of risking an opinion as to the precise amount of income which may be enough for persons who wished to be married. But if we must defer to the manners of the day it is evident that the requisite sum will approach rather to the highest than to the lowest of the figures which have been calculated. A scale of expenditure has been put forward suited to an income of £300 a year, and the analysis of it shows a ridiculous incompatibility with modern habits. At the same time it must be remembered that incomes of that amount often maintained in comfort the great-grandfathers and grandmothers of those who are now straitened on twice or thrice the sum. And yet the scale of prices is not now higher on the whole; some articles of daily consumption having greatly fallen, though others have advanced.'[1]

This brings us to a point made by one of *The Times* correspondents and attacked ferociously some years earlier by the author of *Social Aspects*, viz. the prevailing attitude of mind that 'younger members of a house, when commencing on their own account, should rival the old family establishment'.[2]

'A young man must plunge into married life at full gallop;

[1] 'Morals and Manners' in *The Guardian*, 27th January 1858.
[2] Letter from 'A Friend of Jones' in *The Times*, 15th January 1858.

begin where his father ended. He must have a house replete with elegancies, with plate, pier glasses, pictures, and all the paraphernalia of a drawing-room of fashion; and he must be prepared to give an extensive entertainment, once or twice a year, to all with whom he is on speaking terms; or if he will not do this, if he will not be bound down by such conventionalisms, he must submit to sink his status in society, and be considered a plebeian and a boor by his former associates.'[1]

Indeed, stated *The Times* on 2nd July 1861, the fact that 'newly married couples expect to begin where their fathers and mothers ended' is the root cause why early marriages are becoming less common than they formerly were. 'The luxuries which a bachelor can command at his lodgings and in his club on an allowance of £300 a year, are altogether out of proportion to those which a prudent father of a family would afford himself out of a joint income of thrice that amount, and it is not every man who will make the sacrifice.'[2]

It is to be remarked, however, that the other point of view had some weight:

'Whatever may be said to the contrary, it does cost a great deal of money to be a gentleman, and a great deal more to be a lady. Where the mistress of the house has to be a nurse and domestic servant as well as a wife, she will be almost sure to sink the last character in the first. Unless a woman has extraordinary health and vigour, her husband will enjoy very little of her society if she is always looking after the children or the dinner, and if both he and she are forced to spend a great deal of time and thought in contriving ways to make their income cover their expenses, their minds will be very apt to assume a petty cast, and to be fixed for the most part on small and somewhat sordid, though important, objects. The obscure difficulties and struggles of such a mode of life are, in plain truth, great enemies both to refinement and to high aims in life. A couple to

---

[1] J. S. Smith: *Social Aspects* (1850), p. 45.

[2] See also the correspondence raised by the Belgravian Lament that young men were refusing to marry, in *The Times*, 27th, 28th, 29th June, and 1st and 2nd July, 1861: letters from 'A Sorrowing Mother for Seven of Them', 'A Father of Six', 'Primogenitus', 'N' (or 'M'), 'A Mother', and 'Grandmama'.

whom every sixpence is an object, have to think and talk a great deal about sixpences. Although it is perfectly right that they should do so, it would be better for them both to be free from the obligation.

'It follows from all this, that the desire to keep up appearances is neither an empty nor a vulgar one, for the appearances so kept up cover substantial realities. It is quite true that the first, and perhaps the most obvious result of the sort of marriage which is so warmly advocated is a loss of social station; but the reason why that loss is incurred is, that such marriages almost always render possessions of great importance extremely precarious. They endanger the independence and the refinement of those who contract them, and they make it probable that they will become the parents of children who will hold a position in life altogether different from their own.

'Almost everyone who has the ear of the public, and who writes upon the subject, falls into the error of arguing as if the sacrifice required for the sake of such marriages was no more than a sacrifice of personal luxury and enjoyment. *The Times*, for example, proceeds on the assumption that it is a question of carriages, fine clothes and expensive amusements. But the vanities which are derided as the rivals of marriage, champagne, stalls at the opera, and expensive dinners, are not the real difficulties.

'For £100 a judicious man may get a great amount of that sort of enjoyment; but if he wants to keep a roomy house, and to provide clothes, food, washing, attendance, change of air, doctors, repairs, and furniture for a wife and several young children, his £100 will go much faster than it would in any prudent and reasonable kind of personal indulgence. A married man must be prepared either to meet these expenses on a constantly increasing scale, or to cut them down at the expense of converting his wife into a drudge, and allowing his children to grow up in unwholesome and dirty habits.'[1]

The plain fact of the matter was that the middle classes were now faced by rapidly rising standards of *domestic* expenditure. The prudential considerations which by the thirties had come to be regarded as essentially involved in any attempt to deter-

[1] 'Keeping up Appearances' in *The Cornhill Magazine*, September 1861.

mine the proper time to marry, were by the fifties being made to embrace the calculation of chances as to how far the proposed partnership would be able to live up to the patterns of behaviour required of it. This was, of course, always logically entailed in the notion of the immorality of marrying without the means of supporting a family, but what made the situation especially acute in this later period was the constant expansion in expenditure being made by married and single alike. The unmarried were faced by the possibility of losing status if they did not conform, in a period when ever-increasing expense was the order of the day. In a state of domesticity where 'before a man is fairly out of his honeymoon—for the honeymoon of your "happy man" lasts at least a twelve-month—there is a baby',[1] postponement of marriage was obviously the only way out.

[1] 'The Ethics of Early and Frugal Marriages' in *Tait's Edinburgh Magazine*, February 1858.

CHAPTER IV

The Pattern of Expenditure

THE average age of those clergymen, doctors, lawyers, members of the aristocracy, merchants, bankers, manufacturers, and 'gentlemen' generally, who married between 1840 and 1870 was 29·93 years.[1] It would thus appear that the claims of the writers to *The Times* in 1858 and 1861 had some foundation in fact. There was a tendency for middle- and upper-class men to marry at a late age. The correspondence, however, as we have seen, went further than the mere assertion that postponement of marriage was taking place; it tried to explain it, and almost every letter-writer attributed the cause to the rapidly rising standard of living which confronted the young middle-class men and women of the day. If, therefore, we wish to establish this in a rather more precise way than has been employed so far, some estimation must be made of the more detailed changes involved, and this can best be done in monetary terms.

At the same time, the contrary views put forward in the 1858 and subsequent discussions on the middle-class *minimum* income demonstrate that it is no easy matter to arrive at what might be called a representative set of figures. While it must be admitted that £300 a year was the sum most often quoted in all kinds of places about this time, even for the bank clerks of fiction,[2] the treatment meted out to the details submitted to *The Times* by 'Another Happy Man' shows quite conclusively that what one

---

[1] C. Ansell, Jnr.: *On the Rate of Mortality at Early Periods of Life, the Age at Marriage, the Number of Children to a Marriage, the Length of a Generation, and other Statistics of Families in the Upper and Professional Classes* (1874), p. 45.

[2] See, for example, 'Frugal Marriages' in *The Temple Bar*, Vol. 3, 1861, p. 140 et seq.

middle-class person might consider to be perfectly adequate for the good life, another would find intolerable.

Another example of the same difficulty is to be seen in the estimations of furnishing outlays. Clearly it would be of assistance to us to know the kind of expenses involved in setting up house, faced by middle-class couples at different periods. Unfortunately they appear somewhat reticent on this issue and what little information we have is hardly comparable. Thus, in 1857, J. H. Walsh could furnish a house consisting of a hall and staircase, kitchen, dining-room, drawing-room, library (or breakfast room), three bedrooms, two servants' rooms, and a nursery for £585.[1] Yet we are told of illustrated catalogues issued by some of the cheap furnishing warehouses of London in the early sixties which offered to furnish a ten-roomed house for as little as £289 10s. 6d.,[2] that is, for less than half the cost. In these catalogues a six-roomed house could be equipped for £67 17s. as opposed to £221 on Walsh's scale, while an alternative source some years later reckoned it would cost £98 2s.[3]

This last estimate is more valuable to us because, like Walsh's figures, it was related to income. The six-roomed house, according to Mrs. Warren, was appropriate for those living on £200 a year. Walsh had put it into his £250 range; but that was in 1857, twelve years earlier. In his second edition, in 1873, only four years after Mrs. Warren's book had appeared, he raised this income to £350.[4] The relationship between size of house and income could hardly be decided from these figures. On the other hand, if the cost of furnishing is related to the *income* ranges, Mrs. Warren's £98 2s. estimate works out at 49 per cent of her £200, while Walsh's £192 15s. (his second edition estimate) is 55 per cent of £360. There is a certain amount of correspondence here.

Walsh's estimates, in fact, are useful in a number of ways. In the first place, his book was planned for four grades of income and every aspect of middle-class domestic life was considered

[1] J. H. Walsh: *A Manual of Domestic Economy; suited to families spending from £100 to £1,000 a Year* (1857), p. 211.

[2] 'Our Furniture' by A.W. in *Once a Week*, 16th July 1864.

[3] E. Warren: *A House and its Furnishings* (1869), p. 81.

[4] J. H. Walsh: *A Manual of Domestic Economy; suited to families spending from £150 to £1,500 a Year* (new ed., 1873), pp. 195–204.

under the four headings. Thus, for the £100 per annum group the cost of furnishing was estimated at £83 in 1857. For the £250 group, the comparable figure was £221; for £500, £584; and for £1,000, £1,391. In terms of percentages of annual income these estimates may be set out as follows:

Income £	Furnishing Costs £	Per cent
100	83	83
250	221	88
500	584	117
1,000	1,391	139

showing as a general pattern that he expected not only that the lower-income groups would have much less capital to spare on furnishing their homes than the upper-income groups, but also that they would be able to spare less of their current annual income for it.

In the second place, Walsh completely revised his book in 1873, keeping the same division into four ranges of income, but raising them to £150, £350, £750, and £1,500 respectively. Now he provided the following pattern:

Income £	Furnishing Costs £	Per cent
150	64	43
350	193	55
750	671	89
1,500	1,578	105

which repeated the reasoning of the earlier edition. At the same time, it is to be noticed that the percentages of annual income to be spent on initial furnishing were made much lower in 1875 than they had been in 1857, especially for the lower income groups. If Walsh is to be trusted at all, therefore, there must have taken place some kind of scaling down (about one-third less) during these fifteen years. Indeed, for the wealthiest group, even the addition of a grand piano and stool in 1873 (£123 3s.) —an item not allowed for at all in the lists of 1857—failed to raise the proportion above the earlier estimates (113 per cent as opposed to 139 per cent). Some important variations in standards and prices had obviously occurred over the period.

In his preface to the second edition Walsh wrote: 'During the fifteen years which have elapsed since this book was written, very considerable changes have occurred in several departments of the subjects treated of in its pages. Concurrently with an increase in the demand for luxuries by the classes for whose use it was written, has been a rise in the prices of some of the articles most important to their due development . . . (he specifically mentions food, rent, horses, and clothes). For these several reasons, the lowest range of income to which the book extends has been raised from £100 to £150 a year, while the highest is now £1,500, instead of £1,000.'[1] We are doubtless meant to regard the two sets of income ranges as more or less comparable, with the conclusion that for Walsh, at any rate, the lower-income groups of the middle classes were not prepared to spend so large a sum on furnishings as their older siblings had been, and *all* groups were spending a smaller proportion of their income on it. The percentage changes over time appear as follows:

Income £	Increase Per cent	Furniture £	Increase Per cent
100– 150	+50	83– 64	−25
250– 350	+40	221– 193	−13
500– 750	+50	584– 671	+15
1,000–1,500	+50	1,391–1,701	+22

What are we to make of these figures?

It seems very likely that the original ranges were chosen for reasons of mathematical simplicity and that the increases were dictated by a general impression of a rise in expenditure, and possibly of incomes, of 50 per cent over the fifteen years. The furnishing estimates, on the other hand, were based on detailed price lists of the furniture considered appropriate for those classes of income. It is not unreasonable to suppose, therefore, that the 25 per cent decrease at the lowest range was based on a real fall in the price of household articles considered essential for any middle-class home, whilst the changes at the other ranges made allowance for some increase in the amount the middle classes were prepared to spend on less essential items,

[1] *Op. cit.*, Preface, p. iii.

such as the grand piano. There is, in fact, some evidence that furniture had increased in costliness as a result of becoming 'elegant and tasteful',[1] but on the whole the main rise in outlay required was the result of a general expansion in conspicuous consumption.[2] The best bedroom, for example, had become a show-room 'into which one's wife inveigles lady visitors to look at the full-length mirror let into the wardrobe, and other gorgeous fittings',[3] and a complaint was also made that books were being bought and libraries established merely as a form of decoration.[4]

Contemporary opinion, moreover, did not consider that this new extravagance was confined to domestic furnishing:

'The accommodation, the fitting up, and the decorations of the shop, offices, or counting-house, are now all after a style necessitating the expenditure of as much capital as would, a few years back, have purchased half a tradesman's stock-in-trade; and men say, and very truly, that they have no chance of succeeding if they do not, in these things, keep pace with their neighbours. Men, in many positions, must advertise largely at this time at a vast expense, and incur various other inevitable charges. The medical practitioner cannot drive himself about in a dusty old gig purchased for a few guineas from his predecessor, but must have a neatly appointed brougham and an exceptionally attired man-servant. The young solicitor cannot receive his clients in a dingy den festooned with cobwebs, its bare boards foul with ink; there must be tapestry, carpeted floors, morocco-topped writing-tables, and well-stuffed velvet-covered arm-chairs. In other professions the same necessity obtains; and all struggling in the race, echo the tradesman's assertion of the absolute necessity of show, appearance, style. If, therefore, the mere outlay necessary to procure clients or customers now costs a man nearly as much as would formerly have sufficed for both his business and household expenses, and left him a moderate sum to lay by or add to his trading capital, it is unreasonable to maintain, as some do, that a mere dread of

[1] *Ibid.*, p. 206.
[2] 'The Fashion of Furniture' in *The Cornhill Magazine*, March 1864.
[3] 'A Home of One's Own' in *Chambers's Journal*, 30th May 1863, p. 338.
[4] 'Furniture Books' in *Fraser's Magazine*, January 1859.

personal sacrifice, or desire for domestic luxury and display, are the sole causes of the present unpopularity of early marriages, or of the increasing dislike to marriage which is said to exist among young men in general, but especially among the more refined and educated of the middle classes. One is not justified in saying, on the one hand, that it is mere selfishness which makes a young man, under these circumstances, *prefer* not entering on the responsibilities of wedded life; nor may we declare that he is *frightened* from marrying by the larger demands made by young women for domestic purposes in the particulars of house, servants, dress, furniture, or entertainments.'[1]

From this writer's point of view the real problem was that it was simply far more difficult to manage the new and *more expensive* standards on the old incomes.

One check on this claim that there was an expansion in conspicuous expenditure on household fittings is to be found in the extension in the range of advertisements to be seen in magazines like *The Family Friend* about this time. While continuing to preach economical housekeeping, as in the article 'Domestic Economy' which appeared in November 1864, it nevertheless began to carry a growing number of illustrations of sewing-machines, and kitchen grates of various descriptions and prices. The significance of this lies in the fact that, unlike Mrs. Beeton's *Englishwoman's Domestic Magazine* which was always quite frankly worldly, R. K. Philp's aim in his monthly was to infuse the home with a 'permanent Christian atmosphere'[2] which for him appears to have meant emphasizing the virtues of frugality and economical management to housewives. Everything savouring of extravagance and vain ostentation was attacked at some time or other, and for this reason the advertisements were almost solely confined to domestic articles; but the fact that in the sixties the magazine began to give more space to the existence of these presumably not undesirable things, may have

[1] 'Marriage' in *The Englishwoman's Domestic Magazine*, March 1865. The italics were in the original.

[2] *The Family Friend*, December 1858, Preface—a review of ten years' progress. The average circulation of the magazine over the decade had been 40,000 copies a month.

helped to expand expenditure in this region amongst its readers; it certainly could hardly have worked in the opposite direction.

Moreover, with the inception of schemes of instalment purchasing which appear to have been started about this time, members of the lower-income ranges in the middle class who might not have been able to afford the ready money but who, unlike most members of the working classes, could probably have found the initial 5–7 per cent deposit, were enabled to purchase articles which had possibly been beyond the reach of an older generation in receipt of an equivalent income. Thus pianos could be obtained on a three-years' system of small payments, and an article of 1873 waxed enthusiastic about the General Furnishing Company's new system of hire-purchase.[1] Unfortunately, there still remains to be written a history of instalment trading in this country and we have no way of estimating how widespread the custom was during this vital period. Credit trading in furniture was already an accepted thing in the country districts, if George Eliot is any guide;[2] but we are told that ready money was usually demanded in London.[3] There was always, of course, the alternative of buying second-hand furniture, advocated by Walsh in 1857; and it is also possible that many did not furnish completely at the outset, but carried it out over a period of time from savings made from their current incomes, 'a slow process of doing a room a year, as funds could be saved'.[4] All these possibilities go to explain how difficult it is to arrive at anything like a representative set of figures which may be used as an index to what was happening. The most that can be maintained is that Walsh's estimates are *not disproved* by the general impressions culled from reading the literature.

Fortunately, the problem of tackling most of the changes made in the pattern of general family outlay is much less com-

---

[1] 'How to Furnish' in *Once a Week*, 27th September 1873, p. 270.

[2] In *Middlemarch*, 1873 (Bk. 6, especially Ch. 58) the doctor, Lydgate, who had obtained £400–£500 of credit in furniture and plate to marry with, finds that he has almost ruined himself because of it. Note that the story is set in 1832 and that one reviewer wrote that it 'seems to us to belong to a somewhat older form of our society than that'. (*The Edinburgh Review*, January 1873, Art. 10, p. 248.)

[3] 'How to Furnish' in *Once a Week*, 27th September 1873, p. 271.

[4] *Ibid.*, p. 271.

plicated owing to the fact that throughout the whole of the nineteenth century, and certainly from the fifties onwards, there was a steady expansion in the output of books and magazines on domestic economy. These tend, on the whole, to supplement one another; and it is therefore possible to deal with them in the same kind of way as the works on the population controversy were dealt with earlier, viz. by documenting as fully as possible all statements made and by referring the reader to a detailed list of sources for a further, more comprehensive, investigation of the problem.[1] It must be emphasized, however, that at present our knowledge of this field is far less precise than it is of the population controversy. It has never been worked over before by sociologists and consequently there are no good bibliographies to assist the researcher in his work. Moreover very many of the books listed in publishers' catalogues are no longer available, some having been lost altogether and others destroyed by public libraries who thought them out of date and no longer valuable, completely failing to realize their potential worth as historical documents. It must, nevertheless, be pointed out that the residue, as given in Appendix I to this book, consists of the most influential and undoubtedly the best known of the genre.

As a point of departure, let us begin by looking at the following principles of expenditure 'by which Gentlemen might regulate their outlay' as set out in 1823 by the author of *A New System of Practical Domestic Economy*:[2]

		Per cent	Per cent
1. Household Expenses, viz:			
	Provisions	26	
	Coals, Candles, Soap, etc.	7	36
	Extra, for Entertainments	2	
	Medicine and other Incidentals	1	
2. Servants and Equipage, viz.:			
	Horses and Carriages	10	
	Male Servants	8	22
	Female Servants	4	

[1] See p. 19 and Appendix I: Domestic Economy, p. 208.

[2] *A New System of Practical Domestic Economy; founded on modern Discoveries, and the Private Communications of Persons of Experience* (3rd ed., revised and greatly enlarged, 1823). 'Appendix of Practical Estimates of Household Expenses', p. 49.

3. Clothes, etc., viz.:

Gentleman's Clothes	4	
Lady's ditto	5	
Three Children's ditto	2½	12
Haberdashery, etc.	½	

4. Rent, Taxes, and Repairs, viz.:

Rent	8	
Taxes and Repairs	4	12

5. Extra Expenses, viz.:

Education	4	
Pocket Expenses	2	8
Private Expenses	2	

6. Reserve or Saving		10
	Total	100

This was intended for the income range, £1,000 to £5,000, and covered a man, his wife, servants, and three children, the last being taken as the average size of the family.[1] The question at issue here is: how far can such estimates be taken as a guide to the expenditure of *actual* persons within such ranges? and this applies to all the estimates given in any of the works on domestic economy produced during the century.

It must be recognized from the first that, quite apart from the fact that these books were written by members of the middle classes who, presumably, had their own experience to call upon, most of them claim, especially when they run into second and third editions, that they have been corrected and revised in the light of suggestions and criticisms made by readers and acquaintances. Some, indeed, like the works of Mrs. Beeton, R. K. Philp, and Mrs. Panton, were publicly contributed to through the medium of letters to *The Englishwoman's Domestic Magazine*, *The Family Friend*, and *The Lady's Pictorial*, who had, as it were, a vested interest in promoting discussion on the works of their editors and chief contributors. For this reason it could even be claimed that the estimates which appear in their books give a better picture of the *general pattern* of middle-class expenditure than isolated family budgets about whose representativeness we know nothing. Moreover, these books were sold and used by the thousand. Their influence, therefore, can hardly have been

[1] *Ibid.*, p. 5.

negligible, so that although it would be claiming too much to say that percentages like those set out above were strictly adhered to, it may safely be said that the whole idea of rationally planning one's outlay on the basis of keeping regular accounts did become part of the middle-class domestic atmosphere. Ruled and printed account books were sold for that purpose, and it is to be expected that where these were divided up into the various departments of expenditure, e.g. 'Beer, Malt & Hops', 'Bread, Flour, etc.', 'Butter, Cheese, etc.', 'Books and Stationery', 'Fish', 'Rent, Taxes, etc.', 'Servants' Wages', 'Wearing Apparel',[1] attempts to regulate spending would tend to be made in terms of such categories. We can, therefore, make use of these manuals and guides to give us some indication of the way in which the middle classes actually set about the task of laying out their money.

The most common figure given for the amount to be spent on rent is one-eighth of the total income, or, say, 12 per cent. This is the figure given above when taxes and repairs are included; it is given by Mrs. Beeton, with the proviso that 'circumstances alter cases', in 1861, and again in 1892;[2] it is given by Walsh in 1857 and 1873,[3] and by *Cassell's Book of the Household* in 1890.[4] This proportion is, however, only to be regarded as very rough for Walsh includes taxes within his figure, whereas *Cassell's Book* allows a further one-sixteenth for rates, taxes, and railway fares. There is also some indication of a general feeling that the proportion to be allowed had increased, at any rate for London, during the period. *Cassell's Book*, for example, says: 'In former times, when rents were not so high as they now are, it used to be an understood thing that, when householders were prudent, rent must not exceed one-tenth of the income; and an individual who was known to be living in a house of which the rent exceeded this limit, was looked upon by his neighbours as

---

[1] These items are taken from among the twenty-four divisions of the *Domestic Account Book, 1843*, published by C. Penny & Son, Cheapside, at 2s. each. The British Museum still has, in spite of wartime damage, a number of these blank account books in its collections.

[2] I. M. Beeton: *The Book of Household Management* (1861), p. 20. 1892 ed., p. 19.

[3] J. H. Walsh: *A Manual of Domestic Economy*, 1st ed. (1857), p. 606. 2nd ed. (1873) and subsequent editions, p. 677.

[4] *Cassell's Book of the Household: a Work of Reference on Domestic Economy* (n.d. British Museum, 1890), Vol. 2, p. 55.

unthrifty and extravagant. The limit was a wise one, yet house-holders have had to give it up.'[1]

An interesting case of comparison appeared in an article in *The Cornhill Magazine* for April 1875. The author, in an attempt to deal with complaints about the increase in the cost of living which 'have of late been rife in every quarter', hit upon the plan of comparing some household accounts of some 'forty or fifty years ago' with those of his own day. He claimed that in terms of income and tastes the two sets were rather similar and that therefore comparison was possible. In the older accounts £80 was paid in rent (about 8 per cent); in the newer £125 (12·5 per cent, but this was for a larger and more convenient house. The true difference he estimated at £30; that is, an increase from 8 per cent to 11 per cent. These figures, however, did not include rates and taxes, which had risen in the meantime, mainly to pay for such things as drains, light, and police, 'luxuries that our fathers had mostly to do without'.[2] On the whole, it does seem that between the period 1830 and 1875, rents paid by the middle classes were increasing[3] and later, with the growth of suburban London, a new item of expenditure, namely fares for the journey to work, appeared as part of most middle-class budgets.

For the moment, however, we are mainly concerned with what happened before the seventies; although it must not be overlooked that London did grow by half a million people between 1861 and 1871, of whom about 46 per cent went to live in the outer ring.[4] This must mean that a growing number of middle-class men had fares to pay, like 'Another Happy Man', whose season ticket cost him £8 (3 per cent of his salary) in 1857,[5] and there was some complaint that the growth of suburbia raised costs in other respects. By being further away from

[1] *Ibid.*, p. 55. See also 'How to Live Cheaply' (a series of articles reprinted from the *Daily Express* in 1906), p. 76.

[2] 'Cost of Living' in *The Cornhill Magazine*, April 1875, p. 420.

[3] W. R. Greg: 'Life at High Pressure' in *The Contemporary Review*, March 1875, p. 633. M. G. Mulhall: 'The Housing of the London Poor', Sec. 2, 'Ways and Means', in the *Contemporary Review*, February 1844, maintained that rents more than doubled between 1831 and 1881 (p. 223). For details see Note Da, p. 219.

[4] For an excellent account of the expansion, see H. J. Dyos: *The Suburban Development of Greater London South of the Thames, 1836–1914.* Unpublished Ph.D. thesis, July 1952 (Senate House, London) especially Ch. 3.

[5] Letter to *The Times*, 15th January 1858. See p. 42.

the central markets a man of business became more at the mercy
of his tradesmen and had to pay dearer for everything. It was
even estimated that a man could live better in Liverpool on
£600 a year than in London on £1,000.[1] Nevertheless, the real
effect of this is not discernible in the general development of
the pattern in this period.

The *New System of Practical Domestic Economy*, as we have seen,
allowed 26 per cent of income for provisions, plus a further
7 per cent for coals, candles, soap, etc.; but even the writer of
this work, without being aware of the law that later was to be
made famous by Ernst Engel, based his calculations on the
principle that the smaller the family income was, the greater
would be the proportion of it spent on food. The following
table, culled from his estimates, shows the trend.

Family Size *	Income £	Household Expenses £ s. d.	Percentage of Income
5	150	85 16 0	54
6	200	111 18 2	56
6	250	135 6 2	54
7	300	161 17 0	54
7	400	186 19 8	47
7	500	213 10 6	43
8	600	243 6 4	41
9	750	287 14 8	38

(* The basic family consisted of five persons; a man, his wife, and
three children. The increase in family size in the table is caused through
the employment of an increasing number of servants as the income rises.)

Here, in spite of the fact that the size of the household increases as the income scale is climbed, the percentage expenditure on household requirements is reckoned to fall.[2]

Walsh, thirty-four and fifty years later, makes a similar set
of assumptions.

1857

Family Size *	Income £	Household Expenses £	Percentage of Income
6	100	65	65
7	250	150	60
9	500	200	40
11	1,000	350	35

[1] 'Middle-class Housekeeping' in *Tinsley's Magazine*, January 1868, pp. 740–1.
[2] *Op. cit.*, 'Appendix of Practical Estimates', pp. 35–43.

1873

6	150	95	63
7	350	220	63
9	750	295	39
11	1,500	555	37

(* Here the basic family included four children. The additions were formed, as before, by the employment of an increasing number of servants as income rose.)

Indeed, Walsh's detailed lists are worth looking at even more closely.

1857

Housekeeping items	£1,000	£500	£250	£100
Butcher's meat and bacon	75	40	30	18
Fish and poultry	30	10	7	—
Bread	20	16	14	10
Milk, butter and cheese	20	18	16	8
Grocery	30	20	18	8
Italian goods	8	5	3	—
Greengrocery	20	12	10	6
Beer	20	12	10	5
Wine and spirits	50	15	8	1
Coals	25	15	12	5
Chandlery	12	7	7	2
Washing	40	30	15	2
	£350	£200	£150	£65

This table provides the following percentages of the total housekeeping spent on each item.

	£1,000 Per cent	£500 Per cent	£250 Per cent	£100 Per cent
Butcher's meat and bacon	21·4	20·0	20·0	27·7
Fish and poultry	8·6	5·0	4·7	—
Bread	5·7	8·0	9·3	15·4
Milk, butter and cheese	5·7	9·0	10·7	12·3
Grocery	8·6	10·0	12·0	12·3
Italian goods	2·3	2·5	2·0	—
Greengrocery	5·7	6·0	6·7	9·2
Beer	5·7	6·0	6·7	7·7
Wine and spirits	14·3	7·5	5·3	1·5
Coals	7·1	7·5	8·0	7·7
Chandlery	3·4	3·5	4·7	3·1
Washing	11·4	15·0	10·0	3·1
	99·9	100·0	100·1	100·0

From these tables it is clear that an increase in expenditure arising from an increase in income would have resulted in a *greater* proportionate outlay on fish and poultry, wine and spirits, and perhaps Italian goods and washing, part of the last item, no doubt, being required by the increasing size of the household at the higher ranges of income. On the other hand, apart from the expenditure on coals and chandlery, which we may for all practical purposes regard as remaining constant, the outlay on all the other items would have been more than proportionately decreased, as one ascended the income scale. In general, therefore, we may regard fish and poultry, wine and spirits, Italian goods and washing as luxury items from the middle-class point of view; items, that is, which the lower middle class would have regarded as desirable but on which they usually economized. Wine and spirits were, of course, the outstanding examples, but the others should not be overlooked.

It may well be, however, that Walsh was inclined to overestimate the proportion that the middle classes, at least in the lower income ranges, were prepared to spend on food. In *The Times* correspondence of 1858 two letters gave details of their writer's current expenditure. In the first case the man, his wife, one child and two servants spent £230 6s. altogether in the year ending 31st December 1857. Of this £71 18s. (31 per cent) went on food, and £92 7s. 5d. (40 per cent) went on household items of the kind set out above.[1] This compares with £116 (46 per cent) and £150 (60 per cent) in Walsh's £250 column (for a man, his wife, four children, and a maid). In the second case a man, his wife, three children and three servants spent £393 14s. 1½d. in 1856. Of this £119 8s. 8½d. (30 per cent) went on food, and £154 10s. 2½d. (39 per cent) on household expenses generally.[2] This can only be compared with the 30 per cent (£148) and 40 per cent (£200) of Walsh's £500 a year range. In the main, therefore, Walsh may be accepted as a fair guide for the higher income, but may be used only with reservations for the lower groups. Items other than food and general housekeeping may well have absorbed 50 per cent of the income

[1] Letter from 'Another Happy Man' to *The Times*, 15th January 1858. See p. 42.
[2] Letter from M.A.M., *The Times*, 25th January 1858.

of those with less than £500 a year, at least until the very low range of £100 a year was descended to.[1]

In this connection the second of *The Times* letters is useful as the writer, a clergyman's daughter, and mother of three children, gave details of her expenditure for two different years. The following table taken from her figures shows the percentage changes of the main items.

	1852			1856			Increase
	£	s.	d.	£	s.	d.	Per cent
Bread	10	14	7½	21	19	2	100
Butter & cheese	9	1	8	10	15	4½	
Butcher's meat, bacon, etc.	22	5	7	36	8	7	
Fish, poultry, eggs	4	13	4½	7	2	2½	
Groceries	21	18	0	24	3	5	
Milk	5	9	8½	9	10	8	
Vegetables & fruit	8	7	0½	9	9	3½	
Total food	£82	10	0	£119	8	8½	45
Coals and wood	8	15	10	16	12	11	
Gas	5	11	6	6	16	11	
Washing	3	2	4	9	9	4½	204
Mangling		19	11½	2	12	3½	161
Total housekeeping	£100	19	7½	£154	10	2½	43
Wages	18	0	0	27	0	0	50
Dress	29	12	1	60	16	8½	106
Subscriptions, charity	19	3	7	26	15	4½	40
Medical attendance (inc. nurse, etc.)	16	18	0	18	7	0	9
Travelling & Books (inc. summer excur.)	31	3	2	52	12	8	69
Income tax	8	15	0	18	1	10	107
Insurance	13	3	8	35	10	4	169
Total	£237	15	1½	£393	14	1½	66

[1] See also *Economy for the Single and Married; or the Young Wife and Bachelor's Guide to Income and Expenditure . . . etc.* (n.d., British Museum, 1845). The proportions spent by the *married* on food were 70 per cent of £50 per annum, 68 per cent of £100, 44 per cent of £150, 50 per cent of £200, 45 per cent of £250, 41 per cent of £300, 48 per cent of £350, 50 per cent of £400, 44 per cent of £450, and 40 per cent of £500.

In reading this table it is important to bear a number of points in mind. In the first place, as the writer herself pointed out, 'food of all kinds was dearer in 1856 than in 1852'. Wood, in fact, has shown an estimated increase in *retail* prices of some 30 per cent for the two years (i.e. from 97 points to 126 on his scale; base year 1850=100).[1] Bread, in particular, was very sensitive, rising from 6·8d. to 10·8d. for a 4-lb. loaf in London,[2] an increase of 59 per cent. The great bulk of the 45 per cent increase in expenditure on food, therefore, was in response to the rise in prices; and if we allow 50 per cent for this, we obtain a total food bill of £91 17s. 5½d., a figure only 13 per cent over the £82 10s. of 1852. This, moreover, was for a household which had grown by the addition of a further servant and two children.

Secondly, although the rise in prices would have affected the other items too, the effect was probably not so drastic. In the case of washing and mangling, for example, most of the expense arose from the purchase of labour power; and as the table shows that the wage per head of domestic servants did not increase over the two years, it would not be unfair to assume that the increase of 204 per cent and 161 per cent respectively for the two items did represent a real extension in the amount of washing done. The family, it is true, had grown in size, from five to eight, with the employment of another servant and the birth of two children who would perhaps require more washing than the average done for them; yet even when these points are borne in mind, it does look as if Walsh's general thesis is correct. A rise in income was followed by a disproportionately large increase in expenditure on washing and mangling. Part of the middle-class pattern of the standard of living was formed of a general attitude towards cleanliness and the wearing of frequently washed linen.

This table, further, diverges from the general pattern in two important ways. Rent and taxes were not included for the very good reason that a large house was provided for them by the

[1] In W. T. Layton and G. Crowther: *An Introduction to the Study of Prices* (3rd ed. 1938). Appendix E, Table 1, p. 273, col. 3.
[2] Board of Trade Return to the House of Commons, November 1912, p. 3. (*Parliamentary Papers*, 1912–13, Vol. 93.)

company for which the husband worked; and they deliberately abstained from wine and spirits in order to spend more on the summer excursion. On the other hand, the employment of three servants at that range of income was probably excessive,[1] although since they lived out of London the wage rates were low. It is, therefore, possible that the item 'Travelling and books' played a greater part in this household than was usual, and certainly the disproportionate increase in insurance over the four years suggests a thoughtful family with an eye to the future. If, however, we ignore all these considerations and take the figures as they stand, we still find that with an increase in general expenditure there took place a fall in the proportion spent on food (from 34 per cent to 30 per cent) and on housekeeping generally (from 42 per cent to 39 per cent) which bears out the general argument.

Walsh's housekeeping table for 1873 follows a pattern similar to that in his 1857 table.

Housekeeping items	£1,500	£750	£350	£150
Butcher's meat and bacon	110	60	50	30
Fish and poultry	45	15	12	—
Bread	25	20	18	12
Milk, butter and cheese	25	22	20	10
Grocery	35	28	22	10
Italian goods	10	7	5	—
Greengrocery	25	15	12	8
Beer	25	15	12	8
Wine and spirits	80	20	10	1
Coals	40	25	20	10
Chandlery	20	10	9	3
Washing	50	40	30	3
Repairs and extras	65	18	—	—
	£555	£295	£220	£95

From this table we can obtain the following set of percentages of the total housekeeping spent on each item.

[1] See, for example, 'The Greatest Social Evil' in *Tait's Edinburgh Magazine*, February 1858, p. 113.

	£1,000 Per cent	£750 Per cent	£350 Per cent	£150 Per cent
Butcher's meat and bacon	19·8	20·3	22·7	31·6
Fish and poultry	8·1	5·1	5·5	—
Bread	4·5	6·8	8·2	12·6
Milk, butter and cheese	4·5	7·5	9·1	10·5
Grocery	6·4	9·5	10·0	10·5
Italian goods	1·8	2·3	2·3	—
Greengrocery	4·5	5·1	5·5	8·4
Beer	4·5	5·1	5·5	8·4
Wine and spirits	14·4	6·8	4·5	1·1
Coals	7·2	8·5	9·1	10·5
Chandlery	3·6	3·4	4·1	3·2
Washing	9·0	13·6	13·6	3·2
Repairs and extras	11·7	6·1	—	—
	99·9	100·1	100·1	100·0

The pattern of this table is very similar to that of 1857, so that the really striking fact is the general increase all round, about 50 per cent over fifteen years. This is surprising in view of the fact that Wood's retail prices rose from 119 to 122 points only (+3 per cent) for the same period; and even if we take the mean of his eight years up to 1857 and compare that with the similar period up to 1873 in order to allow for yearly fluctuations, the increase works out to only 5 per cent (112 points to 117).[1] Yet there can be little doubt that the members of the middle classes in the early seventies *felt* that the cost of living had been rising considerably over the period.

'The question of payment occupies now a large space in the columns of every journal,' stated the *British Medical Journal* on 10th August 1872, 'and the items of expenditure occupy a larger space than even before in the diary of every household. . . . It is difficult to see why the medical profession alone should consent to pay nearly 50 per cent more for all the necessaries of life than they did a generation ago . . . and should yet approve of an arrest of honoraria at the standard fixed long years ago when different rates of value were current.'[2]

[1] Layton and Crowther, *op. cit.*, p. 273, col. 3. Eight years only were taken because Wood's table does not begin until 1850.
[2] 'Medical Fees' in The *British Medical Journal*, 10th August 1872, pp. 169–70.

'Complaints about the increase in the cost of living have of late been rife in every quarter.' So began an article in *The Cornhill Magazine* in 1875,[1] and comparing a budget of the day with one of forty or fifty years previous, it came to the conclusion that as far as household expenses were concerned 'we should not, perhaps, be far from the mark if we were to reckon the loss in this department at from £30 to £50; that is to say, the son has to pay that annual sum extra in order to keep his table as well furnished as his father's.'[2] The *British Medical Journal* reckoned the increase between 1852–3 and 1872–3 as amounting to 34 per cent,[3] while a letter to the *Englishwoman's Review* thought that the cost of living had well-nigh doubled in the previous fifty years.[4]

Some writers, however, admitted a change of standards over the period. 'Our parents, and certainly our grandparents, lived on half our means with nearly the same amount of comfort. And yet the positive price of the necessaries, certainly of the luxuries of life, has not increased. . . . Our baths and more frequent changes of linen . . . cost money.'[5] This was in 1861. In 1873 the cause was laid at the door of 'Keeping Up Appearances'.[6]

'It is a universal complaint, the substantial truth of which cannot be denied', wrote W. R. Greg in 1875, 'that life to a vast proportion of the middle classes is becoming more difficult and more costly. Without entering on any controvertible points, there are certain things which we all know, and most of us feel. Increased riches among high and low has brought increased demand for most articles, and in those articles consumption has overtaken production, and many of those are articles of prime necessity. Some of these can be brought from abroad, and the price of them has not, therefore, risen in proportion, if at all. But meat and all farm produce has risen so as to cause serious

---

[1] 'The Cost of Living' in *The Cornhill Magazine*, April 1875, p. 412.
[2] *Ibid.*, p. 417.
[3] The *British Medical Journal*, 16th May 1874, p. 656.
[4] The *Englishwoman's Review*, February 1876, p. 94
[5] 'High Living with Low Means' in *The Family Friend*, May 1861.
[6] G. Smith: 'Mr. Greg on Culpable Luxury' in *The Contemporary Review*, June 1873.

inconvenience in most families, and actual privation in many. House-rent, and servants' wages, and servants' maintenance, have also risen most materially. With the general advance on the wages of labour in all trades, on which we have been congratulating the country, the cost of most articles into which labour enters largely as an element has been materially enhanced; and we have to pay more than we used to do for every job we want done. Probably, on the whole, we are within the mark if we say that, among average middle-class families, the actual cost of living is 25 per cent higher than it was twenty-five years ago.

'But this is only half the story. Owing to the increasing wealth of the wealthy, and the increasing numbers who every year step into the wealthier class, *the style of living* as well as the cost of necessaries and comforts of which 'living' consists, has advanced in an extraordinary ratio; and however frugal, however unostentatious, however rational we may be, however resolute to live as we think we ought, and not as others do around us, it is, as we shall find, simply *impossible* not to be influenced by their example and to fall into their ways, unless we are content either to live in remote districts or in an isolated fashion. The result is that we need many things that our fathers did not, and that for each of these many things we must pay more. Even where prices are lower, quantities are increased. Locomotion is cheaper; but every middle-class family travels far more than formerly. Wine and tea cost less, but we habitually consume more of each.'[1]

Walsh himself noted increases in the prices of meat and coal in excess of the *decreases* in groceries and bread;[2] yet he allowed an expenditure on the last two items which was well above the 1857 figure; groceries being up by 33 per cent, 40 per cent,

---

[1] W. R. Greg: 'Life at High Pressure' in *The Contemporary Review*, March 1875, p. 633. The italics were in the original.

[2] J. H. Walsh: *A Manual of Domestic Economy* (new ed., 1873), p. iii. See also W. T. Layton and G. Crowther: *An Introduction to the Study of Prices* (3rd ed., 1938). Table on p. 75. The price of rice fell by 12 per cent between 1846–50 and 1871–5. Sugar fell by 7 per cent, and flour by 3 per cent. Tea rose by 25 per cent, bacon by 25 per cent, mutton by 34 per cent, butter by 40 per cent, beef by 55 per cent, coal by 100 per cent and coffee by 100 per cent during the same period.

33 per cent, and 25 per cent for each of his four classes, reading them in descending order left to right in terms of income, and bread being up by 25 per cent, 25 per cent, 29 per cent, and 20 per cent. As we shall see later, certain other non-food items were very significant in the general rise of the cost of living for the middle classes between 1850 and 1875; but it is clear that an increased expenditure on food was one of the main features, an increased expenditure on food, that is, *greater* than what was in fact required by the rise in prices.

One factor of importance in this respect was the extension of the habit of dining well. 'Gentlemen must have their sumptuous dinners well served, and expensive wines, or they raise the piteous cry they have "nothing to eat".'[1] *Mrs. Beeton* first appeared in 1861, and although cookery books and housekeeping books with sections on food and feeding had appeared before, it is noticeable that from about this time all writers devoted a growing amount of space to the main meal of the day. Wines of all kinds were falling in price and enthusiasts prophesied the day when they would become the normal accompaniment of all evening dining.[2] Certainly the Cobden treaty to encourage the lighter French vintages had a marked effect on the consumption of light wines in the United Kingdom. The annual average figure rose from 6,600,000 gallons in 1858–60, to over 14,000,000 in 1882–4, while the imports of wine per head of population[3] increased by about 200 per cent. They thus became an integral part of the 'little dinners' so marked a feature of the seventies. One writer to the *Englishwoman's Domestic Magazine* was politely but firmly told that the reason why she could not make ends meet was because these cost too much;[4] and another correspondent, who was careful to point out that she rarely had company, put her dinners as costing 16s. per head 'including wine, always good', which compared with her usual expenditure of 14s. 2d. per day for *all* food items,

[1] *Meliora: a Quarterly Review of Social Science*, Vol. 3, 1861, p. 105.
[2] B. J. Mackei: 'Pure Wine versus Port and Sherry' in *The Family Friend*, August, 1866.
[3] M. Bateson: 'Social Life', Ch. 24 of H. D. Traill and J. S. Mann, *Social England* (1897).
[4] Editor's subscript to a letter from 'Housekeeper' in The *Englishwoman's Domestic Magazine*, October 1871, p. 254.

including claret and light wines at dinner, for a family of four adults, three young children and three servants.[1]

In all, therefore, it can be maintained that these twenty years from about the middle of the nineteenth century onwards were a period in which great changes took place in the pattern of middle-class expenditure on food and drink, and on household requirements generally. Although prices rose by only 5 per cent the expansion in standards required an additional outlay of 50 per cent if status was not to be lost. Assuming that these domestic items took up somewhere between 40 per cent and 55 per cent of the income, it is clear that a family whose receipts increased by less than 20 per cent over the period, all other things remaining unchanged, would have been hard pressed to live up to the new levels forced upon it. In general terms, it would seem that proportionately more money was needed to rise in the social scale of domestic consumption in the seventies than had been needed in the fifties; although we have still to look at other items of expenditure, servants' wages, clothes, etc., before this conclusion can be regarded as more than tentative.

[1] See Appendix II: A Middle-class Housewife of the Early Seventies, p. 211.

CHAPTER V

Domestic Assistance

THE 1832 edition of *A New System of Practical Domestic Economy* set out amongst its principles of outlay for 'Gentlemen', 22 per cent for servants and equipage, further subdivided into 10 per cent for horses and carriages, 8 per cent for male domestics, and 4 per cent for females. This, however, was for the income range £1,000–£5,000 per annum; and we have to ask ourselves whether, accepting this formula as a useful one from which to start, we can apply it to middle-class families living on a much lower scale. Should we, in fact, be justified, as B. Seebohm Rowntree obviously thought himself justified in his first survey of York,[1] in taking the keeping or not keeping of domestic servants as marking the division between the working classes and those of a higher social scale?

There can be no doubt about the answer in so far as the handbooks of domestic economy for the middle classes are taken as our guide. All, almost without exception, were unanimous in recording a certain level of income below which no servant could be kept. This did not mean, of course, that all domestic assistance was out of the question, for there would always be some small part of current income which could be set aside for the purpose. What was considered impossible was the regular employment of domestic servants who were 'kept', that is to say, who required not only wages but board.

Nevertheless, Rowntree's method of division is useful in a sense, for it serves to stress the difference in levels of aspiration, so that we might well describe the nineteenth-century middle-class *attitude* as being typically one in which the keeping of domestic servants played a major part. The real mark of differ-

[1] B. S. Rowntree: *Poverty: a Study of Town Life* (1902), p. 14.

ence between the middle-class man and woman and those who were considered socially inferior was an outlook of mind which was not content until at least one servant could be afforded to wait upon them. Above this level the number of servants could be used as a rough index of gradations *within* all ranks of the socially superior; and we are even told of one lady who took this status-function of servants so far as to use it for regulating the precedence of her guests at table, placing them according to the numbers of servants they kept.[1]

This attitude of mind was displayed even in the various articles and chapters in books, addressed to 'young mistresses' on the danger of newly wedded wives using up too large a part of their resources on servants' wages. 'Your parents may have been prosperous, and possessed sufficient means to justify their keeping many servants; but that does not make it either necessary or right that you should do the same.'[2] Here the emphasis was laid upon the number of servants that ought to be kept, but it was always taken for granted that some, or at least one, were essential to middle-class well-being. Indeed, it was not until the end of the century, that, puzzled by the unwillingness of working-class girls to enter domestic service, a few writers began tentatively to suggest that perhaps they could be done without altogether, since they were after all a 'serious' item in housekeeping;[3] but even so the alternative of daily helps at 3s. per week was not overlooked.[4]

From the point of view of this study, therefore, the cost of domestic assistance was important for the middle-class budget, and this involved in the main both wages and board. In the case of the latter item, as we have seen, although standards rose considerably between the fifties and the seventies, prices rose hardly at all. It is to be expected on that account that estimates of the cost of servants' board varied little over the twenty years. Walsh, for example, reckoned the cost of maintenance for female servants at £20–£25 in 1857[5] and this figure remained un-

[1] E. A. M. Lewis: 'A Reformation of Domestic Service' in *The Nineteenth Century*, January 1893, p. 130.

[2] 'A Word to Young Mistresses' in *The Family Friend*, December 1861, p. 334.

[3] R. ff. Blake: *The Greatest Temptation in the World to Man* (5th ed., 1894), p. 45.

[4] Blake, *op. cit.*, p. 46 and J. E. Panton: *Leaves from a Housekeeper's Book* (1914), p. 67.

[5] J. H. Walsh: *A Manual of Domestic Economy* (1857), p. 226.

changed in 1873.[1] Other writers made different estimates but none were widely divergent from his. Thus Philp gave £30 as the lowest all-round figure in 1855, and again in 1860, while the letter to the *Englishwoman's Domestic Magazine* put it as between £25 and £30 in 1871.[2]

Nevertheless, the real figure is not easy to come by because of a very personal factor which ought somehow to be taken into consideration. The relationship between servants and mistresses was a very intimate one in many ways, leading to possibly wide divergencies in cost according to the kind of rule exercised by the employers. From the record of many a nineteenth-century diary, in fact, we might infer a continuous struggle of will between the middle-class housewife and her servants, mainly over the question of waste in the kitchen[3] and we do know of examples of clashes of opinion between members of the middle class themselves over the extent of indulgence which ought to be allowed to their domestics.[4] The norm, however, is not so difficult to fix. Generally speaking, servants were expected to consume the plainer kinds of food. Not for them were there eggs, fish, or ham for breakfast,[5] but coffee and bread and butter. Dinner might consist of meat and pudding and perhaps two vegetables, with beer to wash it down, but certainly the more subtle and expensive kinds of dishes were never expected to appear on their dining-table. Supper consisted of bread and cheese and beer.[6] Thus, the expenses of wine, Italian goods, and so forth, which we have seen increasing as incomes increased, were not the result of employing more servants. 'Some servants appear to live on air,' wrote Walsh, 'but these are rare exceptions; the general run will average about what I have

[1] J. H. Walsh: *A Manual of Domestic Economy* (2nd ed., 1873), p. 224.
[2] R. K. Philp: *The Practical Housewife, forming a complete encyclopaedia of Domestic Economy* (1855), p. 8. Rev. ed. (1860), p. 10. For the letter from Mrs. S., see Appendix II to this book, A Middle-class Housewife of the Early Seventies, p. 211.
[3] See Louisa Bain's diary in J. S. Bain: *A Bookseller Looks Back* (1940).
[4] See F. M. Redgrave: *Richard Redgrave, a Memoir, compiled from his Diary* (1891). Entry for 12th May 1859: '. . . I hear continually of his servants sitting down to salmon, turkey, goose, etc. . . .' and notice Mr. Sheepshanks's (*sic*) objections, pp. 214–15.
[5] Reply to a letter in the *Englishwoman's Domestic Magazine*, December 1871, p. 381.
[6] See Mrs. S's housekeeping in Appendix II: A Middle-class Housewife of the Early Seventies, p. 211.

fixed as the ordinary cost—in such families as those which are here included. The maid-of-all-work is generally supposed to live on little more than the leavings of the table, but in bread and meat alone she must still make a considerable difference.'[1] Taking it all in all, therefore, we shall not be far wrong if we take the cost of a domestic servant to have been about 10s. per week at the middle of the century, and this figure did not change much over the next twenty years.

There does appear, however, an important exception to this conclusion. By 1873, for example, we find Walsh becoming very outspoken on the subject of *male* domestics. In 1857 he had reckoned their maintenance at £30 a year each.[2] Now he wrote:

'There is no doubt that a man-servant in the house is an expensive luxury, adding according to my experience, at least £50 or £60 to the kitchen expenses, and leading to various kinds of annoyance in addition. Those who go much into society, either in London or the country, are, however, almost compelled to inflict this nuisance on themselves, as it is considered by many people one of the tests of their position, and if it is not carried out, they will find themselves excluded from the visiting lists of people with whom they may desire to associate on equal terms. If, however, they are beyond the reach of such considerations, it will be found that a great saving will be effected, and much more comfort secured by the substitution of a good parlour-maid for the man-servant.'[3]

This, it would seem, was indicative of some kind of reaction against the employment of male indoor servants as reflected in the census returns over this period; but what the cause was we have no idea. Indeed, it is not really significant for our purpose, for if middle-class employers were replacing male servants by females in accordance with Walsh's advice, the effect on their budgets would have been to keep board expenses stable over the period and that is all we need to know.

It is, therefore, to the wages bill that we must turn if we wish to see the cost of domestic assistance working itself out. Here there was a definite income range differential laid down in the

---

[1] J. H. Walsh: *A Manual of Domestic Economy* (1857), p. 226.
[2] *Ibid.*, p. 226.   [3] *Ibid.* (2nd ed., 1873), p. 224.

manuals. Thus *A New System of Practical Domestic Economy* departed from its 12 per cent servants' rule in precisely the opposite way from that in which it departed from its 26 per cent provision rule, which we saw was in conformity with Engel's law.[1] That is to say, an increase in income was to be followed by a disproportionate *increase* in expenditure on servants' wages.

Income £	Servants	Wages Bill £ s. d.			Per cent of income
150	Occasional charing	3	0	0	2
200	One maid	9	10	0	5
250	One maid	16	0	0	6
300	Two maids	21	0	0	7
400	Two maids and occasional groom	32	18	0	8
500	One man, two maids	61	4	0	12*
600	One man, two maids	58	4	0	10
700	One man, three maids	81	4	0	11

(* This income range involved the employment of a man-servant living out of the house whose wages therefore were higher because he did not receive board.)[2]

Other writers followed a similar pattern:

1845[3]

Income £	Wages Bill £ s. d.			Per cent of Income
100	4	0	0	4
150	6	10	0	4
200	10	0	0	5
250	15	0	0	6
300	24	0	0	8
400	24	0	0	6
500	74	0	0	15

1857[4]

Income £	Wages Bill £ s. d.			Per cent of Income
100	5	0	0	5
250	18	15	0	7
500	62	10	0	12
1,000	125	0	0	12

[1] See above, p. 59.
[2] *A New System of Practical Domestic Economy* (3rd ed., 1823), Appendix of Estimates of Household Expenses, Pt. 2.
[3] *Economy for the Single and Married* (1845) *passim*.
[4] J. H. Walsh, *op. cit.* (1857), p. 606.

These percentages should not be regarded as having operated quite so strictly as the figures would suggest. They have been calculated here mainly to show the trend which the general tone of the books on domestic economy confirms.

'An income of £1,000, clear of all other expenditure, and devoted solely to housekeeping and rental, will afford the following servants,' wrote Walsh in 1857,[1] '1st, a butler, or manservant out of livery; 2nd, a coachman or groom; 3rd, one or two house-maids; 4th, a cook; 5th, a lady's maid, or a nursery maid, or sometimes both. . . . The income No. 2 (this was his £500 a year class) will only afford three servants, viz. 1st, a page, or a general manservant, or a parlourmaid; 2nd, a housemaid; and 3rd, a cook. This provides also for the keeping of a single horse or pony and carriage. If, however, the family is a large one, a young lady's maid must be kept for the purpose of making their dresses at home, and in that case a horse cannot be afforded. . . . The income No. 3 (his £250 a year class) will not allow even of the above domestics, and a maid-of-all-work must be the means of doing what is required, aided in some cases by a girl, or in others, by the younger members of the family. . . . The income No. 4 (his £100 a year class) is barely sufficient to provide what is required for the family in the shape of lodging, food and raiment, and therefore no servant can be kept, or, at all events, only such a young girl as it is quite useless here to allude to.'

One of the difficulties here arises from the fact that the wage rates themselves for certain domestic servants covered quite a wide range. The butler, for example, in a nobleman's family received a very high salary, according to his responsibilities, and knowledge of his duties 'including such an acquaintance with the wine trade as would fit him to conduct the business of a wine merchant',[2] but for Walsh's set of incomes, although a butler by name, he was 'really a man-servant-of-all-work, often undertaking an immense number of duties, from cleaning shoes

[1] *Ibid.* (1857), p. 210. See also the 2nd ed. (1873), p. 221. Here the incomes are raised to £1,500, £750, £350, and £150. Compare T. Webster: *An Encyclopaedia of Domestic Economy, comprising such subjects as are most immediately connected with House-keeping* (1844), pp. 330–1.
[2] J. H. Walsh, *op. cit* (1857), p. 221.

and knives and forks up to the cellar management'. His wages, therefore, ranged from £30 to £45 only (£50 in 1873);[1] or from £25 to £50 on Mrs. Beeton's scale where £40 to £80 was allowed for a 'house-steward'.[2]

There was, nevertheless, an understood pattern in building up a household of domestic servants. Beginning with a girl or an occasional char to do daily work, the first really permanent servant, living in, was the general servant or maid-of-all-work, assisted by a young girl occasionally. Her wages ranged from £9–£14 in 1861.[3] At £300 a year an extra servant was considered possible, a nursemaid, according to Mrs. Beeton;[4] but clearly where there were no children, another housemaid (£8 to £12) took her place. The next step was to add a cook.[5] Here the range of incomes was quite considerable, £14 to £30, according to Mrs. Beeton,[6] and any attempt to arrive at an average figure of wages now begins to look very strained. With these three servants, cook, parlour-maid and housemaid, or cook, housemaid and nursemaid, a household was considered complete in all its functions.[7] Further extensions were merely variations on this theme.

'The cook obtains the assistance of a kitchen-maid, and as the kitchen-maid rises into an under-cook, a scullery-maid becomes necessary to do the dirtiest work. Beyond this division development cannot go in the kitchen department, except in having two or more cooks and a proportionate number of underlings, unless there is added a "hall boy", a sort of servants' servant. The parlourmaid's work is the same as that undertaken in grander establishments by the butler and his assistants; she has the care of plate and glass and the place where she works is

[1] J. H. Walsh, *op. cit.* (2nd ed., 1873), p. 223.
[2] I. W. Beeton: *The Book of Household Management* (1861), p. 8.
[3] *Ibid.*, p. 8.
[4] *Ibid.*, p. 8.
[5] Mrs. Pedley: *Practical Housekeeping, or the Duties of a Housewife* (1867), Chs. 25 and 26.
[6] I. W. Beeton, *op. cit.* (1861), p. 8.
[7] Even where there were no servants the Housewifery Association divided domestic work into 'parlourmaid's work', 'housemaid's work', and 'kitchen work'. See 'Domestic Work' in the May 1890 issue of *Little Women*, the quarterly organ of the Association, p. 34–35.

always called the pantry. As to housemaids, there is no development except that where there are several they are classed as
upper and under. In the same way, the nursery maid is in effect
the same for all classes. The essential wants of a baby or of
young children are always alike, and are supplied in much the
same way by rich and poor. The mother plays a part in every
nursery more or less important, rather according to her character than to her place in the social scale.'[1]

The lady's-maid, however, was to be found only in wealthy
households.

At the top end of the scale, therefore, there existed a veritable
army of servants waiting on one another and on the family in
the homes of the aristocracy. 'The premises constituted a settlement as large as a small village,' wrote Layton in 1908, 'carrying coals, making up fires and attending to the vast number of
candles and lamps required in such houses necessitated the
employment of several footmen. Every department was under
the general supervision, as regards the men, of the house
steward, and of the women, the housekeeper.'[2]

On the other hand, at the bottom end of the scale, since a
household to be complete required *three* female servants, there
was a definite pattern of anticipation laid down involving the
expenditure of some £30 to £60 per annum on domestic service
alone; that is to say, on the kinds of scale set out above, involving an annual income of some £400 to £600. A middle-class
household, therefore, could not be regarded as complete until
its income was somewhere in this range, enabling it to afford
the *minimum* of complete domestic service. £300 a year, looked
at from this point of view, was clearly insufficient, and so was
any figure below it. 'Why should a young couple be content to
live on £200 a year!' exclaimed the *Englishwoman's Domestic
Magazine* in its attack on Mrs. Warren, 'instead of trying by
every mode of honourable industry open to them, to double at
least, their income?' A household of 'gentility', which was the
ultimate aim, was not possible where the womenfolk were too

[1] C. Booth and J. Argyle: 'Domestic Household Service' in C. Booth ed.: *Life and Labour of the People in London* (1896) Vol. 8, Pt. 2, Ch. 1, p. 218.
[2] W. T. Layton: 'Changes in the Wages of Domestic Servants during Fifty Years' in the *Journal of the Royal Statistical Society*, September 1908, p. 514.

worn out with housework to give that necessary touch to personal toilet and to the layout of the meal table.[1] To manage on an income of £200 or even £250 with one woman-servant and one nursery-girl to look after the infant meant that the housewife must be 'a head nurse or head housemaid only without wages'.[2]

This increase in the number of servants involved, furthermore, a disproportionate increase in the wages bill, for as has been mentioned already, there was a range of wages for every class of labour and it does appear that an increase in staff involved paying more money for each of the specialists. This is apparent in the books on household economy referred to above; and for the end of the century we have the following table from the Labour Department of the Board of Trade which clearly shows the situation.[3]

AVERAGE AGES AND WAGES

Households by number of servants	London Ages	Wages £ s. d.			England and Wales Ages	Wages £ s. d.		
1	25·2	14	9	0	23·1	13	2	0
2	25·7	16	6	0	25·9	15	9	0
3	27·5	18	8	0	27·9	17	8	0
4	28·2	20	7	0	27·2	18	4	0
5	28·0	21	3	0	27·5	19	1	0
6	28·5	24	4	0	28·6	20	3	0
More than 6	28·9	25	3	0	28·2	23	2	0

This was partly caused by the employment of male servants in the larger and richer households, and partly, as is obvious from the table, by the employment of older servants. Indeed the importance of the age of the servants as a factor in cost can be seen from the following table.[4]

[1] 'Marriage' in the *Englishwoman's Domestic Magazine*, March 1865.
[2] Letter from 'A Bad Housekeeper' to *The Times*, 28th January 1858.
[3] Report by Miss Collet on 'The Money Wages of Indoor Domestic Servants 1899' (*Parliamentary Papers*, 1899, Vol. 42, p. 12). The information was collected between 1894 and 1898. All mean figures throughout except where otherwise indicated.
[4] *Ibid.*, p. 11.

Age	London			England and Wales		
	£	s.	d.	£	s.	d.
Under 16	7	9	0	7	1	0
16	9	3	0	9	0	0
17	10	6	0	10	6	0
18	12	8	0	12	2	0
19	14	1	0	12	7	0
20	15	7	0	14	4	0
21–	17	5	0	16	5	0
25–	20	6	0	19	5	0
30–	23	2	0	21	5	0
35–	27	0	0	23	1	0
40–	27	8	0	24	7	0

This doubtless resulted from the promotion to more specialized posts as the domestic servant became older and more experienced. There is no doubt that age and specialization (and wage rates) were closely linked.

	By Class of Work (Modal Age)[1]					
Class of Work	*Age*	*London Wages*			*England and Wales*		
		£	s.	d.	£	s.	d.
Between maid	19	12	4	0	10	7	0
Scullery maid	19	13	7	0	13	0	0
Kitchenmaid	20	16	6	0	15	0	0
Nurse-housemaid	21	14	9	0	16	0	0
General	21	14	9	0	14	6	0
Housemaid	25	17	5	0	16	2	0
Nurse	25	21	0	0	20	1	0
Parlourmaid	25	22	2	0	20	6	0
Laundrymaid	25	27	3	0	23	6	0
Cook	25	21	8	0	20	2	0
Lady's maid	30	28	1	0	24	7	0
Cook-housekeeper	40	41	6	0	35	6	0
Housekeeper	40	34	3	0	52	2	0

It would appear from these figures, therefore, that we are entitled to claim that a growth of the household as measured by the number of servants employed, involved a greater than proportionate increase of expenditure on domestic assistance because it entailed the employment of more expensive forms of

[1] *Ibid.*, p. 13. Age Z=Modal Age=Most frequently stated age. The strange variation in wages of cook-housekeepers and housekeepers when London is compared with England and Wales as a whole is not explained in the Report. It is probably due, however, mainly to a difference in terminology in the different parts of the country.

labour, the result of specialization by older servants. As she was usually younger and less experienced than her fellow workers, the first servant to be taken on, the general, was unable to obtain the higher rates demanded by the specialized house-maid, parlourmaid, laundrymaid or cook. The regularly ac-cepted pattern of growth, moreover, required that the house-hold should not become larger merely through a multiplication of general servants. The second employee should be a house-maid, a parlourmaid or a nurse, and the third should be a cook. Hence, in so far as the expansion of the household was a function of increased income, it led automatically to the kind of ex-penditure differential worked out from the domestic manuals above, viz. a disproportionate increase of expenditure on dom-estic service; but this would not have arisen had the employ-ment of domestic assistance not played such a major role in the norm of middle-class family life. The importance of the domestic servant in the problem with which we are most nearly concerned cannot be over-emphasized.

It has been necessary, in order to make this perfectly clear, to pass beyond the period 1850–70 and to examine in some detail the report by Miss Collet, published in 1899, since her work was the first to give any detailed and reliable information about the wages of domestic servants in the nineteenth century. An attempt was made, apparently without much success, to collect some statistics in 1886[1], but otherwise very little interest was shown in the subject until 1908 when W. T. Layton obtained sets of figures from the wages books of Lady Bateman's family and compared them with rates for jobs advertised in *The Times* and the *Christian World*. For our purpose the following figures, taken from Layton are of some interest.[2]

Lady Bateman's Servants

Period	Cooks			Housemaids			Nursemaids		
	£	s.	d.	£	s.	d.	£	s.	d.
1848–1852	16	6	0	11	13	0	12	0	0
1853–1857	14	12	0	12	0	0	12	0	0
1858–1862	15	14	0	12	4	0	12	0	0
1863–1867	18	4	0	12	0	0	12	6	0
1868–1872	18	4	0	12	0	0	12	6	0

[1] J. H. Clapham: *An Economic History of Modern Britain: Free Trade and Steel, 1850–1866* (1932), p. 464 n.   [2] W. T. Layton, *op. cit.*

Domestic Assistance

The Times Advertisements

Period	Cooks			Housemaids			Nursemaids		
	£	s.	d.	£	s.	d.	£	s.	d.
1848–1852	15	0	0	11	0	0	11	0	0
1858–1862	16	0	0	12	13	4	12	10	0
1868–1872	19	6	8	14	2	6	17	2	6

These provide the following sets of index numbers (1848–52 =100) for comparison, where it is seen that the Bateman household increases lagged behind what would appear to have been the general wage trend of servants in upper-class homes.

Period	Cooks		Housemaids		Nursemaids	
	Bateman	'Times'	Bateman	'Times'	Bateman	'Times'
1848–1852	100	100	100	100	100	100
1853–1857	90	—	103	—	100	—
1858–1862	91	107	103	115	100	114
1863–1867	112	—	103	—	102	—
1868–1872	112	129	103	128	102	156

These figures in turn may be compared with the following indices calculated from Wood's index of women's wages for roughly the same dates.[1]

Period	Textiles	Others
1850	100	100
1855	100	105
1860	109	116
1863 and 1866 (mean)	122	122
1870	135	157

As was to be expected, the lag of the Bateman household behind the general movement of domestic wages appears also as a lag behind the movement of textile and other (non-domestic) wage rates. There was, on the whole, a slight lag too in *The Times*' rates behind the others, except for nurse-maids in 1868–72, and for housemaids and nurse-maids compared with textile workers for 1858–62. In general, however, there was a fair amount of agreement of changes in domestic workers' wages with industrial wages. Over the period 1850 to 1870, the

[1] G. H. Wood: 'The Course of Women's Wages during the Nineteenth Century', Appendix A to B. L. Hutchins and A. Harrison: *A History of Factory Legislation*, (1903), p. 278.

middle-class household could not have been faced with more than a 30 per cent rise in the cost of domestic assistance, at least in so far as female servants were concerned. Allowing, therefore, some 10 per cent of income for this purpose at the beginning of the period, 13 per cent would have been necessary at the end, to cover the rise in wages alone. The complaint that the increases in wages ate up a large part of the middle-class income does not appear to have much foundation in fact.

What was true of female domestic wage rates also seems to have been true for males. In Lady Bateman's wage books Layton found the following wages paid to *indoor* man-servants.

	£	s.	d.
1858–1862	16	8	0
1863–1867	18	0	0
1868–1872	18	10	0

We have no comparable figures from any other source. These, however, provide the following indices, compared with Wood's wage-rate indices to show the lag behind the general trend.[1]

	Bateman	Wood
1858–1862	100	100
1863–1867	110	130
1868–1872	114	120

The 30 per cent rise in the wages of domestic servants allowed for above from a scrutiny of the movement of female wage rates would appear to err on the side of generosity.

There can be no doubt, however, that the middle class felt the cost of domestic assistance to be rising during the period. By 1875 Greg, it will be remembered, thought that servants' wages had risen 'most materially'[2] and even earlier there were complaints to the same effect. In fact, Lord Shaftesbury, at a meeting on 'Domestic Service' in London, maintained, in 1863, that it was the increase in the numbers of people who could afford to keep servants that was the real cause of the trouble, leading to an ever-increasing burden on the family income and

[1] The indices given here are from the means for the five years calculated from G. H. Wood: 'Real Wages and the Standard of Comfort since 1850', in the *Journal of the Royal Statistical Society*, March 1909, Appendix.
[2] See p. 67.

Domestic Assistance

to independence in the servants themselves.[1] Certainly the census figures showed a tremendous increase in the number of servants employed. In this we are fortunate that the three years 1851, 1861 and 1871 are strictly comparable in this respect, for although the numbers each time are swollen by the inclusion of 'retired' servants among the 'occupied', it is unlikely that the interconsal *increases* are much affected by this peculiarity of classification.

Domestic Servants (England and Wales)[2]

Females	1851	1861	1871
General servants	575,162	644,271	780,040
Housekeepers	46,648	66,406	140,836
Cooks	44,009	77,822	93,067
Housemaids	49,885	102,462	110,505
Nursemaids	35,937	67,785	75,491
Laundrymaids	—	4,040	4,538
Total	751,641	962,786	1,204,477

This table provides the following percentages:

Increases

	1851–1861 Per cent	1861–1871 Per cent	1851–1871 Per cent
General servants	12·0	21·1	35·6
Housekeepers	42·4	112·1	201·9
Cooks	76·8	19·6	111·5
Housemaids	105·9	7·8	121·5
Nursemaids	88·6	11·4	110·1
Laundrymaids	—	12·3	—
Total	28·1	29·3	56·6

For the same periods the total population increased as follows:[3]

1851–1861 Per cent	1861–1871 Per cent	1851–1871 Per Cent
11·9	13·2	26·7

[1] Reported in the *British Mother's Journal and Domestic Magazine*, August 1863.

[2] See *Census of Great Britain, 1851*, Tables 2, Vol. 1, Table 25. *Census of England and Wales, 1861*, Vol. 2. Summary tables xix and xx. *Census of England and Wales, 1871*, Vol. 3. Summary tables xviii and xix.

[3] *Census of England and Wales, 1951*, Preliminary Report, Pt. 3, Table 1, p. 1.

Female domestic servants are thus seen to have been increasing at a rate more than double that for the population as a whole, but this comparison is apt to be misleading, because it does not take into consideration the age structure of the population. What we really want to know is how rapidly the number of families employing domestic servants increased, and none of these figures help us much in that. The 1871 Census, however, did publish the numbers of separate occupiers over the preceding twenty years.[1]

1851	*1861*	*1871*
3,712,290	4,491,524	5,049,016

Taking these figures to represent the number of separate families, we have the following percentage increases over the period:

1851–1861	*1861–1871*	*1851–1871*
Per cent	Per cent	Per cent
21·0	12·4	36·0

These rates, although greater than those for the total population, are still less than for total domestic servants. They have, further, the added advantage that they show clearly that the period 1861–71 was the period of most rapid comparative increase. These ten years, in fact, were the ten years in which the middle-class households (here defined as the servant-employing households) most rapidly increased as compared with those in the rest of the community. At the same time, over the twenty years it was the most expensive form of domestic labour, nurse-maids, cooks, housemaids, and housekeepers, whose numbers grew at the most rapid pace. In so far as the census figures are an indication of effective demand as well as of supply, the clamour of the middle classes for domestic assistance of the more specialized variety may be taken as an indication of their rising standards in this respect. 'Wives and daughters at home do now less domestic work than their predecessors; hence the excessive demand for female servants and the consequent rise of wages', stated the Census of 1871;[2] but it forgot to add that

[1] *Census of England and Wales, 1871*, General Report, Vol. 4 (1873), Tables 9 and 11.
[2] *Ibid.*, p. xlii.

concomitant upon this development was an increase in the size of this leisure class of middle-class women than for the population as a whole, and that this disproportionate increase itself depended upon a disproportionate capacity to pay. The middle classes had grown in numbers and in wealth.

The situation with regard to the cost of domestic assistance between 1850 and 1870, therefore, was very similar to that for the pattern of household spending generally. Although wages rose by about 30 per cent, this in itself added only about 3 per cent of the total income to the proportion set apart to be spent under this heading. Hence the real cause of the expansion in the outlay on servants was a widening in the *normative* standard of life. In order to maintain the level of expenditure required of them, especially if they aspired to rise in the social scale, middle-class men and women were obliged to employ more expensive forms of labour in larger quantities. At the same time they were being called upon to drink wine regularly with their meals, to give little dinners occasionally, and to spend far larger sums of money on their household needs. When together with these developments there are taken into account those to be described in the next chapter, it may readily be seen that the middle-class standard of living, understood as a concept embracing the norm of ostentatious display, broadened considerably in the fifties and sixties of the nineteenth century. The range of satisfactions considered appropriate for civilized existence expanded at an alarming rate and involved all those who numbered themselves among the middle classes in habits of expenditure which they would not find it easy to give up should they be called upon to do so.

CHAPTER VI

The Paraphernalia of Gentility

THE seventeenth-century model of a middle-class household is considered to have been composed of a cook-maid, a chambermaid, and possibly a waiting-woman, a housemaid, a man-servant, and an odd-job boy; and although their names changed and their duties changed, these kinds of domestics were still in demand in the nineteenth century.[1] It is important to emphasize this, partly because in the last chapter the pattern described was confined almost exclusively to female servants, and partly because the Census figures are easily misread on this issue. During the period up to 1871, for example, the recorded number of indoor male servants actually showed a decline, but it should not be inferred from this that fewer male servants were employed, for the function of footman and groom were to some extent always interchangeable, and we must consider them together if we wish to understand the situation as a whole. At the same time, the function of the coachman, while not interchangeable with that of the footman, sometimes involved that of the groom. Indoor and outdoor male domestics, therefore, should strictly speaking, be dealt with as a single class, and although below the three categories are shown separately, it is the total alone which gives the most accurate impression of change.

	1851	*1861*	*1871*
Indoor general servants	74,323	62,076	68,369
Grooms	15,257	21,396	21,202
Coachmen	7,030	11,897	16,174
Total	96,610	95,369	105,745

[1] D. Marshall: *The English Domestic Servant in History* (1949), p. 7.

This table provides the following percentage changes:

	1851–1861	1861–1871	1851–1871
Indoor general servants	−16·5	+10·1	−8·0
Grooms	+40·2	−0·9	+39·0
Coachmen	+69·2	+36·0	+130·1
Totals	−1·3	+10·9	+9·5

The rates for the increase in the numbers of separate households, it will be recalled,[1] were 21·0 per cent, 12·4 per cent, and 36·0 per cent for the same three periods respectively, showing as a general pattern a falling-off in the number of male servants employed.

The numbers of gardeners have been left out of these calculations, partly because it is unlikely that there was much transference in occupation in their case, and partly because to some extent they did not represent a significant factor in terms of finance. As far as the books on domestic management are concerned, gardeners are always regarded as a probable source of income rather than as an item of expenditure. 'Espoir', for example, living in a country village, employed a kitchen gardener at £3 12s. a year, out of a total income of £100. This allowed him to cut down the household expenses for rent, wages, food, soap, coals, and wood to £73 10s. 6d, a ridiculously low figure for the kind of living described.[2]

The employment of male domestics, then, suffered a decline between 1851 and 1871 when the figures are compared with the growth of the number of households; but the number of coachmen, considered separately, increased at about three times the rate of that of households. This is important, because it represents an expansion in expenditure by the middle class on a carriage and horses, on what one writer has aptly named 'the paraphernalia of gentility'.[3] This represented quite a considerable outlay per year and was the symbol of the enjoyment of a higher rather than a lower middle-class income.

[1] See p. 84.

[2] 'Espoir': *How to Live on a Hundred a Year, Make a Good Appearance, and Save Money* (n.d., British Museum, 1874), p. 41.

[3] H. Hookham: *The Class Structure of Society as illustrated by the Novels of Jane Austen* (1938), unpublished prize essay in the Library of the London School of Economics, p. 43.

Thus, for those in receipt of £1,000 a year or more, *A New System of Practical Domestic Economy* allowed 10 per cent for horses and carriage alone, the wages of the coachmen and groom being met out of the 8 per cent set aside for male servants.[1] Below £1,000 a year, the possibility of expenditure on horses was not entirely dismissed, but £400 a year was the very minimum, and here the groom could only be employed occasionally. At £600 a year two horses were possible but the groom would also have to act as footman. At £750 a gig, or some other two-wheeled carriage came into the picture, so that from this author's point of view, £750 was the very minimum income at which a carriage could be kept. If, however, we take the detail costs as he gave them, and attempt an estimate of the upkeep of a one-horse carriage, a gig, say, or a tilbury or a chaise, employing an occasional groom to look after the animal, we get the following table:

	£	s.	d.
Food for one horse	24	10	0
Duty on horse	1	8	9
Shoeing, stable rent, etc.	8	3	3
Duty on gig	3	5	0
Repairs, wear and tear, etc.	8	15	0
Occasional groom	7	18	0
	£54	0	0

An income, therefore, of some £550–£600[2] was the very minimum practical standard for those who wished to keep their own carriage, although no doubt some economized in some other departments of expenditure to make a lower income afford a vehicle.

There were, of course, other ways of obtaining carriages than by outright purchase. They could be hired for a few weeks or a few months at a time, when the hirer could terminate the arrangement if the expense became too great; but this was not

---

[1] *A New System of Practical Domestic Economy* (3rd ed., 1823), Appendix of Practical Estimates, pp. 40, 43, 71 and 74.

[2] This figure is arrived at from the fact that the estimates allow for an expenditure on the equipage of £42 for an income of £400 and £65 17s. for an income of £600.

considered to be the best method by any means. It was 'at once the most expensive, and at the same time the most inconvenient, as they are generally inferior carriages, and charged at a high rate to make up for the uncertainty of their being occupied except at intervals'.[1] Kate Amberley paid £20 a month for such a carriage and a horse in 1866.[2] In any case, the wear and tear had to be met, as well as the cost of the horses.

Alternatively, carriages could be leased for a term of years, usually four or five, when the lessee paid only for accidents, all other running expenses, painting, repairs, etc., being met by the lessor. Here again, however, the cost of the horses and the groom had to be met, as well as the initial lease price which was usually about the same as what would have been required to purchase a carriage outright.[3] Obviously this part of the 'paraphernalia' of gentility was an expensive item of budgeting.

Nevertheless it was not always simply a question of ostentatious display which impelled members of the middle classes to keep a carriage. The doctors in particular, if they aspired to build up a lucrative practice, were almost duty bound to obtain one. As J. C. Jeaffreson wrote:

'In our own day an equipage of some sort is considered so necessary an appendage to a medical practitioner, that a physician without a carriage (or a fly that can pass muster for one) is looked upon with suspicion. He is marked down *mauvais sujet* in the same list with clergymen without duty, barristers without chambers, and gentlemen whose Irish tenantry obstinately refuse to keep them supplied with money. On the whole, the carriage system is a good one. It protects stair carpets from being soiled with muddy boots (a great thing) and bears cruelly on needy aspirants after professional employment (a yet greater thing! and one that manifestly ought to be the object of all professional etiquette). If the early struggles of many fashionable physicians were fully and courageously written, we should have some heart-rending stories of the screwing and scraping

[1] W. B. Adams: *English Pleasure Carriages* (1837), p. 246.
[2] B. and P. Russell: *The Amberley Papers* (1937), Vol. 1, p. 466. Kate Amberley's Journal, 7th February 1866.
[3] Adams: *op. cit.*, p. 247.

and shifts by which their first equipages were maintained. Who hasn't heard of the darling doctor who taught singing under mustachioed and bearded guise of an Italian count, at a young ladies' school at Clapham, in order that he might make his daily West-end calls between 3 p.m. and 6 p.m. in a well-built brougham drawn by a fiery steed from a livery stables? There was one noted case of a young physician who provided himself with the means of figuring in a brougham during the May-fair morning, by condescending to the garb and duties of a flyman during the hours of darkness. He used the same carriage at both periods of the four-and-twenty hours, lolling in it by daylight, and sitting on it by gaslight. The poor fellow, forgetting himself on one occasion, so far as to jump *in* when he ought to have jumped *on*, or jump *on* when he ought to have jumped *in*, he published his delicate secret to an unkind world. . . . It is a rash thing for a young man to start his carriage, unless he is sure of being able to sustain it for a dozen years. To drop it is sure destruction. . .'[1]

This is anecdotal, yet underlying the witticisms lay the serious question that the carriage for the doctor was an essential part of the equipment considered necessary for the discharge of professional duties. For the unprofessional gentleman it was no doubt a luxury, but for the doctor it was not, and it was often felt that the tax on carriages was an unjust imposition in their case. 'Bona fide articles required for the practice of a hard-working profession' were not luxuries and should be exempt from duty in the way that carts and horses used by farmers and tradesmen were exempt.[2]

The clergy, too, seemed to feel the necessity for an equipage in order to fulfil their duties. Trollope's Dr. Grantley 'kept his carriage as became a bishop' in the days of *Barchester Towers* (1857). This, it would seem, arose in part from the amount of travelling, bishops at any rate, were expected to make. Archbishop Benson at one time hesitated about accepting the Bishopric of Truro on the grounds that the £3,000 a year that it carried did not really seem adequate for a person without a

[1] J. C. Jeaffreson: *A Book about Doctors* (2nd ed., rev. 1861), p. 8.
[2] Letter from William Date to the *British Medical Journal*, 18th May 1867.

private fortune, particularly when the amount of travelling which was required in railway-less Cornwall was taken into account, travelling that was 'scarcely possible without carriage and horses of one's own—and very expensive with them'.[1]

However, for many people carriages were kept for display. In the West End of London, for example, the streets contained 'splendid vehicles—coaches, and chariots—with one, two, and even three powdered footmen, in elegant liveries, clustering behind, with long canes, cockades, and shoulder-knots; crimson, blue, green, bear- and tiger-skin hammer-cloths, with burnished coronets and crests upon them; sleek coachmen with wigs and three-cornered hats, and horses that pawed the ground with very pride'.[2] This was hardly the atmosphere of the middle classes but it is possible that each member lower down in the scale aspired in his humble way at least to a pony and gig.

The actual numbers involved are not easy to come by. One source[3] gave the following table showing the increases over the years:

	4-wheeled	2-wheeled
1814	23,000	36,000
1834	49,000	50,000
1844	62,000	33,000
1854	68,000	137,000
1864	102,000	170,000
1874	125,000	285,000

but these were for vehicles paying taxes, and since the kinds of vehicles exempted from tax were increased by the measures of 1823, 1825, 1830, 1839, 1853, and 1869[4] it is likely that the numbers of horse-drawn vehicles expanded even more rapidly than this. The 10th Report of H.M. Commissioners of Inland

[1] A. C. Benson: *The Life of E. W. Benson* (1899), Vol. 1, p. 413: a letter to Canon Westcott on 4th December 1876. The cost of a house was another of Benson's objections and he took the post when a special fund was raised to provide him with a suitable residence (p. 425).

[2] S. Warren: *Ten Thousand a Year* (1841), Bk. 4, Ch. 1.

[3] G. A. Thrupp: *The History of Coaches* (1877), p. 247. Information from Mr. W. H. Smith of the Treasury.

[4] S. Dowell: *A History of Taxation and Taxes in England* (2nd ed., 1888), Vol. 3, Ch. 3, pp. 203–9.

Revenue, moreover, gave the figures for 1864 as 102,886 and 170,749 for 4-wheeled and 2-wheeled respectively, which suggests that Thrupp's informant was not exactly worried about accuracy.

In 1856 the number of carriages in England and Wales *not* let for hire, and subject to tax, was given as 224,313 owned by 208,272 persons (1·08 per head)[1] which is a fair indication that the number of carriage owners was only slightly below the number of carriages taxed. This would also appear to have been the case with horses owned by certain classes, viz.:

	Horses	Persons	Ratio
Farmers	113,442	113,134	1·00
Rectors, vicars and curates	2,987	2,962	1·01
Roman Catholic priests and Protestant and Dissenting Ministers	1,194	1,194	1·00
Physicians, surgeons and apothecaries	3,397	3,390	1·00

whereas horses kept for riding and drawing, not so classified, were kept in the ratio of 1·32 per head (190,924 horses for 144,273 persons).

Keeping these ratios in mind, we should now look at the only satisfactory set of figures we have, viz. those given in the 10th Report of Her Majesty's Commissioners for Inland Revenue.[2]

England and Wales

Year	Carriages	Riding and Drawing Horses	Surgeons, Farmers and Clergymen
1856	201,394	136,872	110,250
1865	257,823	170,554	122,604
Increase	28·0%	24·6%	11·1%

The greatest expansion is seen to have been in carriages and riding- and drawing-horses. The latter were, of course, animals of conspicuous display, for horses used solely for the purposes of husbandry, stage-coach horses, post-horses and hackney-carriage horses, pit-ponies, and animals in the hands of horse-dealers for

[1] H. M. Commissioners of Inland Revenue, 1st Report, 1857. Table No. 65 (*Parliamentary Papers*, 1857, Vol. 4).
[2] H.M. Commissioners of Inland Revenue, 10th Report, 1866, p. lxv, details for ten years (*Parliamentary Papers*, 1866, Vol. 26).

sale were not subject to taxation.[1] The horses of farmers, clergymen and surgeons were subject to a lower form of taxation because it was conceded that they were, at least in part, necessary for professional duties. It is, however, significant that they increased at about the same rate as the population as a whole. The real expansion was in terms of horses and carriages owned for non-professional purposes. Moreover, although we do not know what the ratios were for the later date, if we assume that those of 1856 still operated, it would appear that the more expensive, two-horse carriages expanded most.

Together with this increase in numbers there seems to have gone on an increase in cost. Walsh, for example, in 1857 reckoned the keep of two horses at £52, a figure which he raised to £82 in 1873,[2] a rise of 58 per cent over the fifteen years. Assuming that all other costs, including wages, remained unchanged, this represented a 17 per cent increase for a carriage and pair (£177 to £207). There is some evidence of an increase in the purchase price of the animals too, for a Select Committee of the House of Lords set up in 1873 was told by horse-dealers that the price had risen by about 30 per cent over the preceding ten years and by 100 per cent over the previous forty.[3] This, moreover, was in a period when railway passenger travel was developing rapidly.[4] Englishmen were definitely travelling more.

In this connection it is perhaps worth while making a note that although for the remaining years of the century the cost of keeping horses did not materially increase, writers on domestic economy, unlike their predecessors in the earlier period, showed on the whole little enthusiasm for expenditure on a horse and gig as a necessary aspect of middle-class outlay. Part of the reason for this was perhaps the higher wages demanded by coachmen and grooms, but it does seem that far more important was the fact that railway travel was both faster and cheaper.

[1] Dowell: *op. cit.*, Vol. 3, p. 229.

[2] J. H. Walsh: *A Manual of Domestic Economy* (1857), p. 604 (2nd ed., 1873), p. 673.

[3] 'Report from the Select Committee of the House of Lords on Horses' (*Parliamentary Papers*, 1873, Vol. 14). Answers to questions 9, 166, 409, 888, 3612 and 3618. Compare the article 'The Horse Question' in *Chambers's Journal*, 25th October 1873.

[4] See Note D, p. 219.

Members of the middle classes appear to have felt it more worth their while to spend money in this way, as and when they wanted, rather than to keep a horse and employ a groom continuously. The 'Equipage' ceased to be a necessary part of the 'paraphernalia of gentility' and in doing without a vehicle and horses, they did without a groom; which may therefore have been a contributory factor in the slackening-off in the employment of indoor male domestics, so many grooms having also acted in fact as footmen. In any case, the horse and carriage had been only really possible for the upper-income groups. The lower groups may have aspired to them—the evidence of the domestic manuals seems to suggest this—but with the extension of cheap railway travel, their aspiration was turned into another direction. Here then was a definite change in the pattern of expenditure brought about by the development of an alternative source of satisfaction. For the outlay of about the same amount of money per year, the horizons of life could be widened and made richer.

At the same time, it must be emphasized that, whereas the horse and carriage had always been beyond the reach of people below a certain level of income, some form of railway travel never was. Inasmuch, therefore, as the pattern of middle-class life came to embrace the desirability of more and more travel, larger and larger numbers of the *lower* middle classes, who hitherto had spent very little in this respect, found themselves faced by small but not unimportant outlays on transport fares, not merely to and from their place of employment, but elsewhere on leisure occasions, on excursions, and especially, for the purpose of their annual holiday. In this respect, the development of the seaside holiday, stemming from the eighteenth-century popularity of the spas[1] had an important role to play. By the middle of the nineteenth century a holiday 'well used' was the sovereign medicine of modern existence and to get the most out of it it had to be well planned. Expense should not be stinted.[2]

Strangely enough, the early works on domestic economy

[1] J. A. R. Pimlott: *The Englishman's Holiday; a Social History* (1947), *passim*.
[2] Cf. *The Tourist's Annual for 1868* '. . . Nowadays the Management of a Holiday is a "Social Science" of no small importance' (Preface, and pp. 66–69).

devoted little space to the question. Excursions were mentioned in some, but they were usually linked with other items of expenditure, such as doctors' fees. Indeed, the holiday away from home, involving not only cessation from work but a certain amount of expense, appears to have been regarded as a therapeutic necessity for the town-dweller and it is remarkable how handbooks on holidays continued throughout the period to contain sections on the medicinal effect of relaxation and change. In estimating the effect of this on the household budget, we should no doubt, as one writer pointed out, 'deduct something from what we pay on this head for the great quantities of medicine swallowed by our forefathers',[1] but since we do not know the real cost of either, this will have to remain an unknown factor in middle-class living costs.

On the other hand, we do know that larger and larger numbers of people came to regard the annual holiday away from home as a necessary part of their lives. The explanation for this lies probably in the expansion of the numbers of salaried workers, the result of the movement from primary and secondary into tertiary industry.[2] These workers, white collar of course, tended to be middle class in outlook, and, what is far more significant, to receive a fixed annual holiday with pay every year. In this they differed both from the professional men and employers who could take their holidays as and when they liked, and from the members of the working classes for whom the holiday with pay did not become customary until the twentieth century.[3]

From 1841 to 1881 the numbers of people employed in commerce, expressed as a proportion of the total number of people employed in England and Wales, rose from 5·7 per cent to 9·2 per cent, and in public administration from 0·6 per cent to 1·1 per cent.[4] For these groups it would appear that the annual

[1] 'High Living with Low Means' in *The Family Friend*, May 1861, p. 261.
[2] C. Clark: *The Conditions of Economic Progress* (2nd ed., 1951), Ch. 9, especially pp. 405–7.
[3] Pimlott, *op. cit.* Chs. 8 and 13. Cf. 'In 1900 the annual holiday had hardly begun to attract the attention of sociologists, still less of politicians. It was taken for granted as a luxury which could be enjoyed at a certain level of income but which there was no special hardship in going without.' (Pp. 211–12.)
[4] Clark, *op. cit.*, Table on p. 408.

holiday was an established thing. Bank clerks, for example, were usually allowed a week, ten days, or a fortnight per year, according to their length of service with the firm,[1] while senior clerks at some banks obtained three weeks.[2] They were, it was thought,[3] better off in this respect than clerks generally, for whom the maximum appears to have been a fortnight, although again some senior clerks were given three weeks and occasionally a month.[4] One firm of solicitors indeed, also gave gratuities ranging from £2 to £25 for the holiday period.[5]

Granted that the upper middle class had already set the fashion by their regular trips to English spas and foreign watering-places in the seventeenth and eighteenth centuries, the opportunities offered to the lower middle classes in the form of cheap railway travel and holidays with pay ensured that they too would add this form of behaviour to their pattern of what they considered the right and proper things to do. A certain proportion of the annual income to be set aside for holidays and excursions, therefore, became part of the accepted standard of life of the growing middle class during the middle years of the nineteenth century.

In arriving at this conclusion, it has become apparent that the fairly precise nature of the earlier two chapters has been more or less abandoned. As with the problem of estimating the expenditure on furnishings, the amount of information on which we have to work is exceedingly meagre. The middle-class writers of the fifties and sixties had little to say as a rule about the outlay on those aspects of the paraphernalia of gentility with which we have been concerned so far. On the other hand, in the case of dress, which was clearly another item on which a significant proportion of the income was spent, the problem is less one of a lack of information as of arriving at some kind of golden mean between the various estimates which were offered.

[1] Report from the Select Committee on the Bank Holidays Bill, 1868 (*Parliamentary Papers*, 1867–8, Vol. 7) Qq. 159, 160, 453, 874–6, 960.
[2] *Ibid.*, Qq. 453, 825, 855, 960.
[3] *Ibid.*, Q. 2272.
[4] *Ibid.*, Q. 241–3. First Report of the Civil Service Inquiry Commission (*Parliamentary Papers*, 1875, Vol. 23). Appendix G, details from four insurance companies, five firms of solicitors, the L.N.E.R., the Railway Clearing House and the Mersey Docks and Harbour Board.
[5] *Ibid.*, Appendix G.

Ward and Lock's Home Book in 1880, for example, laid down £18 5s. a year as the mean minimum for a married lady, and £15 a year for the unmarried girl;[1] but there were no doubt many at that time who thought such a small sum ridiculous. As the authoress of *How to Dress on £15 a Year* wrote:

'I fancy I hear my readers, should any be found to open my little book, altering the text and asking, "How can a lady dress on fifteen pounds a year?" Well, this question vexed me much, as no doubt it has vexed and is vexing many others to whom, may be, it is of the greatest moment. Of course, anyone *can* dress on this sum, this is not questioned; but the gist of the matter lies in three words, "like a lady". . . It sounds as if it must be a hard task to do this on such a little sum, almost a hopeless one, you think to yourself; and you are perhaps inclined to throw aside my poor little book, exclaiming: "What a scrubby notion! Fifteen pounds a year! Why, one's gloves and odds and ends alone come to more than that!" . . .'[2]

This reference to gloves brings to mind the other point that there could be no limit to the expense that might be showered on a single outfit.

'I saw her dancing in the ball. Around her snowy brow were set five hundred pounds; such would have been the answer of any jeweller to the question: "What are those diamonds?" With the gentle undulation of her bosom there rose and fell exactly thirty pounds ten shillings. The sum bore the guise of a brooch of gold and enamel. Her fairy form was invested in ten guineas, represented by a slip of lilac satin; and this was overlaid by thirty guineas more in two skirts of white lace. Tastefully down each side of the latter were six half-crowns, which so many bows of purple ribbon had come to. The lower margin of the thirty-guinea skirts were edged with eleven additional guineas, the value of some eight yards of silver fringe, a quarter of a yard in depth. Her taper waist, taking zone and clasp together, I calculated to be confined by thirty pounds sterling.

---

[1] *Ward and Lock's Home Book: a Domestic Encyclopaedia, forming a Companion Volume to Mrs. Beeton's Book of Household Management* (n.d., British Museum 1880), p. 783.
[2] *How to Dress on £15 a Year as a Lady, by a Lady* (1874), pp. 1–2.

H

Her delicately rounded arms, the glove of spotless kid being
added to the gold bracelet which encircled the little wrist, may
be said to have been adorned with twenty-two pounds five and
sixpence; and putting the silk and satin at the lowest figure, I
should say she wore fourteen and sixpence on her feet. Thus,
altogether was this thing of light, this creature of loveliness,
arrayed from top to toe, exclusive of little sundries, in six
hundred and forty-eight pounds eleven shillings.'[1]

Another difficulty arises from the fact that the amount to be
allowed for dress varied considerably according to the extent
to which clothing was made at home. Thus, Orchard, in his
study of the clerks of Liverpool, gave two kinds of budget, one
from those clerks who thought it was not possible to marry on
£80 or £150 a year, and one from those who thought that it
was; and it is striking that the latter were married to wives who
made much of their own clothing and sometimes even their
husband's shirts.[2]

It may perhaps be thought that too much is being made of
this point here. After all, in every department of domestic outlay a great deal of the actual level of living was determined by
the efficiency of the household manager. Nevertheless, whereas
it is true that throughout the nineteenth century, books, articles
and letters to the magazines and newspapers constantly refer to
the inefficient housewife as the reason why ends were not always
made to meet, the norm of expenditure laid down in the manuals was not affected by that point. A sum was given for household expenses which was considered usual and appropriate for a
certain income range. If it was spent unwisely, that was un-
fortunate, but it could not be allowed for. On the other hand,
dress was in a slightly different position. It was taken for granted
that every housewife would do a certain amount of home sew-
ing, especially after the introduction of the sewing-machine on
a large scale in the late fifties, and it was readily accepted that
she would perhaps make, or get her servants to make, most, if

[1] 'The Cost of a Modern Belle' in *The Family Friend*, September 1858, p. 164.
[2] B. G. Orchard: *The Clerks of Liverpool* (1871), pp. 64–65. The comparison is of
B (£150) and D (£80) on the one hand with C (£80) and A (£150) on the other.
A was unmarried.

not all, of her children's clothes; but she was not expected to make her husband's outer clothing and it was not always agreed that she could make her own. Indeed, some of the exigencies of fashion made this well-nigh impossible. The crinoline, in particular, because of its wire frame, required the use of special clamps to fix the claws firmly on the steel and of large blocks to keep the shape. Delicate hands could hardly be considered capable of managing these operations[1] and it is doubtful whether the employment of seamstresses inside the home could have competed successfully in terms of the appearance of the finished product with the tempting articles displayed in the shop windows.

At the same time, the success of the Beetons' paper-pattern schemes, imitated by many other magazine proprietors in the early sixties,[2] showed that many middle-class women married and unmarried, were only too keen to follow the fashion as cheaply as possible. In view of these difficulties, therefore, it is perhaps not surprising that there was a reluctance on the part of most books on domestic economy to tackle this item at all seriously, and they seem in the main to have left it as a residual. What was left over after the proportion for rent, household expenses, and wages were fixed, might be spent in a number of ways, of which one was dress. This seems to be the explanation why it is not possible to see a fairly consistent proportion allowed for this item in the various manuals used as the basis for the conclusions drawn in the last two chapters.

Nevertheless, it is true that from the period after the Crimean War, when it was complained that 'crinoline fashions are ruinously expensive',[3] complaints of the growing expense of women's

---

[1] See the reply to Maria S.P. in the *Englishwoman's Domestic Magazine*, September 1861, p. 264.

[2] N. Spain: *Mrs. Beeton and her Husband* (1948), Bk. 1, Ch. 2, p. 138. The Beetons had to enlarge their staff to deal with the tremendous demand.

[3] Quoted in C. W. Cunnington: *English Women's Clothing in the Nineteenth Century* (1937), p. 170. Cunnington gives details of prices for every year of the century. His book is an excellent survey of the subject, full of quotations from magazines and newspapers, but unfortunately hardly usable as he rarely gives a reference except for an occasional mention of the year of appearance. His otherwise excellent *Feminine Attitudes in the Nineteenth Century* (1935) is also marred by this same defect. Cunnington apparently does not realize that later workers will want to cover the same ground.

clothing continued to appear. This was partly caused by the extension of the wardrobe (the afternoon dress in the fifties, the walking-out dress, the large trousseau of twelve to eighteen of each of the garments and the more diverse underclothing of the sixties, the tennis dress in the seventies, other sports costumes in the eighties, and the bicycle dress in the nineties) and partly by the use of more costly materials or elaborate finishings. At the same time it also appears that, as the century wore on, yard for yard the cost of materials fell. It is possible, therefore, on the one hand to quote people who in the seventies could claim that the expense of dressing 'has nearly trebled in the last forty years'[1] and on the other, people at the end of the century who were surprised that there had been little change since their grandmother's day.[2] Cunnington, in fact, in summing-up the developments of the hundred years concluded that the technical improvements had so multiplied and cheapened materials that an ever-increasing number of women were enabled 'to indulge in following the fashion'.[3] One is left with the general impression that some 16 per cent to 20 per cent of the total income was set aside for dress and that it remained between these limits, far too wide to mean very much, throughout the whole of the century.

It is perhaps worth while to pause at this point for a general evaluation of the information collected together so far. In the ordinary course of procedure for a study of this kind, it is usually considered unnecessary to set out such a mass of detail as we have gone through here. But this is virtually an untouched field of sociological research. Books have been written on the middle classes certainly, and social histories often abound with generalizations on their way of life; but unlike the working classes, about whom there is a whole wealth of material based

[1] *Ibid.*, Ch. 8, 'The 70's', p. 295. The quotation is from some time in 1879. See also J. H. Walsh: *A Manual of Domestic Economy'* (1873), Preface, p. iii. Walsh's discussion of expenditure on dress between two limits demonstrates the kind of difficulty referred to in estimating this department of expenditure (1857), p. 340–1. (2nd ed., 1873), pp. 368–9.

[2] F. Harrison: 'A Grandmother's Budget' in the *Cornhill Magazine*, February 1904. The article was based upon the details given in some old account books of the authoress's grandmother.

[3] Cunnington, *op. cit.*, 'Retrospect', p. 426.

on the investigations made for the many Commissions on Labour and Labour Conditions throughout the nineteenth century, the middle and upper classes remain practically an unknown quantity. No one has in effect thought fit to put together a really detailed and documented study of the facts about their way of life. It has been necessary, therefore, to go to the sources of the information direct and to dig deeply into the books and magazines on these domestic matters produced by and for the middle classes themselves. This has involved a great deal of tiring and unrewarding effort, and it cannot be claimed that the above materials, and those which are yet to follow, form anything other than a pioneer investigation of what needs still to be done. To a certain extent, therefore, the conclusions drawn in the last three chapters can only be regarded as tentative. They represent the impressions which have arisen from contact with what have appeared to be the most likely sources of representative fact.

Nevertheless, it does seem fairly well established that the period up to the 1870s was one in which the middle-class standard of living was rapidly changing. Something in the order of a 50 per cent increase in outlay was expected over the 1850 level on food, drink, and household requirements generally, although retail prices rose by only 5 per cent. Servants' wages rose by less than 30 per cent, but wives and daughters consistently did less in the home so that the employment of housekeepers, housemaids, cooks, and nurse-maids more than doubled over the twenty years. Coachmen, too, found their services in greater demand and more money was spent on travelling about the country. There can be little doubt, moreover, that although it did cost the middle classes much more money now to live than it had in the 1850s, the greater part of that added outlay was the result of a richer standard of life. The underlying cause of the regular stream of complaints appearing in the books and magazines of the period was not so much a rise in the price of the material ingredients of the middle-class way of living but an extension of the number and form of those ingredients. Should at any time these newly established wants become more difficult to satisfy, a critical situation would develop which might well affect matrimonial and family practices . . . but before we can go on to discuss that, we must pause to look at the other side of the picture. How far did the standards expand as a consequence of a greater power to obtain the good things of life? What was happening to middle-class incomes?

CHAPTER VII

Incomes

WE have no really trustworthy information about the incomes received by the members of the middle and upper classes between 1850 and 1870. This may seem surprising in view of the fact that Returns of Income Tax were presented to Parliament annually almost without intermission from 1847, and that the Reports of the Commissioners of Inland Revenue, including a secton on Income Tax, were published regularly from 1857. The details given in these documents, however, were not collected for the purpose of statistical manipulation; nor were they designed to give an impression of what was happening over time. They were merely the by-product of a system of taxation explicitly contrived to raise the maximum revenue with the minimum of inconvenience. Consequently, their adequacy as a record of the incomes received by income-tax payers is impaired not only by the unknown degree of tax evasion[1] but also by the idiosyncracies of their compilation. A single individual, for example, was frequently assessed under more than one schedule, as an owner of property perhaps (Schedule A, Property Tax) and as the recipient of an earned income (Schedule D, Incomes from Trade, Manufacture, Profession, Employment, or Vocation) and hence appeared in the returns in two places, that is, as two persons. Moreover, joint-

---

[1] Contemporary writers considered the amount of tax evasion to be quite considerable. Thus R. D. Baxter (*National Income: the United Kingdom*) (1868) reckoned a loss of revenue of one-sixth under Schedule D to be a 'very moderate estimate' (p. 33). See also the 12th Report of H.M. Commissioners of Inland Revenue (*Parliamentary Papers*, 1868–9, Vol. 18, p. 22), L. Levi: 'On the Reconstruction of the Income and Property Tax' in the *Journal of the Statistical Society*, June 1874, pp. 161–2, and J. C. Stamp: *British Incomes and Property* (1916), pp. 325–9.

stock companies assessed under the same schedules as individual people were not usually classified separately, so that we can never be certain how much of the income assessed for taxation was in fact available for purchasing the kinds of domestic comforts described in the last three chapters.[1]

Nevertheless this does not rule out the possibility that the figures given in the taxation returns may be used to indicate trends, and indeed an examination of Table G.4 in J. C. Stamp's *British Incomes and Property* is rewarding in this respect. This table, based on the returns given in the official reports, provides the total income which *would* have been taxed in every year between 1842–3 and 1913–14 had the system of assessment applied in 1876–93 and in 1894–1913 been operated throughout. That is to say, the table gives the results of Stamp's calculations of two different sets of figures both of which allow for the discrepancies in the original totals caused by the changes in the method of assessment which were introduced from time to time. For our purpose here, however, the differences between these sets are insignificant in so far as they both show a remarkably similar expansion in the total amount of taxable income assessed under all schedules; and no great misrepresentation will be incurred if to simplify the analysis we confine ourselves to Stamp's first, i.e. to the conditions of 1876–93 when the exemption limit was £150 per annum.

The following estimate, therefore, has been derived from the fourth column of Stamp's table.[2] It consists of the *total* amount of income assessed during the five-year periods centred on the Census years, 1851, 1861 and 1871, standardized to the conditions of 1876–93.

Total Income Assessed (United Kingdom and Ireland)

Census Date	Assessment Period	Income above £150
1851	1848–9 to 1852–3	£1,051·1 millions
1861	1858–9 to 1862–3	£1,299·1 ,,
1871	1868–9 to 1872–3	£1,882·1 ,,

[1] For a more detailed discussion of the difficulties, see Stamp, *op. cit.*, pp. 1–9, and J. A. Banks: *The English Middle Class Conception of the Standard of Living* (unpub. M.A. thesis, London University, 1952), Ch. 7.

[2] Stamp, *op. cit.*, p. 318.

This is equivalent to increases of 23·4 per cent over the ten years between 1851 and 1861; 44·9 per cent over the ten years between 1861 and 1871, and 79·2 per cent over the twenty years between 1851 and 1871.[1] It would thus appear that incomes over £150 expanded at a considerable rate during the third quarter of the nineteenth century.

We cannot, however, simply assume that this was so from the figures given. What we still need to know is whether this increase was caused by a real net gain per head, or whether it arose from a growth in the *numbers* of those assessed for receiving more than £150 per annum.

One way of looking at this problem is to estimate the growth in the numbers of middle-class occupations. Between 1841 and 1881, as we have already seen,[2] the numbers employed in commerce expressed as a proportion of the total number occupied in England and Wales, rose from 5·7 per cent to 9·2 per cent and in public administration from 0·6 per cent to 1·1 per cent. This is a general indication that the proportion of white-collar workers was growing in the community. Indeed the total number of commercial clerks, accountants and bankers alone, over twenty years of age, increased from 44,000 in 1851 to 67,000 in 1861, and to 119,000 in 1871,[3] increases of 52·3 per cent and 77·6 per cent respectively.

Nevertheless not all of these would have been assessed for income tax. In Manchester and Salford in 1860, for example, only salesmen and buyers received as much on average as £150 a year. The average for cashiers was no more than £100 and for book-keepers and clerks, £60.[4] In 1875, of the 215 clerks employed by the Mersey Docks and Harbour Board, 179 received no more than £150, and 96 of these were in receipt of less than

---

[1] A similar calculation based on Stamp's fifth column gives 24·1 per cent for 1851–61, 45·7 per cent for 1861–71, and 80·8 per cent for 1851–71. These percentages are for the increases in taxable incomes over £160.

[2] See p. 95.

[3] C. Booth: 'Occupations of the People of the United Kingdom, 1801–81' in the *Journal of the Statistical Society*, June 1886, p. 336.

[4] D. Chadwick: 'The Rate of Wages in Manchester and Salford, and the Manufacturing Districts of Lancashire, 1839–59' in the *Journal of the Statistical Society*, March 1860, p. 29.

£100.[1] Even in the Civil Service, 70 clerks in 1868–9 could hope for a *maximum* salary eventually of no more than £150; and 447 were commenced with a *minimum* of less than £150 rising by £5 and £10 annual increments to a maximum ranging from as low as £100 to no more than £400.[2] These incomes moreover were for established clerks only (a total of 892 in 1868–9, excluding chief and principal clerks). Supplementary, copying, extra and temporary clerks apparently received on average less, although even their remuneration was higher than that given in private employment.[3]

We have no very precise idea, therefore, of the extent to which the great increase in commercial and administrative employment resulted in raising the numbers of the middle classes who were in receipt of more than £150 a year. Much of the expansion shown in the Census returns might well have arisen from the employment of a growing number of poorer-paid clerical workers. If it were indeed the case, as one writer put it, that the pay of the great majority of clerks was not equal to that of a good mechanic,[4] and that their prospects of rising much above £180 were remote,[5] it can readily be understood that a very large proportion of the white-collar occupations growing in the middle years of the nineteenth century were staffed by persons whose incomes allowed them very few of the

[1] First Report of the Civil Service Inquiry Commission (*Parliamentary Papers*, 1875, Vol. 23, Appendix G). Apprentice clerks received up to £80. B. G. Orchard: *The Clerks of Liverpool* (1871), p. 26, gave the comparable figures for 1871 as 160 in receipt of less than £100 per annum, and 200 in receipt of less than £150, out of a total of 264.

[2] H. Mann: 'Some Statistics Relating to the Civil Service', Appendix A, Scales of Salary assigned to Established Clerkships, in the *Journal of the Statistical Society*, December 1868, p. 416.

[3] *Ibid.*, p. 411.

[4] Letter from 'A Parent' to the *Daily News*, quoted in *Good Advice, Part One: How to get on in the World; or, the Sure Guide to Independence and Wealth* (1871), p. 197.

[5] *Ibid.*, Letters from 'A Tradesman' (quoted p. 196) and 'G.J.' (quoted p. 198). The pamphlet itself reckoned that a clerk's starting salary was £80, advancing by stages to £150. See also C. Mitchell (?): *Advice to Clerks, and Hints to Employers, showing the Road to Preferment and Comfort, by an Experienced Clerk* (n.d., British Museum, 1848) where the range was put at £70–£80 to £150 (pp. 6–7). B. G. Orchard: *The Clerks of Liverpool* (1871) considered that 'at least one-fourth of the clerks in this town are engaged in businesses where not one of all the number can scarcely hope to ever receive £300 a year, however useful he may be' p. 25. 'In the usual course a bank clerk at thirty earns about £200 a year', p. 29.

comforts considered essential by those writers whose estimates
formed the basis of the preceding chapters.

At the same time it is unlikely that many wage-earners were
receiving sufficient per annum to lift their incomes above the
tax-exemption limit. The average earnings of a working-man's
family of four and a half persons was reckoned at about 30s. a
week (£78 a year) in 1882.[1] In Wood's indices of money wages
this appears as something of a depression year as far as wage
rates are concerned, but even so they stood at 47 per cent above
the level for 1851 and at no time between 1851 and 1871 were
the average wage rates more than 38 per cent above the 1851
level.[2] An alternative estimate reckoned 15s. per week as the
average wage in 1860.[3] This was compared with averages of
£150 per annum for the middle classes (further described as
merchants, lawyers, artists and clerks) and £900 per annum
for the upper classes. Even the better-paid, skilled manual
workers rarely received more than about £100 a year,[4] so that
it is doubtful whether any significant number of wage-earners
were included amongst the people assessed for income tax. In so
far as the estimates are to be trusted at all, the great expansion of
taxable wealth between 1851 and 1871 was confined almost, if not
exclusively, to the middle and upper classes. This must not be
taken to mean that working-class incomes were not also rising,
for they clearly were,[5] but they still remained below the income-
tax exemption limit and hence may hardly be regarded as effect-
ively participating in the drive towards the higher middle-class
standard of living which was so marked a feature of the period.

[1] L. Levi: 'On the Statistics of the Revenue of the United Kingdom for 1859–82,
in relation to Taxation' in the *Journal of the Statistical Society*, March, 1884, p. 21.
[2] G. H. Wood: 'Real Wages and the Standard of Comfort since 1850', Appendix,
in the *Journal of the Statistical Society*, March 1909.
[3] L. Levi: 'The Distribution and Productiveness of Taxes with Reference to the
Prospective Ameliorations in the Public Revenue of the United Kingdom' in the
Journal of the Statistical Society, March 1860.
[4] Chadwick: *op. cit.*, Appendix of Tables—Average Return of Weekly Wages,
pp. 23–29. Only five classes of wage workers received at least 40s. per week, viz.
Hand Mule Spinners in Cotton, 40s.; Die Makers for Calico Printing, 45s.; Wall-
paper Printers, 40s.; First Class Domestic Glass Workers, 55s.; Silk Hatters, Teppers
Off, 40s.
[5] The following increases calculated from Wood's indices of money wage rates
show the trend: 1850–3 to 1859–63, 11·8 per cent; 1859–63 to 1869–73, 22·4 per
cent; 1850–5 to 1869–73, 37·0 per cent.

On the other hand, it must not be overlooked that by far the largest proportion of the personal incomes appearing in the returns were given as falling just around the £150 per annum range. Thus of the 49,287 people assessed in 1851 under Schedule E (Income from any public office or employment) 21,897 were on record as being in receipt of less than £150 per annum, and a further 8,346 were receiving more than £150 but less than £200.[1] That is, more than 60 per cent of those assessed earned less than £200 a year, while only 1,418, or less than 3 per cent, had incomes of £1,000 a year and over. By 1871 the proportions had changed to more than 70 per cent and less than 2 per cent respectively,[2] although this variation is strictly speaking meaningless since the exemption limit in the latter year was only £100 as compared with £150 on the former occasion and the later method of assessment gathered in a larger proportion of the smaller incomes into the statistics.

Because of this and similar changes in the exemption limits, it is perhaps wiser to exclude all the incomes below a certain figure, say £200, when attempting to estimate the number of taxpayers under a given schedule. This eliminates the great variations from time to time observable among those in receipt of incomes just around the exemption limit. Other purely temporal fluctuations may also be allowed for by taking the averages for three consecutive years as the index of the number assessed. Certain irregularities in the details will still remain, but these can hardly be avoided, and for that reason the figures given below, taken as they are from a *single* schedule should not be regarded as anything more than a tentative indication of what was happening between 1851 and 1871.

Taxpayers assessed under Schedule E for incomes of £200 and over[3]

	Number of taxpayers	Total income assessed
Average for 1849–51	19,217	£8,513,271·3
Average for 1859–61	24,569	£10,684,722·0
Average for 1869–71	35,567	£14,946,050·3

[1] Income Tax Return, 15th June 1852 (*Parliamentary Papers*, 1852, Vol. 28).

[2] Income Tax Return, 4th August 1873 (*Parliamentary Papers*, 1873, Vol. 39). The fact that a large number of taxpayers were assessed on more than one schedule explains why figures were given of a number of incomes *below* the exemption limit.

[3] For details and references, see Note E, p. 221.

Incomes

Increases[1]

	1851–1861 Per cent	1861–1871 Per cent	1851–1871 Per cent
Taxpayers	20·8	44·8	85·1
Incomes	25·5	39·9	75·6

From these figures it is clear that a very large increase took place over the twenty years in the number of salaried and other persons assessed under Schedule E for incomes of at least £200. This becomes especially marked if we compare the growth with that of the population as a whole and with that of the total occupied *male* population aged twenty and over.

Taxpayers assessed under Schedule E for incomes £200–£999[2]

Increases

	1851–1861 Per cent	1861–1871 Per cent	1851–1871 Per cent
Taxpayers	29·3	45·4	88·0
Incomes	33·4	42·7	90·3

The general impression obtained earlier that the middle-class groups were growing far more rapidly than the rest of the population appears to be borne out here.

Moreover, from the increases in the incomes assessed, it is also clear that in the 1860s, at any rate, the number of the lower-paid salaried workers assessed under Schedule E grew at a faster rate than did the number of higher-paid salaried workers. That is to say, the fact that the incomes themselves were not expanding quite so rapidly as the numbers of people receiving them, is an indication not simply that some people were receiving less per annum than they had been, although there may have been a few in this unhappy position, but rather that every year more and more people were added to the numbers of those just above the exemption range. This can perhaps best be seen if we confine ourselves to those assessed for receiving between £200 and £1,000. Roughly 90 per cent of the assessments were for people in this category and their growth was marked as follows:

---

[1] Calculated from the three-year totals and not from the means which have been rounded off.

[2] See Note E, p. 221.

Incomes

Growth of population and occupied males

	1851–1861 Per cent	1861–1871 Per cent	1851–1871 Per cent
Total population	11·9	13·2	26·7
Occupied males (20 and over)	10·9	12·2	24·6

Here the same kind of comparison between taxpayers and incomes may be made as in the earlier table, and in addition we can see that this £200-£999+group grew more rapidly than the £200 and over group, where incomes of £5,000 and even more were included.

In general it does appear, therefore, that the greatest growth in numbers took place amongst the lower middle classes, amongst clerks and administrative workers earning about £100 to £200 per year, or just a little more; but this fact should not cause us to overlook another of even greater significance. At every level the numbers assessed increased considerably, at a far more rapid rate indeed than the population as a whole. This can be seen quite distinctly in the distribution of those assessed under Schedule E for the single years 1851 and 1871. The figures appear in the reports as follows:[1]

£	1851	1871	Percentage increase
£200–	8,885	17,529	97·3
£300–	4,135	8,213	98·6
£400–	1,993	4,092	105·3
£500–	1,090	2,072	90·1
£600–	603	1,253	107·8
£700–	423	788	86·3
£800–	293	624	112·6
£900–	204	353	73·0
£1,000–	1,125	1,832	62·9
£2,000–	235	356	51·5
£5,000–	58	80	37·9
All £200 and over	19,044	37,192	95·3
Occupied males (aged 20 and over)	4,717,013	5,866,168	24·6
Total population	17,927,609	22,712,266	26·7

[1] Figures obtained from the Income Tax Returns given in footnotes 1 and 2 above, p. 108. For a similar distribution comprised of the details from Schedules D and E taken together, see J. A. Banks: *The English Middle Class Concept of the Standard of Living* (unpub. 1952), pp. 161–2. The tables given there allow in part for the transference from Schedule D to Schedule E as joint-stock company registration proceeded, but they have the disadvantage of treating both firms and individuals together as though their respective incomes were equally available for spending on the kind of consumption patterns relevant to the problem of the middle-class standard of living.

This could be explained on the assumption that many incomes remained little changed while others increased by quite large amounts; but a much more plausible explanation seems to be that there was a very extensive movement up the income scale over the twenty years. A comparison of the numbers assessed for incomes of £200–£299+ in 1851 with those assessed for £300–£399+ in 1871, for £300–£399+ in 1851 with those for £400–£499+ in 1871, and so on throughout the various levels, suggests that over the twenty years many people had received increases in their salaries and annuities of about £100 per head. That is to say, it is possible that most of the 19,044 persons assessed under Schedule E for incomes of £200 and over, in 1851, appeared in the 1871 returns as assessed for incomes of £300 and over, and that the 18,148 extra persons assessed at the later date had been in receipt of less than £200 a year on the earlier occasion. This interpretation of the growth in numbers does not allow for deaths during the period, nor for the quite considerable transference of individual assessments from one schedule to another, in particular from Schedule D to Schedule E as a result of the spread of joint-stock enterprise, and to that extent it over-emphasizes the degree of mobility up the income scale, but it is valuable in that it brings out the point that quite possibly a large number of individual incomes increased by not inconsiderable amounts.

Furthermore, it is to be noted that this rise in the incomes received by members of the middle and upper classes represented a clear gain in terms of purchasing power. Real wages were indeed rising very rapidly during this period and we may therefore conclude that middle- and upper-class *real* incomes rose accordingly. From Wood's table of average retail prices the means of the five-year periods centred on the census year show an increase of 10 per cent for 1851–61, and only 5·6 per cent for 1861–71.[1] The total of 16·2 per cent for the full twenty years would thus seem to be well below the possible increase in salary and income received by those assessed for income tax, except perhaps in the very highest ranges.

Hence, no matter how careful we may be to avoid drawing

[1] Increases calculated from W. T. Layton and G. Crowther: *An Introduction to the Study of Prices* (3rd ed., 1938), Appendix E, Table 1, p. 273, col. 3.

too many fixed conclusions from the evidence of the income-tax returns, we cannot escape the impression that the years of mid-Victorian prosperity were marked by a more than proportionate increase in the number and incomes of those people receiving sufficient per year to pay for some of the domestic comforts, the servants, and the paraphernalia of gentility, described in the last three chapters. At the same time as there took place a rise in the standard of living, regarded as a norm to which middle-class men and women aspired, there occurred a rise in the standard of living, regarded as a level which they attained. It is not unlikely, therefore, that this growing capacity of the middle classes to consume great quantities of goods and to employ large numbers of servants was one of the reasons, if not the major reason, why they came to think them so vitally necessary for a truly civilized life. Those who wished to retain their middle-class status, equally with those who strove to acquire it, felt it incumbent upon them to follow the example of those who set the pace and who, in this period, had a rising income to spend. It is only against the background of such a social situation that it makes sense to talk of the impact of growing world competition on English prosperity in the later Victorian years as the chief factor impelling the middle classes towards the acceptance of family limitation.

CHAPTER VIII

A Case Study—Anthony Trollope

So far the attempt has been made to describe the twenty years leading up to the Great Depression as a period in which there took place a striking expansion in the numbers of the English middle classes, in their wealth, and in their level and standard of living. Already it had become customary for them to consider prudently the expenses of married life before embarking upon a marriage and to estimate carefully the extent to which their incomes would be sufficient to support a family, and it has now to be shown how the changed attitude towards family limitation which was so marked a feature of the last twenty years of the nineteenth century was directly produced by the alleged financial stringencies of those years.

Before we go on to do this, however, let us endeavour to embody the bare statistical details of the last four chapters in some more specific form. Ideally, this would best be done by describing the life history of a 'typical' middle-class family living at the time, but in practice this ideal is unattainable owing to a real lack of autobiographical data having relevance to our theme. We are not, nevertheless, completely prevented from doing something in this direction, for Anthony Trollope was writing his best novels in the 1850s and 1860s, and we are fortunate that more than any other man of his time he was prolific in expressing the opinions common to the intelligent 'Philistines' of the middle-class world. His eye was keen in discerning the routine details of their everyday lives, and in his way he became a kind of champion of domesticity, observing and recording in some fifty full-length novels and collections of short stories the ordinary, regular manner of behaving of the comfortably-off classes of London and the English shires. His is not a complete account, of course, mainly because he seems blissfully unaware of the commercial and industrial developments which were so rapidly transforming the family lives of our northern towns. Nor would one ever guess from a familiarity with his works that Newman and Arnold, Darwin and Huxley, John Stuart Mill and Ruskin, were carrying on a revolution in ideas as tremendous in its impact on the age as the coming of industrialization had been. But for all that, Trollope does describe with loving faithfulness the day to day problems of the farmer, the squire, and the landowner, the doctor, the lawyer, and the clergyman, which still remained the problems of the middle-class man for whom the manuals and domestic handbooks used as the basis for this study were produced. Getting on in one's career, making money, finding a life's partner and marrying her, these are the ever-present concerns of his characters, as they were of the average professional and upper middle-class men of London and the southern counties; and what theme could be more relevant to us here?[1]

Anthony Trollope, born in London in 1815, was himself the son of an unsuccessful lawyer who gave up his practice to become an even more unsuccessful farmer. Educated at Winchester and Harrow as a day-boarder, the future novelist failed consistently to obtain either an exhibition, a sizarship or a scholarship to a university, and left school eventually at nineteen with apparently little talent and no future. His father went bankrupt soon afterwards, and the family took flight to Bruges where Mrs. Trollope maintained them by writing successful novels.[2] For his part Anthony strove for a time to fill the role of a classical usher at a school in Brussels but, finding the work painfully uncongenial, he eventually returned to London where employment was found for him by family influence as a clerk in the Post Office.

'My salary', he wrote long afterwards,[3] 'was to be £90 a year,

---

[1] See the excellent introduction to M. Sadleir: *Trollope: a Commentary* (1927). Other sources of information on Trollope are given in Note F, p. 221.

[2] 'Her career', wrote her son, 'offers great encouragement to those who have not begun early in life, but are still ambitious to do something before they depart hence.' Her first book was written when she was fifty and she went on writing until she was seventy-six, producing in all 114 volumes.

[3] A Trollope: *An Autobiography* (1883), Ch. 3.

and on that I was to live in London, keep up my character as a gentleman, and be happy.' Enthusiastic at first, he soon found that it was not enough for him to live on. 'I came up to town purporting to live a jolly life upon £90 per annum. I remained seven years in the General Post Office, and when I left it my income was £140. During the whole of this time I was hopelessly in debt.' Often he went without meals. Regularly he was behind with his lodging-house keeper, and if it had not been for his mother's ready assistance he would probably have gone the way of his own creation, Charley Tudor of *The Three Clerks*, who spent a short period in a debtor's prison.[1] On one occasion a tailor took from him an acceptance for some £12 which found its way into the hands of a money-lender. 'With that man, who lived in a little street near Mecklenburgh Square, I formed a most heart-rending but a most intimate acquaintance. In cash I once received from him £4. For that and for the original amount of the tailor's bill, which grew monstrously under repeated renewals, I paid ultimately something over £200. . . .' The experience went deep, for the money-lender with his wheezy emphasis on the need for punctuality in payment, appeared later in two of his novels, *The Three Clerks* and *Phineas Finn*.[2] Small wonder that one of his early characters is made to feel that the life he was leading 'contracting debts which he could not pay, and spending his time in pursuits which were not really congenial to him', was unsatisfactory and discreditable.[3]

It is interesting to read what his characters in a similar situation thought about the subject of marriage. Johnny Eames, for example, in the *Small House at Allington* was a civil servant, clerk, employed at £80 a year. Although in love with Lily Dale, he had not dreamed of asking her to be his wife. John Eames was about to begin the world with eighty pounds a year, and an allowance of twenty more from his mother's purse. He was well aware that with such an income he could not establish himself as a married man in London.[4] Indeed, ten times that

[1] A. Trollope: *The Three Clerks* (1858), Ch. 28.
[2] *Ibid.*, Chs. 17 to 20. A Trollope: *Phineas Finn* (1869), Ch. 21.
[3] A. Trollope: *The Kellys and the O'Kellys* (1848) quoted in L. P. and R. P. Stebbins: *The Trollopes: The Chronicle of a Writing Family* (1946), p. 133.
[4] A Trollope: *Small House at Allington* (1864), Ch. 4.

sum was insufficient for most. When Alaric Tudor married Gertrude Woodward he was receiving £600 a year 'and though this was to be augmented occasionally till it reached £800, yet even with this advantage it could hardly suffice for a man and his wife and the coming family to live in an expensive part of London and enable him to "see his friends" occasionally, as the act of feeding one's acquaintances is now generally called'.[1] In attempting to reach higher, Alaric in fact over-reached himself, but the problem of the expenses of married life faced everyone of Trollope's civil servants irrespective of their grade. Even Adolphus Crosbie, a senior clerk with £700 a year plus £100 or so patrimony, living the life of a West End swell, began to have some qualms once he had become engaged to Lily Dale as she had no money. 'He must give up his clubs, and his fashion, and all that he had hitherto gained, and be content to live a plain, humdrum, domestic life, with eight hundred a year, and a small house, full of babies. . . . Could he be happy in that small house, somewhere near the New Road, with five children and horrid misgivings as to the baker's bill?'[2] The case could hardly have been better put.

Of course, this did not prevent Trollope from making his characters marry for love. 'Frank must marry money', asserted the Countess de Courcy on learning of the state of the Gresham family's finances and that imperative became the dominant note of the novel.[3] Yet Frank refused to give up his penniless sweetheart Mary Thorne and his creator was obliged to kill off Sir Roger Scatcherd and his only son, Sir Louis, in order to make her a wealthy heiress and so permit the marriage to go through. In one form or another the *deus ex machina* of a satisfactory middle-range income comes into all Trollope's plots. The choice in fact before his characters never worked itself out as between riches and poverty, but between wealth and sufficiency. Crosbie would not have been a poor man if he had not forsaken Lily Dale for the opulent hand of Alexandrina de Courcy; and George Vavasor, Phineas Finn, and Frank Greystock were not faced with the dilemma of love in a cottage

---

[1] A. Trollope: *The Three Clerks* (1858).
[2] A. Trollope: *Small House at Allington* (1864), Chs. 2, 5, 6, and 15.
[3] A. Trollope: *Doctor Thorne* (1858), Ch. 4, *et seq.*

versus luxury in the hall, but riches and a political career on the one hand as opposed to love and a struggle to make good but on a competence on the other.[1]

Trollope's own career was not very different from the world of his fancy. In the Civil Service in London his prospects were not good. As a clerk his salary increased by less than £10 a year and even if he had stayed there for twenty-one years his maximum at the grade would not normally have risen above £260.[2] In 1840 he applied for and obtained the post of surveyor's clerk in the Irish branch of the Post Office at a salary of £100 a year; but the work entailed a great deal of travelling and at 15s. per day subsistence allowance plus 6d. per mile in a country where travelling was done at half the English prices, his income after paying his expenses became at once £400. 'This was the first good fortune of my life.'

The second was when at Kingstown, the watering-place near Dublin, in one of his journeys he met Rose Heseltine. 'The engagement took place', he wrote, 'when I had been just one year in Ireland; but there was still a delay of two years before we could be married. She had no fortune, nor had I any income beyond that which came from the Post Office; there were still a few debts.' In 1844 they were married. 'We were not very rich, having about £400 a year on which to live. Many people would say that we were two fools to encounter such poverty together. I can only reply that since that day I have never been without money in my pocket, and that I soon acquired the means of paying what I owed.'[3] Living in Ireland was cheaper than in England and Trollope was able to spend a great deal of his time hunting. Nevertheless, for some years they lived in lodgings and his two sons were born there.[4] Yet it could hardly be claimed that they lived in poverty. £400 a year was a competence.

By this time moreover he was trying in real earnestness to become a writer; and there is no doubt about his reasons for

[1] A. Trollope: *Small House at Allington* (1864), *Can you Forgive Her?* (1864), *Phineas Finn* (1869), and *The Eustace Diamonds* (1873).
[2] See E. Yates: *Edmund Yates: his Recollections and Experiences* (1884), Vol. One, p. 123.
[3] A. Trollope: *An Autobiography* (1883), Ch. 4.
[4] Henry Merivale, March 1846, and Frederick James Anthony, March 1849.

attempting a double career. 'My first object in taking to literature as a profession was that which is common to the barrister
when he goes to the Bar, and to the baker when he sets up his
oven. I wished to make an income on which I and those
belonging to me might live in comfort.'[1] In 1853 promotion in
the service came. He was made a surveyor at £800 a year plus
expenses.[2] *The Warden, Barchester Towers, The Three Clerks,* and
Dr. Thorne were written soon afterwards. For the last he received £400 and he now began to calculate his chances for the
future. 'If I wrote a novel, I could certainly sell it. And if I
could publish three in two years . . . I might add £600 a year
to my official income. I was still living in Ireland, and could
keep a good house over my head, insure my life, educate my
two boys, and hunt perhaps twice a week, on £1,400 a year. If
more should come, it would be well; but £600 a year I was
prepared to reckon a success. It had been slow in coming, but
was very pleasant when it came.'[3]

We are fortunate that Trollope was so preoccupied with the
financial aspects of life, for it comes out very well in his novels
and supplements what we have learned elsewhere. Take, for
example, the question of the equipage. On £400 a year he
clearly felt that horses were questionable, although he had two
hunters and employed a groom. He was obliged therefore to
cover as much ground as possible at 6d. per mile, to pay for
them, and was not happy unless he did. His characters were
made to feel similarly. Thus on £900 a year Mark Robarts gave
his wife a pony-carriage, kept a saddle-horse for himself and
had a second horse for his gig. 'A man in his position, well-to-do
as he was, required as much as that.' He had a footman too, a
gardener and a groom. 'The two latter were absolutely necessary, but about the former there had been a question.' When he
made himself responsible for Nathaniel Sowerby's £400 debt,
'he pronounced to himself the doom of that footman, and the
doom also of that saddle-horse. They at any rate should go.
And then he would spend no more money on trips to Scotland.'[4]

[1] A. Trollope: *An Autobiography* (1883), Ch. 6.
[2] See Note G, p. 222.
[3] A. Trollope: *An Autobiography* (1883), Ch. 7.
[4] A. Trollope: *Framley Parsonage* (1861), Ch. 9.

This last point is interesting in that it directly reflects upon Trollope's personal experience. His own family was living in Florence all the time that he was working in Ireland but it was not until April 1853, after his promotion to the rank of surveyor, that he was able to take his wife to see his mother and brother.[1] In the next five years, however, they visited them in Italy three times.[2]

We saw earlier how £300 a year was a much-discussed income in the late 1850s. Here is how Trollope regarded it in 1870. Miss Sarah Marrable, with £300 a year, took a small house in the respectable part of the county town of Loring where rents were cheap, 'and here Miss Marrable was able to live, and occasionally to give tea-parties, and to provide a comfortable home for her niece, within the limits of her income'.

She apparently did not stint herself over clothes for she was always nicely dressed and always wore silk at and after lunch.

'She dressed three times a day, and in the morning would come down in what she called a merino gown. But then, with her, clothes never seemed to wear out. . . . She was never seen of an afternoon or evening without gloves, and her gloves were always clean and apparently new. . . . She was as grand a lady to herself, eating her little bit of cold mutton, or dining off a tiny sole, as though she sat at the finest banquet that could be spread. She had no fear of economies, either before the two handmaids or anybody else in the world. She was fond of her tea, and in summer could have cream for twopence; but when cream became dear, she saved money and had a penn'orth of milk. She drank two glasses of Marsala every day, and let it be clearly understood that she couldn't afford sherry. But when she gave a tea-party, as she did, perhaps six or seven times a year, sherry was always handed round with cake before the people went away. There were matters in which she was extravagant. When she went out herself she never took one of the common street flies, but paid eighteen pence extra to get a brougham from the Dragon. And when Mary Lowther—who had only fifty pounds a year of her own, with which she clothed herself

[1] L. P and R. P. Stebbins: *The Trollopes* (1946), p. 141.
[2] A. Trollope: *An Autobiography* (1883), Ch. 6.

and provided herself with pocket money—was going to Bull-hampton, Miss Marrable actually proposed to her to take one of the maids with her. Mary, of course, would not hear of it, and said that she should just as soon think of taking the house; but Miss Marrable had thought that it would, perhaps, not be well for a girl so well-born as Miss Lowther to go out visiting without a maid. She herself rarely left Loring, because she could not afford it; but when, two summers back, she did go to Weston-super-Mare for a fortnight, she took one of the girls with her.'[1]

Here the family was small, consisting of two maiden ladies and their two servants, and one of the ladies had a further £50 to herself, making £350 in all. Yet there is a similarity in this to the pattern laid down by Walsh in 1873 which is striking. This novel is also interesting in that the question of £300 a year and marriage was raised in it, when Walter Marrable, old Sarah's nephew, fell in love with Mary Lowther, his cousin. At the time he was an army captain, receiving a captain's pay, and optimistic about his prospects of receiving a further £300 a year. Told by an uncle that of course he could not think of marrying on such a figure, his reply was scornful:

' "Half the fellows in the army are married without anything beyond their pay; and I'm to be told that we can't get along with £300 a year! At any rate, we'll try."

"Marry in haste, and repent at leisure," said Uncle John.

"According to the doctrines that are going now-a-days," said the Captain, "it will be held soon that a gentleman can't marry unless he has got £3,000 a year. It is the most heartless, damnable teaching that ever came up. It spoils the men, and makes women, when they do marry, expect ever so many things that they ought never to want."

"And you mean to teach them better, Walter?"

"I mean to act for myself, and not be frightened out of doing what I think right, because the world says this and that."

As he spoke, the angry Captain got up to leave the room.

"All the same," rejoined the Parson, firing the last shot, "I'd

---

[1] A. Trollope: *The Vicar of Bullhampton* (1870), Ch. 9.

think twice about it, if I were you, before I married Mary Lowther." '[1]

In this case, the course of true love, as usual with Trollope, ran smooth, for although for a time Walter lost his £300 and decided that without it marriage was impossible, another uncle Sir Gregory, worth about £3,000 a year accepted him as his heir when his only son died. Thus the *deus ex machina* appeared according to custom, although it is noticeable that the standard was higher by 1870.

In all the novels of Trollope dealing with this kind of thing there is a clear recognition of class differences in the extent to which any given income was conceived to be appropriate. It came out first in his treatment of clergyman and curates. To a certain extent this appeared in *Barchester Towers* where Mr. Quiverful's fourteen children were made fourteen good arguments for his obtaining the post which most people felt should go to Septimus Harding[2] and the struggle of his wife to manage on £70 was most sympathetically portrayed, but it was in *Framley Parsonage* that the comparison with the working classes really showed. Josiah Crawley received no more than £70 per annum for ten years during which time his wife had several children, of whom only three survived. Their plight was described as follows:

'And so they had established themselves, beginning the world with one bare-footed little girl of fourteen to aid them in their small household matters; and for a while they had both kept heart, loving each other dearly and prospering somewhat in their work. But a man who has once walked the world as a gentleman knows not what it is to change his position, and place himself lower down in the social rank. Much less can he know what it is so to put down the woman whom he loves. There are a thousand things, mean and trifling in themselves, which a man despises when he thinks of them in his philosophy, but to dispense with which puts his philosophy to so stern a proof. . . . And then children had come. The wife of the labouring man does rear her children, and often rears them in health,

---

[1] *Ibid.*, Ch. 21.
[2] A Trollope: *Barchester Towers* (1857), Ch. 25.

without even so many appliances of comfort as found their way into Mrs. Crawley's cottage; but the task to her was almost more than she could accomplish.'[1]

A later novel recognized the difference in outlook between the classes as an explanation of their different approaches to the question of marriage. Frank Greystock and Arthur Herriot, puzzled by the problem of the lack of inducements to the middle-class man to marry, discussed how it might nevertheless be brought about that they should.

' "We can't do it by statute."

"No, thank God."

"Nor yet by fashion."

"Fashion seems to be going the other way," said Herriot.

"It can only be done by education and conscience. Take men of forty all round—men of our own class—you believe that the married are happier than the unmarried? . . ."

"I think the married are happier. . . ."

". . . If morality in life and enlarged affections are conducive to happiness it must be so."

"Short commons and unpaid bills are conducive to misery. That's what I should say if I wanted to oppose you."

"I never came across a man willing to speak the truth who did not admit that, in the long run, married men are the happier. As regards women, there isn't even ground for argument. And yet men don't marry."

"They can't."

"You mean there isn't food enough in the world."

"The man fears that he won't get enough of what there is for his wife and family."

"The labourer with twelve shillings a week has no such fear. And if he did marry the food would come. It isn't that. The man is unconvinced and ignorant as to the source of true happiness, and won't submit himself to cold mutton and three clean shirts a week—not because he dislikes mutton and dirty linen himself—but because the world says they are vulgar. That's the feeling that keeps you from marrying, Herriot." '[2]

[1] A. Trollope: *Framley Parsonage* (1861), Ch. 16.
[2] A. Trollope: *The Eustace Diamonds* (1873), Ch. 24.

One final example: Gerard Maule, with £800 a year wanted to marry Adelaide Palliser who had a fortune of only £4,000.[1] His father said he looked on it as an 'act of simple madness'.

' "Yet sir, married men with families have lived on my income."

"And on less than a quarter of it. The very respectable man who brushes my clothes no doubt does so. But then you see he has been brought up in that way." '[2]

The complete unreadiness of men like Gerard Maule for the exigencies of married life was also emphasized in this passage.

' "I suppose that you as a bachelor put by every year at least half your income?"

"I never put by a shilling, sir. Indeed, I owe a few hundred pounds."

"And yet you expect to keep a home over your head, and an expensive wife and family, with lady's maid, nurses, cook, footman, and grooms, on a sum which has been hitherto insufficient for your own wants! I didn't think you were such an idiot, my boy!" '

This particular novel is interesting in that it contains a list of the economies which Trollope conceived would be necessary if Adelaide and Gerard were to make a success of their married life on £800 a year. To begin with they would have to lay out her fortune on repairing and furnishing Maule Abbey, where no one was living at the time.

'Then, if Gerard Maule would be prudent, and give up hunting, and farm a little himself—and if Adelaide would do her own housekeeping and dress upon forty pounds a year, and if they would both live an exemplary, model, energetic, and strictly economical life, both ends might be made to meet. . . . After all there could be no such great difficulty for a young married couple to live on £800 a year, with a house and a garden of their own. There would be no carriage and no man

[1] A. Trollope: *Phineas Redux* (1873), Ch. 3.
[2] *Ibid.*, Ch. 21.

123

servant till—till old Mr. Maule was dead. The property would be Gerard's some day.'

We may compare this with the standard of living proposed for the £750 per annum range set out by Walsh in the same year that the novel appeared. This income, he thought, would permit of a page or general man-servant, a parlourmaid, a second housemaid and a cook, total wages, £95. £75 might be put aside for the equipage, one horse or a pony and gig; while £50 for the wife's clothes and £45 for the husband's should suffice.[1] Thus the standards allowed by the household economist permitted of a greater expenditure on what has been called 'the paraphernalia of gentility' than Trollope would tolerate for his characters, but in general the patterns agree.

Indeed, the explanation for the novelist's tendency to scale upwards probably lies in the fact that by this time he was living well above this level himself. Towards the end of 1859 he had been appointed surveyor in England, a step which must have reduced his income a little as English travelling was more expensive than Irish, but it could have been a reduction of very little significance, for by now his novels were selling for a fair sum of money. So far he had had nine published altogether and one book of travels, amounting in all to £2,819 17s. 5d. for twelve years' work.[2] In the following year Smith and Elder offered him £1,000 for the copyright of his next three-decker novel. This was more than double anything he had yet received and he felt himself able to take on a Georgian house at Waltham Abbey on which he spent £1,000 in improvements. He lived there for the next twelve years and it was, as he said, a period of great prosperity.[3] Thus between 1860 and 1870 he wrote twenty-one books and issued four collections of tales for which he obtained £35,620, or more than £3,000 a year.[4] In addition to his salary as surveyor this total raised him well into the ranks of the upper-middle classes; and although he resigned from the Post Office in 1867, it was in order to take over the post of

[1] J. H. Walsh: *A Manual of Domestic Economy* (2nd ed., 1873), pp. 221, 369 and 677.
[2] For the details see Note H, p. 222.
[3] A. Trollope: *An Autobiography* (1883), Ch. 8.
[4] See Note H, p. 222.

A Case Study— Anthony Trollope

editor to the newly issued *St. Paul's Magazine*, for which he obtained £1,000 a year, and this lasted him until May 1870.[1] Now some of the entertainment he was describing in his novels was made possible for him,[2] especially since the house at Waltham Abbey produced its own vegetables, pork and butter.[3]

It is at this point that we must leave him, for in the early 1870s, as his biographers point out, Anthony Trollope suffered a gradual disillusionment, the fruit of which was his satirical attack on the bad new times of England in *The Way we Live Now*.[4] It is tempting, of course, to carry this over as illustrative of the change of atmosphere which lies central to our theme. Anthony Trollope was the product of his time, and with the greater difficulties which came upon the middle and upper classes in the seventies, it is to be expected that he would reflect the growing anxiety and bitterness of his generation in a severe castigation of the intrigues of girls who desperately wanted to get married and of young men who dearly preferred to remain single, even if, as with Sir Felix Carbury, there was every pressure on them to embark upon the matrimonial state because the lady was an heiress. In his portrayal of the mentality involved in this arrangement of alliances between aristocracy and plutocracy, Trollope was brutally frank.

' "Business is business," Sir Felix said to his mother. "You want me to marry the girl because of her money."

"You want to marry her yourself."

"I'm quite a philosopher about it. I want her money; and when one wants money, one should make up one's mind how much or how little one means to take—and whether one is sure to get it."

"I don't think there can be any doubt."

[1] L. P. and R. P. Stebbins: *The Trollopes* (1946), p. 263.

[2] The house parties are most prominent in the political novels, viz. *Can You Forgive Her?* (1864), *Phineas Finn* (1869), *The Eustace Diamonds* (1873), *Phineas Redux* (1874), *The Prime Minister* (1876), and *The Duke's Children* (1880).

[3] A. Trollope: *North America* (1862). 'Out of my own little patches at home I have enough for all domestic purposes of peas, beans, brocoli, cauliflower, celery, beetroot, onions, carrots, parsnips, turnips, seakale, asparagus, French beans, artichokes, vegetable marrow, cucumber, tomatoes, endive, lettuce, as well as herbs of many kinds; cabbages throughout the year, and potatoes.' (New ed., 1867), Vol. 1, p. 183.

[4] L. P. and R. P. Stebbins, *op. cit.*, Ch. 19, and A. Trollope: *An Autobiography* (1883), Ch. 20.

"If I were to marry her, and if the money wasn't there, it would be very like cutting my throat then, mother. If a man plays and loses, he can play again and perhaps win; but when a fellow goes in for an heiress, and gets the wife without the money, he feels a little hampered you know." '[1]

This is a far cry from the emphasis on love and a competence so prominent in the earlier novels; but Trollope was an ageing man. In February 1875, when the first instalment of the story appeared, he was a month or two off fifty-nine, with less than eight more years to live. This in itself may have affected him, quite apart from the tenor of his day. His eyesight was beginning to fail, so that he became dependent upon his wife's niece to take down his books to dictation. He was forced to give up hunting, which had always meant so much to him, although he was able to keep on riding until the end. His popularity was on the wane, notwithstanding the fact that his writings still sold well; and all in all this decade was not a very pleasant one for him personally. For these reasons, it would not be wise to rely too much upon his novels as reflecting without distortion what was happening to his fellow men. To the middle-class way of life of the 1850s and 1860s he is an excellent guide, as his fortunes were waxing as those of the middle classes waxed and his powers as a chronicler were at their height; but in the 1870s we cannot be so sure of him, because although his star was waning in a period of economic depression, his powers were waning too, and it is not easy to distinguish between Trollope the man and Trollope the mirror of a class. For our purpose, however, the novels of the earlier period will suffice, since we see portrayed in them the problems of a career, of marriage, and of money, as they appeared to that section of the community whose standard of living was developing in the way our earlier chapters have described; and there can be very little doubt that the people of real life whose day-to-day activities he used as the setting for his imaginary characters were just the people who most felt the impact of the Great Depression when it came.

This excursus into the life and writings of Anthony Trollope raises the interesting question of how far novels may be taken

---

[1] A. Trollope; *The Way We Live Now* (1875), Ch. 23.

as documents for social history. In this chapter it has been assumed that quotations from Trollope's novels are illustrative not only of his personal views on the problems of marriage and the standard of living, but also of those of the members of the middle classes generally. That is to say, his voice has been regarded as an echo of the people of London and of the English shires where he was born and reared and where he lived and worked and recorded his everyday experience. But, it may be asked, has not the implication been wider than this? Has it not been suggested that, for instance, the conversation between the clergyman and the officer, taken from the *Vicar of Bull-hampton*[1] was in some way typical of what a middle-class uncle might well have said to his nephew, or what the member of one professional group might well have said to the member of another round about the year 1870? And is this valid? Can we accept Trollope's novels as a record of what was more than merely generally true? Are we justified in treating the actions and words of his characters as specifically representative of the actions and words of the different sexes, of the different age groups, of the people of the different occupations, and of the members of the different social classes, which is what they purport to be?

There is, of course, no simple answer to this charge. Novels must at least be treated like all other sources used as material for the reconstruction of the past. As with the report of a middle-class government inspector on the conditions of life of the labouring classes, the data has to be carefully sifted for evidence that its author was a reliable observer of matters of fact. To a considerable degree this means taking into account the background of the man himself so that we may allow for the distortions which arise from personal idiosyncrasies and from those social presuppositions which are the product of a special kind of education and upbringing. But that is all. The imaginative aspects of fictional writing which supposedly make it suspect to a historian who wishes to get at what was 'really' happening, are no more difficult of appraisal than any other aspect of documentary content—no more difficult, that is, provided we know as much about our source to distinguish between what the

[1] See pp. 120–1.

author may well have known and what he must have invented. In this sense a novel by a Victorian set in the Middle Ages is of as much value, or of as little value, to us as any other book on the Middle Ages written during the Victorian period. As material for information on the mediaeval way of life, it would be merely secondary, and we might do much better to go to the sources used by the novelist, or the historian, direct.[1] But as a document on the outlook of the Victorian period itself, either would have some specific value as a primary source. This does not mean that every novel has the same worth—no more than every history, or every government report, has the same worth —but it does mean that each *in its own way* bears the imprint of the times in which its author lived.

Every novel, therefore, is a sociological novel, except perhaps those which set out deliberately to be so. For this reason we should hesitate to rely on middle-class novelists for our information on contemporary working-class life, if we had good grounds for believing that they had relied for their information not upon experience of working-class behaviour but on government reports; but just because they were middle class themselves, those novelists who set their plots in the way of life of that class among whom they customarily moved and whose everyday behaviour they had every opportunity of observing, may well be regarded as sources of primary information for the social historian. In this way we may claim that Trollope was a writer of 'reports', the details in which are as reliable as those produced by government inspectors on whose word we are dependent for much of our knowledge of the nineteenth-century working class; and it is absurd to refuse to use what his novels can supply, on the grounds that they are 'purely imaginative', at the same time as having no qualms whatsoever about almost every other kind of writing merely because it is 'serious'. All this is merely to say that novels may be used as historical documents provided that they are used intelligently; and this means no more than treating them as we ought in fact to treat any other kind of record whatever its form.

[1] A good example is George Eliot's *Romola*, for the sources of which see her Journal of 17th December 1861, as given in J. W. Cross: *George Eliot's Life as Related in her Letters and Journals* (1885), Vol. 2, Ch. 11, p. 325.

CHAPTER IX

The Eighteen Seventies and After

IN recent years economic historians have more and more inclined to the view that there is something enigmatic about the 'Great Depression'. While it is freely admitted that from about 1873 onwards the leaders of English business enterprises certainly avowed their affairs to be regularly subject to a series of grave reversals, it is emphatically maintained that it was the business men themselves and the politicians rather than the economists and statisticians who were the most vociferous in expressing the current uneasiness. It is not for a moment denied that this was indeed a period of economic restriction but, it is pointed out, the really fundamental facts about the situation were falling prices and a continued elusiveness of profits. In no sense of the term could conditions be described as actually retrogressive. Businesses, it is true, found themselves hard pushed to make the profits they had made earlier, but they made some nevertheless, and for this reason the age might better be known as one of 'lean years' in contrast to the preceding 'good years'.[1] Hence the 'Depression' appears as a psychological reaction to a field of narrowed opportunity rather than as an objective description of what was economically the case.

Even as early as 1886 a Royal Commission had expressed a similar conviction.[2] Although, as the Majority Report pointed out, complaints from all sides were in agreement that business

---

[1] See, for example, H. L. Beales: 'The Great Depression in Industry and Trade' in the *Economic History Review*, October 1934. W. W. Rostow: *British Economy in the Nineteenth Century* (1948), Ch. 3.

[2] Final Report of the Royal Commission 'appointed to Inquire into the Depression of Trade and Industry' (*Parliamentary Papers*, 1886, Vol. 23).

was being conducted with the smallest possible margin of profit and in very many cases 'with no profit at all' the statistics of income tax did not appear to provide evidence that this was so. Assessments per head of the total population had risen from £15 3s. in 1872 to £17 7s. in 1876, and they still stood at £17 6s. in 1884–5. Under Schedule D, the figures of commercial profits alone had remained surprisingly stable, being £8 2s. per head in 1875, £8 3s. in 1876, £8 2s. in 1884 and £8 1s. in 1885. It was thus worthy of remark that the amount of profits brought to the notice of the tax collectors had actually increased with great steadiness throughout the preceding five years—'a period which the universal testimony of those best qualified to form an opinion pronounces to have been the least profitable in the commercial history of this country'. What had really happened was a redistribution of wealth. 'A smaller proportion falls to the share of the employers of labour than formerly.'[1]

This conclusion was nowhere rejected by the writers of the Minority Reports. Although in some cases critical of the uses made of income-tax statistics, they were concerned to demonstrate that their fellow Commissioners had drawn invalid inferences from the situation rather than to argue that their facts were wrong. In no case did they maintain that incomes had not continued to rise. This they considered to be somewhat beside the point. Their main topic of interest was with total profits and hence with returns on capital, and here the situation was certainly far less favourable.[2] From our point of view, however, the facts are hardly in doubt. While there was certainly no retrogression, the *rate* of progress had slackened off. The general prosperity of the mid-Victorian years had received a serious check.[3]

This is clearly shown in the totals of income assessed under all schedules, calculated from Stamp's tables, for the five-year periods centred on the Census years.[4]

---

[1] *Ibid.*, paras. 31, 44–48, 52–55, 92 (pp. xi–xxiii).
[2] *Ibid.* See in particular the report by R. H. I. Palgrave (pp. xxxvi–vii) and also parts of the rest (pp. xxxi–iii, xliv–l).
[3] See A. Sauerbeck: 'Prices of Commodities and the Precious Metals' in the *Journal of the Statistical Society*, September 1886, p. 623.
[4] J. C. Stamp: *British Incomes and Property* (1916), Table G.4, pp. 318–19.

Total Income Assessed (United Kingdom and Ireland)

Census Date	Assessment Period	Income over £150
1871	1868–9 to 1872–3	£1,882·1 millions
1881	1878–9 to 1882–3	£2,506·3 ,,
1891	1888–9 to 1892–3	£2,916·2 ,,
1901	1898–9 to 1902–3	£3,673·7 ,,
1911	1909–9 to 1912–13	£4,556·1 ,,

From this table we have the following ten-year increases:

	Per cent
1871–1881	33·2
1881–1891	16·4
1891–1901	26·0
1901–1911	24·0

Here there is evidence that the decade 1881–91 witnessed a considerable abatement in the growth of incomes over £150 and at no time during the forty years under review was there a return to the remarkable expansion of the 1860s (44·9 per cent for 1861–71)[1]. In so far, therefore, as the great expansion in taxable wealth in the earlier decades had been the main factor in the rise in middle-class standards, the period after 1873 may well be regarded as one of quite serious limitation and hence of re-assessment of the cost of raising children.

This argument, however, should not be accepted without further question. There was, after all, a continued growth of taxable wealth during the forty years, and the movement of retail prices may well have operated to offset the falling-off in the rise of incomes—at least, until the end of the 1880s. This indeed would appear to be borne out by a study of Wood's indices of retail prices. Between 1871 and 1881 these fell by about 10 per cent and between 1881 and 1891 by 13 per cent. Thereafter the fall was checked and the new century witnessed a considerable movement in the opposite direction. (A fall of 1·5 per cent for 1891–1901 and a rise of 11·6 per cent for 1901–11.)[2] Certain commodities, of interest to us here, were very sensitive. Thus, between 1871–5 and 1894–8, the price of sugar

[1] See p. 105.
[2] The retail price increases have been calculated from the indices of average retail prices given in W. T. Layton and G. J. Crowther: *An Introduction to the Study of Prices* (3rd ed., 1938), Appendix E, Table 1.

fell by 58 per cent, tea by 54 per cent, flour by 41 per cent, potatoes by 39 per cent, coal by 38 per cent, rice by 35 per cent, pork by 33 per cent, beef by 29 per cent, bacon by 26 per cent, butter by 25 per cent, mutton by 25 per cent and coffee by 10 per cent.[1] It is not surprising, therefore, that we find no complaints from the middle classes about the cost of food during this period, and it was not until the turn of the century that the periodical press began to repeat the arguments of the 1870s about the rising cost of living. At the same time, it must be emphasized that even during the difficult first decade of the twentieth century when *real wages* fell,[2] it is likely that *real* middle-class incomes continued to rise.

The evidence for this is frankly conjectural, and is derived from a comparison of Stamp's figures of taxable incomes with Wood's indices of retail price movements. By correcting the increases observable in the former in accordance with the variations of the latter a set of figures may be obtained which certainly *seem* to suggest a continuation of middle-class progress. The details are given below.

Increases in incomes, prices, and real incomes, 1851–1911

Period	Incomes over £150 Per cent	Retail Prices Per cent	Real incomes[3] Per cent
1851–1861	23·4	10·0	12·2
1861–1871	44·9	5·6	37·2
1871–1881	33·2	—10·0	48·0
1881–1891	16·4	—13·0	33·8
1891–1901	26·0	—1·5	27·9
1901–1911	24·0	11·6	11·1

From these figures it would appear that for the thirty years up to 1881 each decade experienced an even more rapid expansion in middle-class *real* wealth than had been experienced in the previous decade. After 1881 the movement was in the opposite direction. We are, of course, as yet remarkably ignorant of the mechanism by which such variations in economic circum-

---

[1] *Ibid.*, Table P. 88.

[2] Wages rose by only 3·4 per cent between 1901 and 1911 (calculated from Layton and Crowther, *op. cit.*, Appendix E, Table 1).

[3] Calculated directly from the figures given in the text by dividing the income increases by the retail price changes.

stances make their influence felt upon the outlook of individual human beings, but it does not appear unwarrantable to suggest that there might be some correlation between this fact of steadily narrowing opportunity after 1880 and the spread of family limitation. Granted that ideas about prudential marriage had already become closely associated with a concept of the standard of living, itself derived from the growing power of the middle classes to purchase socially peremptory goods and services, a change in the circumstances producing this ever-rising standard of living would in time affect the general conception of marriage and its consequences. That is to say, the fact that the so-called 'Great Depression' had no perceptible influence on the middle-class *level* of living, except perhaps to raise it through the lower prices which prevailed, is of far less importance to us here than its concomitant impact on the growth of incomes, and hence on contemporary ideas of what was required by a civilized way of life. What appears to be the operative factor in this connection, therefore, is the *comparison* members of the middle classes were able to make of their own levels of living at different times with those of their immediate neighbours and acquaintances; and in so far as this had any influence whatever on the strength of their aspirations, it is not unlikely that the period after 1880 by reducing the extent to which men found it possible to scale the income ladder, also resulted in their seeking alternative ways of achieving social mobility or 'social promotion'[1] by cutting down in some departments of expenditure, especially those not directly relevant to their appearing affluent to the eyes of the world.

All this, however, depends upon the degree to which the *total* income figures as given in Stamp's table are an indication of the amounts individual members of the middle classes were able to spend on socially desirable goods and services. As we saw in

---

[1] This is the term favoured by the Royal Commission on Population (Report, *Parliamentary Papers*, 1948–9, Vol. 19, para. 100). In general the present argument follows that of the Report and of A. Dumont: *Dépopulation et Civilisation* (1890), especially Ch. 6 *passim*. Dumont calls the force which causes social mobility alternatively *capillarité sociale* and *attraction capillaire* and regards it as dependent upon the psychological 'fact' that 'when the goal dreamed of is not too disproportionate to the means of attaining it the strength of the aspiration multiplies man's powers and hastens his progress' (p. 109).

Chapter VII, the attempt to arrive at a reliable estimate of the incomes received by income-tax payers is beset with considerable difficulties. Moreover for the period after 1873 the factual data presented in official publications is even less tractable than for the preceding twenty years. Nevertheless what evidence there is[1] generally seems to support the view that from about 1873–5 onwards the lower middle classes grew more rapidly in numbers and in comparative wealth than did their richer neighbours, and if we assume that it was the latter group who first began to limit their families, once more it would appear that it was the felt threat to their social superiority which was the operative factor in bringing about the decline in fertility.

It is interesting in this connection to consider the problem of domestic service as it appeared in the last quarter of the nineteenth century. As we have already seen, a middle-class household to be complete in all its functions required a minimum of three domestic servants whose wages in consequence formed a not inconsiderable burden on the middle-class budget. Between 1871 and 1900, moreover, female domestic servants' wage rates rose by some 30–37 per cent[2]—a remarkable increase when compared with the 19 per cent for women's wages generally.[3] Part of this, of course, arose from the ever-growing demand for them produced by the still-growing number of those in receipt of middle-class incomes, but part also arose from a movement of labour out of the industry. Girls no longer showed themselves eager to take up housework as a career, and the lack of supply drove wage rates up.

To establish this quantitatively requires that we should treat the Census returns with considerable care as the system of classification was changed at each successive Census. However, the figures for 1881, 1901 and 1911 are not incapable of direct comparison and these show an increase in the number of female

[1] See J. A. Banks: *The English Middle-Class Concept of the Standard of Living* (unpub. 1952), pp. 196–200.

[2] W. T. Layton: 'Changes in the Wages of Domestic Servants during the Fifty Years' in the *Journal of the Statistical Society*, September 1908.

[3] G. H. Wood: 'The Course of Women's Wages during the Nineteenth Century', Appendix A to B. L. Hutchins and A. Harrison: *A History of Factory Legislation* (1903), p. 278.

domestics of 0·41 per cent per annum for the first twenty years and 0·21 per cent per annum for the last ten, as compared with 1·26 per cent and 1·09 per cent per annum for the total population for the same two periods respectively.[1]

The Census of 1901, indeed, commented on this comparative decline and went on to point out that the increase in the number of domestic servants was 'limited to women aged twenty years and upwards'. The numbers in this group had risen by 23·5 per cent over the previous twenty years whereas among girls under the age of twenty there had been a decrease during the same period of 12·3 per cent. The following table, taken from the report, shows the increase (+) or decrease (-) per cent for the different age groups over the twenty years:[2]

Under 15	15–	20–	25–	45–	Over 65	Total
−34	−7·3	+16·5	+33·1	+20	+1·2	+8·2

Part of the cause for the reduction in the proportion of the under fifteens employed was no doubt the introduction of compulsory education in 1876 and the progressive raising of the school-leaving age in the years that followed, but as the Census Report pointed out, this cannot have accounted for the decline between the ages of fifteen and twenty. 'The decrease of 7·3 per cent in the number of domestic servants at ages between fifteen and twenty years, notwithstanding an increase of 28·1 per cent in the number of females living at these ages, suggests the conclusion that young women are preferring other employments.'[3]

The period 1901–11 witnessed a continuation of the trend:

10–	14–	15–	20–	25–	35–	45–	55–	Over 65	Total
−62·7	−17·2	−2·1	−1·7	+7·3	+19·3	+22·9	+12·0	+4·3	+2·1

Once again the Census Report commented on the 'increasing disinclination on the part of young women to enter indoor domestic service'.[4] It was, as a writer put it in the 1890s, 'no

---

[1] For a more detailed account of the use and difficulties of these statistics, as well as of those for male domestics, see J. A. Banks, *op. cit.*, pp. 202–4.

[2] *Census of England and Wales, 1901*. General Report with Appendices (1904), p. 95.

[3] *Ibid.*, p. 96.

[4] *Census of England and Wales, 1911*, General Report (1917), Vol. 4, p. 106. The table is from Vol. 10 (1914), p. xxvi.

longer regarded as honourable' to enter domestic service.[1] The
day when the daughters of the working classes would cease to
work for the middle and upper classes, foretold by the *Westminster Review* fifty years since,[2] had arrived. There was a rebellion
in the ranks of the employees in 'the *unpopular* industry'.[3]

The importance of this for our study of expenses and standards is twofold. As we have seen, the employment of older
servants required the payment of higher wage rates. One of the
effects, therefore, of the movement of young girls away from
domestic service into other forms of employment[4] was to throw
a greater burden on the middle-class budget. This was true not
only for those who were lucky enough to obtain servants, but
for the unlucky ones, for in comparison with the low rate of
increase in indoor domestic female servants from 1881 to 1911,
the Census tables show an increase in the number of charwomen
of 13·3 per cent for 1881–91[5], 6·7 per cent for 1891–1901, and
12·7 per cent for 1901–11.[6] Part of this increase, it is true, can
be explained in terms of the expansion of commercial offices
requiring cleaning during this period, but part also represents
the increased demand for cleaners on the part of those middle-
class households which were unable to get full-time labour.

The other effect was one of a change of standards. Having
less servants to rely on meant that certain essential functions
had to be performed in a different way. Washing, for example,
was put out.[7] The smaller suburban house came to be regarded
less unfavourably when less of its room space was taken up by

---

[1] A. S. Swan: *Courtship and Marriage* (1893), p. 130.

[2] 'Helix': 'Human Progress' in the *Westminster Review*, October 1849. He thought
that the only remedy for the middle class was to increase the number of mechanical appliances and labour-saving processes 'to make themselves self-dependent as
fast as their domestic servants become independent'. (P. 22.)

[3] A. A. Bully: 'Domestic Service: a Social Study' in the *Westminster Review*,
February 1891. Articles on this subject were legion at the close of the century and
the beginning of the next.

[4] It is not necessary for our purpose to discuss why this happened when it did,
but we may note in passing Ensor's interesting suggestion that it was due to the
drift from the land. The great bulk of the domestic servants of an earlier age had
come from the families of agricultural labourers. R. C. K. Ensor: *England, 1870–
1914* (1936), p. 272.

[5] *Census of England and Wales, 1891*, Vol. 4 (1893), p. 40.

[6] *Census of England and Wales, 1911*, Vol. 10 (1914), p. xxxi.

[7] *Cassell's Book of the Household* (1890), Vol. 2, p. 138.

the servants, every additional one of which made 'one more person to cook and provide for, one more person to wash dishes and clothes for, one more person to use the family goods, one more temper to be conciliated'. There was, after all, something in the view that the multiplication of servants did not lead to the work being better done.[1] At the same time, the status-function of servants began to disappear. In London two servants were, for the professional classes, at least, still a *sine qua non*; in suburbia one was enough.[2]

There nevertheless continued for a long time to exist a strong body of feeling that there was a limit to this process. A lady, after all, could not be expected to do household chores,[3] and a middle-class housewife who was, if only temporarily, 'without' was an object of general sympathy.[4] In any case the rationale had been worked out long before. A mother was in charge of immortal beings. She must therefore have the time to devote her first strength and utmost effort to the highest duties.

'But how can she be adequate to this if the whole attention to the personal comfort of several young children devolves upon her? If she is to make and mend their articles of dress, bear them in her arms during their period of helplessness, and exhaust herself by toils throughout the day and watchings by night, how can she have leisure to study their various shades of disposition, and adapt to each the fitting mode of discipline, as the skilful gardener suits the seed to the soil? . . . The remedy is for the mother to provide herself with competent assistance in the spheres of manual labour, that she may be enabled to become the constant directress of her children, and have leisure to be

[1] *Ibid.*, p. 137. This argument had already been made in the article: 'A Word to Young Mistresses' in the *Family Friend*, December 1861, quoting a rhyme of 1721 to bear out the point. The point of view was quite old. The new circumstances merely resuscitated it and gave it added force.

[2] J. E. Panton: *Nooks and Corners, being a companion Volume to 'From Kitchen to Garret'* (1889), p. 191.

[3] F. P. Cobbe: 'Household Service in *The Fortnightly Review*, January 1868. See also the various references to the servant problem scattered through this chapter. There was a symposium on the subject in *The Lady's Realm*, June 1897 (p. 212 *et seq.*) entitled 'The Domestic Servant Difficulty'.

[4] W. MacQueen-Pope: *Twenty Shillings in the Pound* (1948), p. 203. He tends to underestimate the servant problem (Ch. 13).

happy in their companionship. This would seem to be a rational economy.'

Throughout this argument there ran the thread that the middle-class mother must perforce be provided with domestic assistance, not that she might indulge in indolence, but that she might be freed to devote all her energies to the proper upbringing of her children.[1]

This view of motherhood, held in both religious and purely secular circles, persisted at least until the end of the century, and for that reason it is likely that the impact of the servant problem was quite considerable. Once it had become established that birth control was not immoral, the fact of not being able to obtain domestic assistance would itself become a salient factor in the fall in family size. If more children implied more domestic assistance, less domestic assistance implied either more domestic appliances or less children.

Taking all these things together, then, it can be seen that in comparison with the period 1851–71, the years of the 1870s and onwards were years of some difficulty for those in receipt of middle- and upper-range incomes. Prices fell, it is true, but incomes suffered something of a setback too. Servants' wages rose and their labour became more difficult to obtain. Hence, in comparison with the lower-middle classes, the better-off sections of society were faced with a greater struggle to maintain and extend the differential standard. The years of what had promised to be inevitable progress had passed away. Some kind of personal planning was necessary now if the social hierarchy was to be preserved; but before we can discuss why it took the form it did, we must return to the population movement and examine what was happening to the attitude towards contraception.

[1] L.M.S.: 'Economy' in *The British Mothers' Magazine*, April 1855, pp. 85–87.

CHAPTER X

Birth Control and the Size of the Family

BY the middle of the nineteenth century, as we saw in Chapter III,[1] the existence of some form of class differential in family size had come to be accepted by most serious writers on population problems, although they were not agreed as to whether this was the result of a reduction in the physical potency of the better-off sections of the community, or of moral restraint on their part acting through postponement of marriage. The writers for the press, however, do not appear to have been so much in doubt; and certainly in their treatment of the French population crisis in April 1857, the sterility of the biological organism was regarded generally as the most obvious explanation of the current trend.

The facts of the matter can be briefly told. In 1857 the French Census, taken in 1856, showed that for two years deaths had exceeded births. In 1854 the figures had been 923,000 births to 992,000 deaths, and in 1855, 902,000 births to 937,000 deaths. Was the French population setting in for an absolute decline? *The Times* immediately jumped to the conclusion that this was so:

'We learn the astonishing fact that at the present time the population of France is actually diminishing, although emigration has almost entirely ceased. War, a succession of bad harvests, the grape-blight, and the diseases of the silkworm, are all pointed to as having a share in producing this startling result; but we cannot but feel that there must be some cause deeper and more abiding than any of these.'[2]

[1] See pp. 37–40.
[2] Leader in *The Times*, 10th April 1857.

For *The Times* 'some deficiency of prolific power' was taken as the main cause without question, and it is interesting that this should have been so since there can be no doubt now that the real cause of the decline at that time was a great rise in the number of deaths. It is true that the number of births had fallen a little below the figures of the previous few years but this was apparently only a temporary recession, dependent upon a slight fall in the marriage rate between 1852 and 1856; for the number of births rose again soon afterwards. The death rates, however, from a figure of about twenty-two deaths per thousand inhabitants previously, leapt to 27·4 for 1854 and were still above twenty-five in 1855, falling below twenty-three in 1856. The Crimean War, starvation, and the cholera outbreak of 1853–4 were the really salient factors, in spite of *The Times'* denial.[1]

This preoccupation with fertility rather than with mortality has been laid by Griffith at Malthus's door,[2] and certainly the whole trend of population thought from the beginning of the century had been biased in that one direction.[3] Whatever the reason, however, the effect is beyond denial. The interest in the state of French population in 1857 was focused on the fall in the birth rate and explanations were made in terms of biological deficiency.

Thus, the number of wars in which the French had participated during the previous fifty years was pointed to by *The Times* as a cause of physical deterioration. 'It is no exaggeration to say that the entire vigorous male population of the country was swept away, leaving only the rejected of the conscription to be the fathers of a future generation.'[4] This, thought *The*

[1] E. Levasseur: *La Population Française* (1889), Vol. 3. 1854 and 1855 were years when 'la guerre, la disette et le choléra ont conspiré contre la population française' (p. 151). See Note I, p. 224.

[2] G. T. Griffith: *Population Problems of the Age of Malthus* (1926), p. 99. 'Although . . . Malthus did lay stress on the importance of the decline in the death rate, it is still true to say that in general estimation his contribution has laid the emphasis on the side of births and marriages more than on the side of deaths and has tended since his time to obscure the importance of the death rate.'

[3] This is also true of nineteenth-century French population opinion. See J. J. Spengler: 'French Population Theory since 1800' in the *Journal of Political Economy*, October 1936 and December 1936; and J. J. Spengler: *France Faces Depopulation* (1938), Chs. 5 and 6.

[4] *The Times*, leader, 15th April, 1857.

Economist, was to overlook 'the recuperative powers of society' by which it meant 'the inherent vitality' of society to sweep away the traces of the ravages brought upon it by war and to plant and sow, and to nourish into vigorous life more men to defend the country. The fact that France had not done this, while other nations had, was therefore proof that wars as such were not the cause of physical deterioration. Taxation and poverty, and the needs of a military regime were the real culprits.

'We can fancy, too, that the mothers of France have had irresistible motives for not caring to provide more generous nourishment for their children when stunted bodies saved them from being the prey of conscription.'

The social system was at bottom at fault but operating through stunting its people in body and mind.[1]

'The want of food superinduces a lesser frequency of marriages, and contributes to sterilize the marriages already contracted.'[2]

'Revolutions, proscriptions, confiscations, delations, banishment, war—these are the civilized fiends which have stricken France with the palsy of inertness; and, superadded to them, the promiscuous intercourse of the sexes has brought on sterility.'[3]

In this manner the whole gamut of possible explanations was run through, to add up to the single factor, failure of the biological organism.

This is not to argue that there was no one at all to voice an alternative point of view. The *Daily News* regarded the French as a very prudent people.

'They have small trust in Providence, and like to confide their future to themselves. They seldom marry without good surety of livelihood, and when events disturb human calcula-

[1] *The Economist*, 25th April 1857, pp. 447–8.
[2] H. Darimon in *La Presse*, quoted with approval by *The Manchester Guardian*, 16th April 1857.
[3] *Reynolds Newspaper*, 19 April 1857

141

tions, and render life a lottery, the French abstain from marriage altogether. . . . The fact is, that the French are a people who will not increase in numbers without an increase in wealth. And this resolve does them infinite honour.'[1]

Even *The Times* did not wonder that, granted the state of the nation, the French 'carry out to the letter the teachings of Malthus and Mill, and deliberately marry with the intention of having only one or two children, or none at all'.[2] This did not mean, however, that any writer, other than Drysdale, was prepared to admit that some form of contraception was commonly being used. Where the explanation of the fall in family size was not given in biological terms, some vague reference to 'moral restraint' was considered sufficient to satisfy the inquiring mind.

This is important in view of the fact that the letters and articles on the cost of married life, referred to earlier,[3] were also appearing in English magazines and newspapers at this time. As far as this controversy was concerned, there was no suggestion that expenses might be kept low by the use of birth-control. Once a marriage was contracted it was assumed that children would follow as a matter of course,[4] and the only alternatives before the impecunious were either not to marry at all or to be prepared for a reduction in the standard of life. Nevertheless, it is likely that the desire for some kind of family limitation was spreading behind the scenes, and we have some evidence that the practice of inducing miscarriages was growing amongst middle-class women in the early sixties. Thus, Greaves, at a meeting of the Manchester Statistical Society in 1863, said:

'I have known a married woman, a highly educated, and in other points of view most estimable person, when warned of

[1] *The Daily News*, 18th April 1857.

[2] *The Times*, 15th April 1857. Drysdale seems to have overlooked this passage in his attack on *The Times* argument in favour of biological sterility. G. Drysdale: *The Elements of Social Science* (1859), p. 475.

[3] See pp. 40–47.

[4] C. Woodham-Smith: *Florence Nightingale, 1820-1910* (1950) records that in 1853 when Arthur Hugh Clough and her niece Blanche were considering marriage, Florence Nightingale 'worked out detailed budgets showing what Clough and Blanche absolutely required to live on, including a scale of provision for children, basing her calculations on the frequency at which they would be likely to arrive at the average birth rate.' (P. 109.)

the risk of miscarriage from the course of life she was pursuing, to make light of the danger, and even express her hope that such a result might follow. Every practitioner of obstetric medicine must have met with similar instances, and will be prepared to believe that there is some foundation for the stories floating in society, of married ladies whenever they find themselves pregnant, habitually beginning to take exercise, on foot or on horseback, to an extent unusual at other times, and thus making themselves abort. The enormous frequency of abortions (amounting, according to one high authority (Dr. Whitehead), to one miscarriage in seven conceptions, and to another (Dr. Granville), to one in three), cannot be explained by purely natural causes. It makes one almost tremble, to contemplate the mischief which such laxity of principle, on the part of those who ought to be the leaders of society, must produce upon their inferiors and dependents, and especially on the class of female domestic servants.'[1]

It must be emphasized that this practice of inducing miscarriages was considered to be growing amongst *married* women, and was not merely a means whereby unmarried mothers might avoid having illegitimate children. Unfortunately, as is to be expected, the nineteenth-century writers are very quiet on this issue, although there is one diary extant which contains a reference in 1807 to a married woman who 'took something when pregnant of her little girl, intended to fall on the child', showing that the practice was not unknown earlier.[2] This diary is interesting too, in that it contains an early expression of opinion on large families.

'What troubles and turmoils people bring themselves into, by burthening themselves with children! Mr. and Mrs. A. might have kept their carriage, had they only the root and stem of the tree to have supported; but they have *foolishly* contrived

[1] G. Greaves: 'Observations on Some of the Causes of Infanticide' in the *Transactions of the Manchester Statistical Society*, Session 1862–3, p. 14. The article was also published separately as a pamphlet (Manchester 1863) and reviewed in *Meliora* (Volume 4, 1864) and *The British and Foreign Medico-Chirurgical Review*, October 1863.

[2] E. Hall (ed.): *Miss Weston. Journal of a Governess, 1807–1911* (1936). Letter to Miss Chorley, 13th December 1807 (Vol. 1, p. 60).

to increase, and multiply, so many branches, that they must deny themselves many a gratification, in order to provide those branches with leaves. A fortnight ago, the eldest of six children completed her seventh year, and another will, I suppose, make its entrance into this comical bustling world by Xmas. I don't suppose the parents are either of them more than thirty, so they may have at least a dozen children yet, in addition to the present number. Heaven help them! . . .'[1]

Strangely enough, the writer was a spinster.

Another spinster of the same social class had already expressed a similar sentiment a few years earlier: 'Poor Woman! how can she be honestly breeding again.' But apparently Jane Austen's horror was less over matters of conspicuous consumption like the carriage as over the effect of child-bearing on the mother. Thus to her niece, Fanny Knight, she wrote of a mutual friend, 'poor Animal, she will be worn out before she is thirty— I am very sorry for her—Mrs. Clement too is in that way again. I am quite tired of so many children—Mrs. Benn has a 13th', and earlier, when Fanny was about to marry, she advised: 'By not beginning the business of Mothering quite so early in life, you will be young in Constitution, spirits, figure and countenance, while Mrs. Wm. Hammond is growing old by confinements and nursing.' Her method of preventing conception, moreover, was quite simple: 'Good Mrs. Deedes!—I hope she will get the better of this Marianne, then I wd. recommend to her and Mr. D. the simple regimen of separate rooms.'[2]

Jane Austen, so far as we know, never mentioned abortion or contraception in this connection; but her opinions are worthy of quotation as an indication that the desire for relief from the burden of child-bearing was at least latent in the first half of the nineteenth century. Unfortunately, we have no idea of the degree to which these scattered expressions of discontent are

---

[1] *Op. cit.*, Vol. 2, p. 61. The italics were in the original. On p. 61 an editorial footnote reads: 'Heaven help them indeed—the poor wretch of a wife was to become the mother of fifteen children! Joseph Armitage spared no one, his wife least of all.'

[2] R. W. Chapman (ed.): *Jane Austen's Letters to her sister Cassandra and others* (1932). Letters of 1st October 1808 (Vol. 1, p. 210); 23rd March 1817 (Vol. 2, p. 486); 13th March 1817 (Vol. 2, p. 483), and 20th February 1817 (Vol. 2, p. 480).

representative of the opinions of the class of women from which the writers came. [1] It does seem fairly clear, however, that even where the desire was felt it was accompanied by the conviction that nothing could be done about it. Queen Victoria's letter, for example, quoted by the Royal Commission on Population in this connection, is a clear indication of this. Her uncle, the King of the Belgians, had written to her saying that he could well understand her astonishment at finding herself within a year of her marriage the very respectable mother of a nice little girl, but he thanked Heaven that it was so and flattered himself that she would eventually become 'a delighted and delightful *Maman au milieu d'une belle et nombreuse famille*'. Her reply was to the effect that a large family would be inconvenient to say the least, as well as a hard task to go through 'very often'; but, she went on, 'God's will be done, and if He decrees that we are to have a great number of children, why we must try to bring them up as useful and exemplary members of society'. [2]

The religiously-minded, indeed, carried this further, quoting the Psalmist to illustrate their view:

'Lo, children are an heritage of the Lord: and the fruit of the womb is his reward.

As arrows are in the hands of a mighty man: so are children of the youth.

Happy is the man that hath his quiver full of them.' [3]

No doubt this sometimes meant a financial struggle, but it was all for the best in the long run. God would provide. [4] In an age when Christian texts still had some weight, the effect of the almost constant reiteration of this kind of belief in the maga-

---

[1] Report of the Royal Commission on Population (*Parliamentary Papers*, 1948–9, Vol. 19, paras. 94–5).

[2] A. C. Benson and Viscount Esher: *The Letters of Queen Victoria: a Selection from Her Majesty's Correspondence between the years 1837 and 1861* (1907). Letters of 26th December 1840 and 5th January 1841. (Vol. 1, pp. 318 and 321.)

[3] Psalm 127, iii. 5. Cf. its use as the caption for the article 'Large Families' in *The British Mothers' Magazine*, January 1849, p. 4.

[4] 'Large Families versus Small Ones' in *The British Mothers' Magazine*, June 1857, and 'Another Mouth to Feed' in *The Penny Post*, February 1866. For a diary expression of these opinions over time, see G. R. Parkin: *Edward Thring; Headmaster of Uppingham School. Life, Diary and Letters* (1898), Vol. I, pp. 114 and 124; Vol. 2, pp. 231 and 264–5.

zines read by the lower middle classes, was probably to inhibit the free expression of the contrary point of view amongst them.

That the actual contraceptive viewpoint was still out of favour can perhaps best be seen in the outcry which was raised against Lord Amberley in the autumn of 1868. A few years earlier apparently, he had been converted to neo-Malthusianism as a result of reading George Drysdale's *Physical, Sexual and Natural Religion* which had been recommended to him by his ex-tutor, J. S. Laurie.[1] Although not won over to the author's 'very materialistic notions' he did think there was merit in protesting against 'the utterly foolish delicacy which prevails over these most important subjects' and consented to take part in a meeting of the Dialectical Society on 'Over-Population and Public Health' at which James Laurie, Charles Bradlaugh and Charles Drysdale also spoke. This was held on 1st July 1868 and continued on the 15th. Amberley, in favour of small families, seemed most bothered by the problem of how they could be kept small without injury to health.[2]

On 1st August, the *British Medical Journal* reported on the meeting and added, 'we believe that our profession will repudiate with indignation and disgust such functions as these gentlemen wish to assign to it,'[3] and *The Medical Times and Gazette* followed this lead with an attack on 'Viscount Amberley's Insult to the Medical Profession'[4]. These journals were indeed very anxious to assure the world that most medical men could not possibly condone such views as were being expressed. When two doctors who had been at the meeting, hastened to repudiate the 'anti-genetic' teachings of the main speakers, the *British Medical Journal* published their letter 'with great satisfaction', feeling it 'honourable to the authors of it'.[5] At this period *The Lancet* did not join in the fray, but in the following spring it was moved to line up with its fellow medical journals

[1] B. and P. Russell (eds.): *The Amberley Papers* (1937), John Russell's *Journal*, 2nd February 1864 (Vol. 1, p. 288).

[2] *Ibid., Journal*, 13th August 1868 (Vol. 2, pp. 167–73). A detailed report of the meeting, by J. Laurie, called 'The Limitation of Families' was published as Malthusian tract No. 3 (1879–80). There was also a detailed, critical account in *The Medical Press and Circular*, 22nd July 1868.

[3] The *British Medical Journal*, 1st August 1868.

[4] *The Medical Times and Gazette*, 8th and 15th August, 1868.

[5] The *British Medical Journal*, 8th August 1868.

on being sent a copy of a French edition of what would appear to have been Drysdale's book.[1] It referred to 'an assemblage of obscure busybodies' which had made itself notorious the preceding year and in addition to 'ambitious lordlings' it attacked medical men who supported this kind of 'nastiness'. By this time the organized medical profession had begun to take action. Already on the 14th November 1868, the Liverpool Medical Institution had unanimously agreed that it was very necessary for the members of the profession to express their opinions on the subject and to show their disapprobation of the suggestions made.[2] The 37th Annual Meeting of the British Medical Association, in the following year, took a similar line and received with great approbation an attack on the 'odious doctrines openly recommended by societies composed of the upper ranks of the people, and presided over by noble senators'. In this attack, Dialectical was made equivalent to 'diabolical'; and *The Lancet* expressed its pleasure that Dr. Beatty had raised his voice against 'beastly contrivances'. The medical profession was certainly not yet ready to accept 'filthy expedients for the prevention of conception'.[3]

While the doctors were thus putting on record their anti-contraception opinions, Amberley himself had become the centre of a storm of invective in Devon. When the news of the Dialectical Society's meeting had first appeared, in the medical press of 22nd July and 1st August 1868, it apparently did not penetrate very far outside medical circles, for during the month of August he was accepted as the Liberal candidate for the constituency of South Devon in opposition to two Conservatives. But the attack on him of the 8th August was read more widely, as the Devon newspapers took it up. On August 13th the *Exeter and Plymouth Gazette* accused him of advocating 'unnatural crimes' and a battle royal began amongst the Liberal and

---

[1] *The Lancet*, 10th April 1869. The reference was to an English book on birth-control by 'a graduate of medicine'.

[2] On the occasion of Ewing Whittle's paper on 'Infanticide and Abortion' in which he said: 'We ought to proclaim loudly that medicine is not the science of the day that points out the way to infidelity and vice; and that as a profession, we abhor the unnatural projects which have been proposed.' Reported in the *British Medical Journal*, 20th March 1869.

[3] The *British Medical Journal*, 7th August 1869, address of T. E. Beatty on 'Midwifery'. See also *The Lancet*, 7th August 1869.

Conservative papers, to last throughout the rest of the election campaign, as the speakers exploited the situation on the public platforms.[1] It is significant that in the very violent controversy that followed, the battle raged not over the pros and cons of contraception, but over whether Amberley had advocated 'infanticide' or not. His supporters eagerly denied the charge and treated it as a political stunt, as an attempt to discredit their candidate in the eyes of the electors by casting dirt.

Of their opponents they claimed:

> '. . . *they took up a ribald pen,*
> *Which they eyed exultingly:*
> *"If abuse won't do," they grinning said,*
> *"We'll try obscenity!"*

> '*A loathsome tale, for prurient minds,*
> *Well spiced they now reprint;*
> *Into each sickening detail plunged,*
> *Without reserve or stint.*'[2]

As part of the election campaign posters were displayed showing Amberley as 'The Quack Doctor' selling 'depopulation mixture' according to 'the New French and American Systems'; and men actually went to the public meetings pretending to offer for sale articles purporting to be useful for contraceptive purposes. Even when all the heat and fervour of an election period are allowed for, it cannot but be felt that the incident shows clearly how little the public expression of opinion at this time was in favour of birth-control.

Amberley lost the election; whether or not for this reason we cannot say, although his ex-tutor claimed that the force of 'public intolerance' was against him.[3] At this time to be an *avowed* Malthusian was, as Austin Holyoake put it, 'detestable'.[4] Yet even for those who, like Amberley, retracted from advocat-

---

[1] For the complete story, see B. and P. Russell, *op. cit.*, Vol. 2, Ch. 11, Sec. B, pp. 166–249.

[2] *Ibid.*, quoted on p. 195.

[3] *Ibid.*. Letter of J. S. Laurie, 10th November 1860, quoted on pp. 245–6.

[4] A. Holyoake: *Large or Small Families? On which side lies the balance of comfort?* (1871), p. 1.

ing 'immoral practices'[1] and remained purposely vague as to what they meant by the limitation of families, there was really no widespread social approval. When, a few years later, a public memorial was proposed for John Stuart Mill who had just died, the revival of his youthful Malthusian activities by Abraham Hayward[2] led Mr. Gladstone, who had earlier intimated his willingness to co-operate, withdrawing his support.[3] Whatever may have been happening in terms of the quiet percolation of contraceptive knowledge,[4] openly the subject was tabu.[5]

On the other hand, there can be little doubt that a real awakening of birth-control *propaganda* had begun in the 1860s. Charles Bradlaugh's *National Reformer* carried articles on the subject written by him and by George Drysdale from its very first number (1861) and although its circulation was limited almost entirely to Freethinkers, many of the articles were re-issued in pamphlet form and probably found a wider audience.[6]

---

[1] See his letter to the Roman Catholic Bishop of Liverpool who had preached a sermon accusing Amberley of 'stifling children in their birth (B. and P. Russell, *op. cit.*, pp. 186–9).

[2] W. D. Christie: *John Stuart Mill and Mr. Abraham Hayward, Q.C.—a reply about Mill to a letter to the Rev. Stopford Brooke, privately circulated and actually published* (1873). G. J. Holyoake: *John Stuart Mill as some of the Working Classes Knew Him* (1873).

[3] J. Morley: *The Life of William Ewart Gladstone* (1903), Vol. 2, pp. 543–4 (2nd ed., 1906, Vol. 2, pp. 151–2). Gladstone wrote to withdraw his name privately, but as Morley writes, 'unfortunately, the withdrawal of such a name could not be other than a public step'.

[4] For the best account for what was going on underground see M. C. Stopes: *Contraception* (6th ed., 1946, Ch. 10); although it does appear that Himes was right in arguing that she makes too much of the influence of Trall's book. (See N. Himes: *The Medical History of Contraception*, 1936, p. 268.)

[5] Cf. the attack of F. W. Newman: 'Malthusianism, true and false' in *Fraser's Magazine*, May 1871, where he pointed out that the Malthusians of his day were *not* followers of Malthus who had believed in moral restraint. They would make marriage 'unholy' (p. 598). Another attack appeared in 'Two Solutions' in *Fraser's Magazine*, April 1871, where 'young startling Amberley sophists' were taken to task for recommendations which were 'inhuman, immoral, unpractical' (p. 453).

[6] The success of the *National Reformer* might well be compared in this respect with George Drysdale's own *Political Economist and Journal of Social Science* which ran from January 1856 to April 1857, and was apparently conducted single-handed by its editor. (See No. 15, April 1857, p. 119.) One difficulty might well have been the handling of sales. Even the *National Reformer* was banned by W. H. Smith & Sons from their bookstalls. (See H. B. Bonner: *Charles Bradlaugh* (1894), Ch. 13, pp. 130–1.) For details of the articles per issue, see N. Himes: *Medical History of Contraception* (1936), pp. 236–7.

The books of Robert Dale Owen, Knowlton and Drysdale were also reissued several times during the next fifteen years and a new work, R. T. Trall's *Sexual Physiology* appeared from America in 1866. In addition, two anonymous pamphlets, *Valuable Hints* (1866) and *The Power and Duty of Parents to Limit the Number of their Children* (1868) were published, as well as M. G. H.'s *Poverty: its Cause and Cure* (1861), Austin Holyoake's *Large or Small Families?* (1871) and the privately circulated Oedipus's *The Marriage Problem*—in reality by Dr. Haslam. Even the *Fortnightly Review* entered the arena with M. Cookson's article, 'The Morality of Married Life', inspired by the issue of the seventh edition of Malthus's *Essay on Population* in 1872. This article was addressed mainly to the middle classes and recommended the use of the 'safe' period.[1] Taken in conjunction with the Amberley affair, the impact of these works, while not yet bringing round the force of middle-class publicly expressed opinion to the contraceptive point of view, nevertheless could hardly have been negligible.

The real test case was, of course, the trial of Charles Bradlaugh and Annie Besant in 1877.[2] On this occasion the legal position of birth-control literature was at issue, but in fact the public debate more clearly divided on the wider pros and cons of the practice itself. The indictment, for example, put the extreme moralist anti-contraceptive point of view. Charles Bradlaugh and Annie Besant, it said, 'unlawfully and wickedly devising, contriving, and intending, as much as in them lay, to vitiate and corrupt the morals as well of youth as of divers other subjects of the Queen, and to incite and encourage the said subjects to indecent, obscene, unnatural, and immoral practices, and bring them to a state of wickedness, lewdness and debauchery, unlawfully . . . did print, publish, sell and utter a certain indecent, lewd, filthy, and obscene libel, to wit, a certain indecent, lewd, filthy, bawdy, and obscene book called *Fruits of Philosophy*.[3] But some of the daily and weekly newspapers were now not so unfavourably disposed.

---

[1] M. Cookson: 'The Morality of Married Life' in *The Fortnightly Review*, 1st October 1872, p. 412. (See also note, p. 760.)

[2] For details see Himes *op. cit.*, Ch. 10, and D. V. Glass: *Population Policies and Movements* (1940), Ch. 1, and H. B. Bonner: *op. cit.*, Vol. 2, Ch. 3.

[3] Quoted in Glass: *op. cit.*, p. 424, n. X.

Thus *Reynolds's News* said, 'The authorities have deemed it desirable to prosecute the London publishers of Dr. Knowlton's pamphlet, *Fruits of Philosophy*. We have carefully perused this treatise, and albeit we may not feel inclined either to fall in with the views it advocates, or to justify its indiscriminate distribution, we still must pronounce it a far less immoral and dangerous book than that which has been privately printed for the delectation of certain Anglican priests.'[1] The reference here was to *The Priest in Absolution*, a book which became a thorn in the side of the authorities, for it gave detailed instructions to guide priests in their probing into the sexual lives of female devotees, both inside and outside marriage; and hence was open to the charge that it contained 'nice sort of questions for a salacious young parson to put to a young married woman!', as *Reynolds's* dramatically put it. Naturally, there were soon found people who were not slow to point out that if *The Priest in Absolution* was fit for circulation, certainly *Fruits of Philosophy* was too.[2] At any rate, whether the court and jury were influenced by the questions raised on the issue in Parliament or were not, they pronounced the publishers of Knowlton's book free of any ill intention, although they found them guilty of issuing obscene literature.

The press reports on the whole were unfavourable although few were so shocked at the lightness of the verdict as *The Englishman*, which described the book as 'the most wicked work that was ever written—one which practically recommends and points out the way to an indiscriminate destruction of human life'. One interesting comment was made by this paper which in view of subsequent events has proved something of a prophecy. 'We should not be wrong', the editor wrote, 'in saying that twenty people will read each copy sold, and that probably some hundreds may be influenced by the teachings of each individual reader or buyer; this would represent millions corrupted by this diabolical work; youths and girls taught not "to restrain nature", but indulge in it, and then murder the helpless offspring.'[3] Whatever we may think of the editor's views on the

---

[1] 'Prying Priests and their Fair Penitents' in *Reynolds's News*, 24th June 1877.
[2] Cf. Forsyth's question in the House of Commons, 21st June 1877 (*Hansard*, 1877, Vol. 235, p. 83). See Note J, p. 225.
[3] *The Englishman*, 30th June and 7th July 1877.

contraception question there can be little doubt that he correctly
foresaw the degree to which the propaganda would spread, even
if the effects of this were not as he thought.

The Times, on the other hand, although less disapproving,
was further from the mark. A leading article read as follows :

'The plea of arresting excessive increases of population ought
not to be allowed to pass without more challenge than it has
received from the Court and the Jury. We may be ready to
admit, for so the doctors and their female coadjutors often
pronounce, that there are many cases in which it is expedient
that the command to increase and multiply ought to be modified in some way or other. But this can only be in most exceptional cases. To make them the law of society, or even the prevalent usage, would be in fact to subordinate all that is good
and healthy and strong in society to all that is bad and sickly
and weak. We might as well treat all the world as incurable
patients because some are out of health, all the world as paupers
because some can hardly earn their own bread, all the world as
mad because some are not quite rational, and all the world as
utterly wicked because some are wanting in stability of character, as believe this is a proper book to be put into the hands of
the majority of people or its advice good for the world generally.
. . . Happily the real truth is that the world is greater than one
man or one opinion and since we have to choose between
Mr. Bradlaugh and Mrs. Besant on the one hand, and certain
reserves and properties surrounding the first law of Nature, and
the domestic hearth on the other, we are glad to find that this
well-intentioned pair are not held to have established a right
to dictate new rules of action and new conditions of existence
to a reluctant, and, as it feels, an insulted world.'[1]

Reynolds's News was inclined somewhat favourably on the
whole and was prepared to give the subject a hearing. Its report
of the case was full and fair, although it declined to comment.[2]
The *Daily News* also gave a full report.[3] *The Times*, on the other
hand, contented itself with a short paragraph on the actual
trial.

[1] *The Times*, 22nd June 1877.
[2] *Reynolds's News*, 1st July 1877.
[3] The *Daily News*, 22nd June 1877.

From our point of view the most obvious and most important effect of the trial was its value as publicity. This was made much of by the *Daily News*, which deprecated not only its fellow newspapers for the treatment of the case, but also the authorities for promoting prosecution.

'In plain words, a few hundred purchasers in the course of many years have been converted into more than a hundred thousand purchasers in a few weeks. More than this, the substance of the book, in a form as open to question as that in which it originally appeared, has been given with illustrative comments, parallel passages, and physiological argument in the very full and candid reports of some of our contemporaries. The reserve which we have thought it right to practise has been nearly peculiar to ourselves. The whole subject has been put, with the morning and evening newspapers on the breakfast table and drawing-room table in thousands of households. Thus the doctrines of this book will . . . form another stage in the popular education of the country. For all this the promoters of an ill-advised prosecution have to thank themselves, and the friends of pure literature and wholesome social doctrine have to consider whether they ought to thank them.'[1]

The Englishman was also concerned at the publicity which the trial afforded. According to its report the defendants received a thousand pounds subscribed to a Defence Fund, and it grew furious at the thought.[2] *The Times* in addition bore witness to the increased sales of *Fruits of Philosophy* as well as to the enthusiasm with which its message was received. On June 25th, seven days after the trial, it contained the following report:

'Last night the new Hall of Science, Old Street, was densely crowded, it having been announced that Mr. Bradlaugh and Mrs. Besant were to deliver addresses. Of the 600 persons who filled the hall, one-third were women, many very young. Prices of admission ranged from 2d. to 2s. 6d. In the streets were some 400 people who were unable to obtain admission. Copies of *The Fruits of Philosophy* were sold by the hundred, young women and lads purchasing largely. When Mr. Bradlaugh and Mrs.

[1] *Ibid.*
[2] *The Englishman*, 30th June and 4th August 1877.

Besant, and Mr. Truelove of Holborn entered the Hall, they were received with great cheering.'[1]

A month later, *Reynolds's* reported:

'At the Hall of Science Mrs. Besant delivered a lecture upon the results, or rather the probable results, of the recent trial in the Court of Queen's Bench. The hall was crowded in every point, a large proportion of which consisted of young females who appeared fully to endorse the opinions enunciated by the lecturer. . . . Speaking of the Malthusian League, which has only been in existence for a week, Mrs. Besant announced that 220 members had already been enrolled.'[2]

By 26th August, Charles Bradlaugh, speaking at a Bristol meeting called to form a branch of the Malthusian League there, said that although the sale of the pamphlet used to be about a hundred a year, since the prosecution over 130,000 had been sold.[3]

Of the subsequent developments of the birth-control movement, little need be said here. Bradlaugh founded the Malthusian League and a journal, *The Malthusian*, was started in 1879. The Bradlaugh-Besant trial was not the last birth-control prosecution, for Edward Truelove was charged while the case was being held, to be tried soon after his colleagues; and two more cases were heard in the 1890s, but at no time afterwards was the movement seriously hindered by the law, and it was able to pour out a continuous stream of propaganda without interference. The details of this 'inundation', as Himes called it,[4] are given in Professor Glass's *Population Policies and Movements in Europe*.[5] Some 3,000,000 pamphlets and leaflets were circulated between 1879 and 1921 all urging family limitation in some form. Of these over 1,000,000 between 1876 and 1891 gave details of contraception. We do not know, of course, how far they were influential, but the mere fact that it was possible for the Malthusian League to carry on this work is an indication

[1] *The Times*, 25th June 1877.
[2] '*Reynolds's News*, 22nd July 1877.
[3] *Reynolds's News*, 26th August, 1877.
[4] Himes: *op. cit.*, p. 238.
[5] Glass: *op. cit.*, Ch. 1, pp. 35–43.

that people generally were much more prepared to support it by buying its publications and sending it donations than they had been before 1877. Looked at in this way, it becomes apparent that to a great extent the Bradlaugh-Besant trial acted as an agency for releasing into the public expression of opinion the forces which had been developing quietly but with some power since 1868 and the Amberley affair.[1]

It is, moreover, significant that this change in outlook took place in spite of the hostility of very many doctors. In 1868 when Amberley joined publicly in the Dialectical Society's discussion on family limitation, it was the medical press which first took up the challenge and attacked his neo-Malthusian views. The doctors allowed the Bradlaugh-Besant trial to pass without comment, but they raised their voices soon afterwards, and for the rest of the century the organized profession, as represented by its official organ, expressed itself consistently opposed to contraception.[2] In some measure, this seems to have been the result of a certain degree of over-emphasis by a few medical men on the more undesirable effects of some forms of birth-control. Thus Routh, at a meeting of the Obstetrical Section of the British Medical Association at Bath in 1878, instanced metritis, leucorrhoea, menorrhagia and haematocele, hysteralgia and hyperaesthesia of the genital organs, galloping cancer, ovarian dropsy and ovaritis, sterility, mania leading to suicide, and nymphomania as being attributable to the use of 'sexual fraudulency' or 'conjugal onanism' by women, and nervous prostration, mental decay, loss of memory, intense cardiac palpitations, and mania leading to suicide, to its use by men.[3]

Yet although he did not confine himself to *coitus interruptus* as

[1] Cf. A. Besant: *An Autobiography* (2nd ed., 1893). Pp. 223–4 where she writes of 'letters from thousands of poor married women—many from the wives of country clergymen and curates—thanking and blessing me for showing them how to escape from the veritable hell in which they lived.'

[2] The *British Medical Journal*, 26th January 1878 (an attack on Charles Drysdale), 13th July 1889 (an attack on Henry Allbut), 14th January 1899 (an attack on the Birth-control movement in particular) and 24th September 1904 (an attack on Neo-Malthusianism generally).

[3] C. H. F. Routh: 'The Moral and Physical Evils likely to Follow if Practices intended to act as Checks to Population be not strongly discouraged and condemned' (1879), reprinted from the *Medical Press and Circular*, October 1878, pp. 8–10. Routh followed the 1877 edition of L. F. E. Bergeret: *Des fraudes dans l'accomplissement des fonctions génératrices* (1st ed., Paris, 1868; 5th ed., 1877).

the method most commonly used and actually referred to 'coverings' employed by males and 'plugs and injections' by females, even including intra-uterine stems designed originally for uterine diseases, it is fairly clear that many of the complaints listed were in the nature of mental disturbances, possibly deriving from the nervous strain involved in *coitus interruptus*.[1] Medical men, in fact, because of their disproportionate familiarity with abnormal and diseased cases, were inclined to see too many dangers in the practice of contraception, and this laid them open to the charge that they shirked the issue of a true inquiry into its physical and psychological effects.[2]

The medical objection, however, was not the only one put forward by the medical press. Even after the Bradlaugh-Besant trials there was a considerable amount of opposition to the alliance of medical men with unqualified people for the purpose of propagating what was referred to as 'obscene and audacious quackery'.[3] This came to a crisis in 1887 when Henry Allbut was cited to appear before the Fellows of the Royal College of Physicians at Edinburgh to demonstrate why he should not be deprived of membership and licence of the College 'for having published and exposed for sale an indecent work entitled *The Wife's Handbook*, and for having published or attached thereto advertisements of an unprofessional character, titled "Malthusian Appliances"'.[4]

The case moved from the Royal College to the General Medical Council, which eventually ordered Allbut's name to be erased from the Register.[5] This act was approved by the *British Medical Journal*, which had earlier attacked the charge against Allbut, but only on the ground that the publicity would have a worse effect than the pamphlet if left alone.[6] Eighteen

---

[1] Routh: *op. cit.*, p. 22 (contribution of Dr. Bennet to the discussion). See also Dr. Sims's remarks, pp. 22–24.

[2] Cf. E. Lyttleton's review of R. Ussher: 'Neo-Malthusianism' in *The Economic Review*, October 1895, p. 567.

[3] 'Obscene Quackery' in the *British Medical Journal*, 31st May 1879. The attack also involved books on venereal disease.

[4] The indictment was cited in these words by Allbut in a letter to the *British Medical Journal*, 2nd April 1887.

[5] Details of the hearing were given in the *British Medical Journal* on 26th November and 3rd December 1887.

[6] The *British Medical Journal*, 28th May 1889.

months later it made the following statement which may be taken as typical of the organized profession at this time:

'An attempt has been made in a certain section of the lay press to represent Mr. H. A. Allbut as a martyr to anti-Malthusian bigotry. What the general opinion of the profession on that subject may be we do not know. It is probable, however, that Mr. H. A. Allbut might have ventilated his views without let or hindrance from professional authority had he been content to address them to medical men instead of to the public.'[1]

This was quite consistent with the way in which the British Medical Association continued to allow Dr. Charles Drysdale to address its meetings year after year when he inevitably brought up the subject of birth-control. Within medical circles the topic was still open to debate and anyone less prominent an authority than Drysdale[2] was likely to be regarded as violating professional etiquette if he was too outspoken in the wider non-medical world.

A few years later in an attack on abortion the *Journal* expressed its hostility to the publicity which birth-control was receiving in the popular press.

'For years we have been accustomed to the advertisements of "female pills" and other remedies, which are guaranteed to remove "obstructions" and to have the "desired effect" without pain or danger. Most of these are mere swindles, for, although some of them undoubtedly contain injurious and poisonous substances, the majority contain nothing more than a little aperient. They are, however, none the less direct incitements to crime, and it cannot be doubted that the women who buy them do so with the direct intention of producing abortion.'

Moreover the advertisements were now becoming more widespread and more plainly spoken . . . 'for the benefit of their readers—and their daughters'.

'From the *Newcastle Evening News* of 4th December, we extract the following: "To Married Ladies (gratis)—Write for my

---

[1] *Ibid.*, 13th July 1889.   [2] On syphilis.

secret Remedy for the Prevention of Large Families. Guaranteed infallible." Again, "Marriage and its Consequences—Advice how to limit your family and valuable information to ladies." Is it not obvious that a public offer of a means of getting rid of the "consequences" of marriage is a direct incentive, not only to undesirable practices among the married, but to all sorts of immorality among the young, by holding out a promise of relief if difficulties should arise.'[1]

At the time of the Allbut case in 1887 it had emphasized its objection to Malthusian literature on the ground that it fell into the hands of young people and of those with insufficient moral and intellectual capacity to deal with it.[2] It repeated that objection now, linking abortion with contraception as practices used by young people *outside* marriage in order to have a life of luxury and pleasure incompatible with the expenses of early matrimony.[3]

It should not be assumed from this, however, that all doctors, with the exception of those known definitely to be in some way linked with the Malthusian League, were hostile to planned family limitation. There is indeed some evidence that over the years the practice was growing amongst an ever-growing number of them to advocate the spacing of pregnancies. At a meeting of inquiry held by the National Birth-Rate Commission in 1914, for example, Dr. J. W. Ballantyne was asked:

'Is it not the case that now it is almost a rule for the medical man to tell parents that there ought not to be another child, say, for two years, and in some cases for three years?'

His reply was:

'I think there is no doubt that doctors do say that; I think so. I am very often asked, and I have always said that the reasonable time for nursing the child, whether the child is nursed by

---

[1] 'Immoral Advertisements' in the *British Medical Journal*, 14th December 1895. Another attack appeared on 22nd August 1896, and again on 22nd June 1901 when the *Journal* castigated *The Railway Review* (organ of the Associated Society of Railway Servants) for advertisements headed: 'A Book for Ladies', 'Family Limitation' and 'Price List of Malthusian Appliances'.

[2] The *British Medical Journal*, 28th May 1887.

[3] *Ibid.*, 14th January 1890.

the mother or not, should be observed, which is about a year.'

And to the question: Would you not say that thirty or forty years ago the advice was much less frequently given by doctors? he replied:

'Yes, when I started practice I do not think we were asked that, or ever gave that advice voluntarily, when the next child should be.'[1]

The fact of the matter was that if the medical profession was not to give this advice it would throw mothers into the hands of quacks,[2] and the trial of the Chrimes brothers at the Old Bailey for attempted blackmail on 12,000 women who had applied to them for abortifacients over a period of two years showed how great the danger could be.[3]

There is no doubt that the use of some form of prevention was growing during this period.[4] This was partly the result of the mass of propaganda put out by the Malthusian League and other interested people, bombarding the parents of every newly born child with literature on how to get no more,[5] and partly the result of a change in the general attitude towards family size. In the most unlikely places references to the subject turned up, so that a sober writer on domestic economy, like Mrs. Panton, is found exclaiming, apparently for no reason at all: 'I have a very strong opinion that people should not bring into

[1] 'The Declining Birth-Rate: its Causes and Effects, being the Report of and the chief evidence taken by the National Birth-Rate Commission, instituted, with official recognition, by the National Council of Public Morals—for the Promotion of Race Regeneration—Spiritual, Moral and Physical.' (1916.) Evidence of the meeting of 21st January 1914 (pp. 178–9). See also the evidence of Dr. M. Scharlieb, 29th April 1914 (p. 272).

[2] I. M. A. MacFadyen: 'The Birth-Rate and the Mother' in *The Nineteenth Century and After*, March 1907, pp. 433–4.

[3] Details of the case were given by the *British Medical Journal*, 14th January 1899.

[4] See the letters of Sidney Webb to *The Times*, 11th and 16th October 1906. S. Webb: *The Declining Birth-Rate* (Fabian Tract No. 131, 1907) based on a survey of members of the Fabian Society. E. M. Elderton: *Report on the English Birth-Rate, Part I* (1914) mainly confined to the incidence of abortion among the working classes of the North. *The Declining Birth-Rate: its Causes and Effects* (1916), Ch. 1.

[5] *The Declining Birth-Rate* (1916), statement by Dr. Schofield, pp. 185–6, and *passim*.

the world any more children than they can reasonably hope to equip in some measure for the fight',[1] and similar sentiments, lacking in the handbooks produced before 1877, were much more common afterwards.[2] Even clergymen were won over, and at least one, Whatham, produced a pamphlet *Neo-Malthusianism*, which advocated 'artificial prevention of child-birth'.[3]

The Church indeed was faced by a rather awkward dilemma. Although the Bishops were moved to pass a resolution in 1908 regarding 'with alarm' the growing practice 'of the artificial restriction of the family', and earnestly calling upon 'all Christian people to discontinue the use of all artificial means of restriction as demoralizing to character and hostile to national welfare',[4] this could hardly have been found satisfactory to many of the more active church workers who had been seriously perturbed for some time as to the line they should take. Their problem had become acute in 1885 when W. T. Stead had revealed how the law actually aided in the purchase of young girls for imprisonment in brothels.[5] For the earnest Christian it was no longer possible to ignore the social evil of prostitution, but to advocate the alternative of early marriages exposed the zealot to the counter claim that this meant large families, and large families meant poverty.[6] One way out of the dilemma was to deny the last premise of the argument on the grounds that God automatically provided for His children,[7] but this was not very plausible in the light of experience, and most Church of England supporters seem to have followed the

[1] J. E. Panton: *Nooks and Corners* (1890), p. 113. See also J. E. Panton: *The Way they should go: Hints to Young Parents* (1896).

[2] For a good example see *Sylvia's Family Management* (1898), pp. 14–16, and 429. This book was addressed to working people.

[3] Quoted in C. R. Drysdale: *The Life and Writings of Thomas R. Malthus* (2nd ed., 1892). Preface.

[4] The resolution was quoted in full in *The Declining Birth-Rate* (1916), p. 388.

[5] W. T. Stead: 'Maiden Tribute to Modern Babylon (1885), reprinted from *The Pall Mall Gazette*, 6th and 12th July 1885. For accounts of Stead's trial see E. W. Stead: *My Father: Personal and Spiritual Reminiscences* (n.d.) and J. W. R. Scott: *The Life and Death of a Newspaper* (1952) Ch. 13. Stead was in favour of 'early marriages and limitation of families' (p. 118) and although he had six children, practised contraception himself (p. 106). Josephine Butler's contribution is well dealt with in M. G. Fawcett and E. M. Turner: *Josephine Butler: her Work and Principles* (1927).

[6] E. R. Chapman: *The New Godiva and other Studies in Social Questions* (1885), especially Chapter 1, 'The Sanction of Pureness'.

[7] R. ff. Blake: *The Greatest Temptation in the World to Man* (1894), p. 42.

lead of the non-conformists in admitting the need for some kind
of family limitation. Eventually, even the Bishops fell in line,
and, while still condemning mechanical contraception, recommended the use of the 'safe' period, where 'the health or
strength of the wife may be unequal to the bearing of more
children; the conditions of the home may give no hope of their
decent housing; or poverty may make it apparent that they
could not be maintained and brought up'.[1]

This attitude of the Church is important because it helps to
explain why during this period the books written specifically on
marriage avoided the subject of family limitation, except in very
general terms. Whatever may have been the case with the
development of rationalism, in the Rationalist Press Association
meaning of the term, they at any rate continued to pay at least
lip service to the argument that married life should be conducted
on strictly Christian lines.[2] We should not, under these circumstances, expect to find them advocating the very thing against
which the Bishops so determinedly set their faces. But, on the
other hand, like their predecessors of the forties and fifties, they
continued to insist on the need for prudence. No man, wrote
one,[3] should marry before he could afford it. To marry without
'sufficiency' of means was to court disaster, wrote another.[4] A
competency and provision for those that follow was a *sine qua
non* of a good match, wrote a third.[5] There were six qualifications necessary for honest matrimony, wrote a fourth, and these
included an adequate income.[6] In fact, if the girls of Trollope's
earlier days seemed to him 'to like propriety of demeanour,
decency of outward life, and a competence'[7] the girls of twenty
years later might well be claimed to have liked the same.

[1] *The Misuse of Marriage* (printed for private circulation amongst the clergy and
workers of the Church of England who desired counsel as to the line they should
take in these matters), Secs. Biii and Biv. (January 1914), reprinted in the *Declining
Birth-Rate* (1916), pp. 382–8.

For the Nonconformist view see *The Christian World*, 15th June 1893, quoted in
D. V. Glass: *Population Policies and Movements* (1940), n. jj, p. 429.

[2] See Appendix III: Books on Marriage at the End of the Century, p. 217.

[3] *Matrimony Made Easy, or How to Win a Lover* (1898), p. 21.

[4] A. W. Thorold: *On Marriage* (1896). Thorold was at one time Bishop of Winchester. He was in favour of large families.

[5] *Hints on Matrimony, by a Practical Man* (1882), Hint 6.

[6] J. Flower: *A Golden Guide to Matrimony* (1882), p. 42.

[7] See his aside in Ch. 11 of *The Belton Estate* (1865).

Birth Control and the Size of the Family

Love, chastity, and precious health.
These must accompany;
With just enough of worldly wealth
To bring prosperity.[1]

One interesting difference is the latter-day insistence on chastity, which although it had appeared before had not been given quite so much prominence. This again was probably connected with the publicity work of Josephine Butler and W. T. Stead. It might have been possible for some before their time to regard the prostitute as 'ultimately the most efficient guardian of virtue',[2] but the revelations of the *Pall Mall Gazette* had turned this into a 'flourish of sublime nonsense'.[3] Behind the Victorian barricade of conventional rectitude the 'vast reality of prostitution' had flourished at a time which 'permitted it, did it, and looked the other way',[4] but that time was passing now that the Social Purity Alliance could boast of a membership of 3,000 (1885). The word 'chastity', so prominent in the books on marriage appearing in the last fifteen years or so of the century had no merely conventional connotation. It had behind it the background of these revelations. Yet we do not know what the effect of this was, although it is clear that *if* middle-class men had been much accustomed to have recourse to prostitution in order to make late marriages bearable or to help keep down the numbers of their children when married, and *if* they were now shamed into discontinuing the practice, some other method of achieving the same results must be found. This, of course, was the uncomfortable dilemma facing the Church, and the recurring theme of 'self-control' demonstrates how the writers on marriage were uncomfortable about it too.

At the same time the writing of this later period shows a greater awareness than was obvious before that the cost of bringing up the children was the real problem.

[1] Flower: *op. cit.*, p. 57.
[2] W. E. H. Lecky: *History of European Morals from Augustus to Charlemagne* (1869), Ch. 5 (10th ed., 1892, Vol. 2, p. 283).
[3] E. R. Chapman, *op. cit.*, Note that the book was dedicated to Josephine Butler.
[4] H. L. Beales: 'Victorian Ideas of Sex' in 'Ideas and Beliefs of the Victorians, an historic revaluation of the Victorian Age—a series of talks broadcast on the B.B.C. Third Programme' (1949).

Birth Control and the Size of the Family

'As a bachelor with seven hundred a year or so, I am well off. As a young married man upon this income, I should be moderately well off. With one child to maintain and educate, my margin would be gone. With two children I should be poor. With half a dozen children I should be an abject slave; haunted by heavy forebodings about the butcher's bill, by dread of ill health, by dread of diminution in my practice, by a thousand apprehensions; and destitute of all the refined and cultured enjoyments that mitigate the torture of the modern struggle for existence.'[1]

'No man should marry who has not a reasonable prospect of being able to bring up and properly educate his children.'[2]

There was, in fact, a much greater consciousness that the future of the child must always be considered.

'Give the boys a good education and a start in life, and provide the girls with £150 a year, either when they marry or at your own death, and you have done your duty by your children. The girls cannot starve on that income, and neither would they be the prey of any fortune hunter; but no one has a right to bring children into the world in the ranks of the upper middle class and do less; misery will come of it if he does; be quite sure of that.'[3]

This writer, it is to be noted, was nevertheless advocating early marriages, while another was pointing out that the cost of education was a serious item for the gentleman and reckoned that £200–£300 a year out of an income of £1,800 (11–16 per cent) should be put aside to provide for the future family.[4]

This is not to imply that the problem had never been looked at in this light before. It had. Gentlemen in the 1860s had expressed their desire to give their children a good education, and their anxiety lest the working classes, through state assistance,

---

[1] 'Why We Men Do Not Marry' in *The Temple Bar*, October 1888, p. 222.
[2] T. L. Nicholls: *Marriage in all Ages and Nations* (1886), pp. 192 and 248.
[3] J. E. Panton: *Nooks and Corners* (1889), p. 187–9.
[4] Mrs. Earle: '£1,800 a year' in *The Cornhill Magazine*, July, 1901, p. 49. This was the fourth article in a series of five on Family Budgets, viz. A Morrison: 'A Workman's Budget', April 1901. G. S. Layard: 'A Lower Middle-Class Budget', May 1901. G. Colmore: '£800 a year', June 1901. Mrs. Earle: £1,800 a year', July, 1901; and Lady Agnew: 'Ten Thousand a year', August 1901.

might do better in this respect than they.[1] But with the extension of the state system of education after 1870, and especially after 1902, the anxiety became much more pronounced. 'We find ourselves possessed of the most ridiculous aspirations in regard to our children's future', wrote seven members of the middle classes in 1906:[2]

'We confess to desiring for them the very best in the way of education that can possibly be had—an education that may fit them for stations in life to which they are not called—the higher Civil Service, the Professions, the Army perhaps, the Navy forsooth; yes, even the Church! And somehow the London Board Schools, with all their excellences, advantages and chances, do not appear to offer quite the kind and quality of education that we deem necessary to give our children a fair send-off on the careers we have marked before them. We confess to sharing the feeling, widely, if not universally, entertained by the middle classes of London, that the Board Schools were never intended to provide education for the children of people like ourselves.'[3]

Perhaps there was more than mere snobbery in this. One of the writers, after all, did try the experiment of sending his boy to a Board school where 'within a year he contracted the following diseases: measles, ringworm, whooping-cough, vermin, ill-manners, bad language, and a cockney accent'. But the main drift of the article is clear enough. At bottom the desire for education sprang from the fundamental aim of preserving the the social differential, in income as well as in status.

In the period after the Great Depression, as we have seen, this became more difficult. Although the actual level of living suffered no setback, and although incomes continued to rise at a time when prices were falling, nevertheless the lower-income groups seem to have benefited more from the changed economic

[1] T. Browning: 'Middle Class Education' in *Transactions of the Manchester Statistical Society*, 10th March 1862, p. 94.

[2] S. F. Bullock (Author), H. Davis (Solicitor), G. H. Seccombe (Employer), H. E. Wilson (Insurance Agent), S. W. Goodyear (Broker), E. D. Malcolm (Journalist), J. L. Murray (Tradesman).

[3] 'The Burden of the Middle Classes' in *The Fortnightly Review*, September 1906, pp. 416–7.

situation than did the higher-income groups. This too was in a period when the general expansion of wealth was preceding at a slower rate than in the 1860s. At the same time there does appear to have been a slowing down in the rate of expansion of living standards, regarded as levels to which the middle classes aspired rather than actually achieved. Thus, a fourth edition of Walsh's *Manual of Domestic Economy* appeared in 1890. It was merely a reprint of the second (1873) edition. If this can be taken as any guide therefore, the seventeen years between had not witnessed anything like the changes in standards of the sixteen years between the first and second editions when it had been found necessary to scale up all estimates by 50 per cent.

Yet there were some departments of expenditure in which changes had occurred for which the new reprint did not allow —an increase for rent in London, for example. Walsh's estimate remained at £95 on an income of £750, whereas Layard in 1888 had put this as £139 (on £700) and Colmore in 1901 reckoned £130 was necessary for an income of £800.[1] If we accept these later estimates as valid, the outlay on this item alone had risen by about £40, entailing the equivalent reduction in the amount to be spent on other things. Again, the expenditure assessment for general housekeeping at first sight does not appear to have changed, being £295 on the £750 income-level in Walsh's schedule and £299 on £800 in Colmore's; but Walsh's was for a family of four children and three servants whereas Colmore's was for no children and two servants. This would suggest that the level had risen during the period, if it were not for the fact that Layard had allowed only £237 on £700 for two children and three servants in 1888. This in fact demonstrates once again the real difficulty involved in dealing with estimates of expenditure, since so many personal subjective factors intrude. Nevertheless the general impression remains that where the proportions allowed for housekeeping were smaller in the later period it was because the assessor had in mind a smaller family to be catered for.

[1] G. S. Layard: 'How to Live on £700 a Year' in *The Nineteenth Century*, February 1888, p. 243. G. Colmore: '£800 a year' in *The Cornhill Magazine*, June 1901, p. 797.

Birth Control and the Size of the Family

In the earlier estimates generally, and in Walsh's in particular, a four-child family was usually taken as standard. In the later estimates this had fallen to two. There are, indeed, some indications that in this later age the two-child family was considered by a growing number of people as ideal.[1] Every woman wanted a son, and a home was incomplete without a daughter, but what need was there for more?[2] An attack on Grant Allen who, writing on the disinclination for marriage among feminists, had maintained that the four-child family was necessary to keep the nation's numbers just stationary,[3] demonstrates how little such a sense of social responsibility was considered to be abroad at the time:

'We certainly never heard before that any theory of obligation to contribute so many individuals to the future population influenced the motives that usually induce men and women to enter into the partnership of marriage, or that any suppositious Mrs. A ever feels herself morally obliged to have six children because her neighbour, Mrs. B, has only two, or eight because Mrs. B has none.'

With great indignation the writer pointed out that the decision on such matters was purely personal and considerations of the society of to-morrow did not arise.[4]

Thus in a very general kind of way the fears of social theorists about declining population which became much more pronounced at the end of the century are seen to have had little influence on actual behaviour, and on popular thinking. Family limitation was becoming deliberately practised on a wider and wider scale, and the current attitude of mind was more concerned with the present happiness of the parents and perhaps the future opportunities of the children than with anything else.[5] Anthony Trollope's advice to a young lady: 'fall in love,

---

[1] *How to be happy though married* (1885), p. 149 *et seq.*

[2] A. S. Swan: *Courtship and Marriage* (1893), pp. 99–100.

[3] G. Allen: 'Plain Words on the Woman Question' in *The Fortnightly Review*, October 1889, p. 448.

[4] M. A. B.: 'Normal or Abnormal' in *The Englishwoman's Review*, 14th December 1889, p. 533.

[5] See *The Declining Birth-Rate*, Ch. 5 and *passim*.

marry the man, have two children and live happy ever afterwards'[1] seems neatly to sum up the outlook of this later period.

In sum, therefore, we may take it that the resistance of both the medical profession and the Church to contraception had little effect on the attitude towards marriage and the family. The kinds of prudential consideration laid down earlier continued to operate, and handbooks on marriage and articles in magazines reinforced the view that foresight was necessary if the standard of living was to be maintained. At the same time, while not openly advocating birth control, they nevertheless implied that the smaller family was a desirable thing. The view that marriage would be all very well if it were not for having so many children, attacked as 'unnatural' and 'unmanly' in the 1850s,[2] had not only been accepted by the turn of the century but modified to the form that middle-class mothers of many children were objects of compassion.[3] The number of children was now clearly recognized as subject to personal choice and the only woman who was willing 'to be regarded as a mere breeding machine' was she who lacked 'the wit to adopt any other role'.[4] The attitude towards the proper time to marry had become fused with a sense of the proper size of family.

The general movement of birth-control opinion may thus be summarized in the following way. In 1868, when Amberley made his political blunder, the middle classes were experiencing a rapid expansion in income and in their standard of living. Family limitation was not an immediate problem, so far as they were concerned, and although some of them were doubtlessly practising it, there was no widespread opinion that it was a necessary thing to do. By 1877, however, they were moving into a period when it was becoming increasingly difficult to preserve

[1] Quoted in L. P. and R. P. Stebbins: *The Trollopes* (1946), p. 255. Note also the title of the last chapter of *Framley Parsonage* (1861) viz. 'How they were all married, had two children, and lived happy ever after.' Trollope himself had two sons. The size of the families in his novels, however, does not show any consistent pattern.
[2] 'Large Families versus Small Ones' in *The British Mothers' Magazine*, June 1857, p. 123.
[3] Lady Bell: *At the Works: a Study of a Manufacturing Town* (1907), pp. 199–200. The contrast here was between the attitudes of middle-class and working-class mothers to frequent conceptions and infant deaths.
[4] 'The Maternal Instinct' in *The Saturday Review*, 8th June 1895, p. 753.

the kind of differential standards to which they had become accustomed, and the Bradlaugh-Besant trials appeared as a 'catalytic agent' bringing into the light of day what was rapidly becoming the conviction behind the scenes. It is noticeable, nevertheless, that the press opinions at this time were still rather hostile than not. It cannot be claimed that there was anything in the nature of a complete reversal of public outlook. Under these circumstances it is possible that had the economic situation returned to the pre-1870 state, the Malthusian League might have withered away and its propaganda missed fire. On the other hand, we cannot be certain that the mere continuation of the depression for another sixteen years was the only salient factor. We still need to know why it was that events took the course they did. Granted that it had become necessary for members of the middle classes to practise some kind of personal planning in order to maintain established standards, why did they choose to cut down the size of their families rather than to economize in some other departments of expenditure? The emphasis on the future of the child, apparent in books and articles on marriage in the last thirty years of the century, is a hint to us here and we need to make a more complete survey of what was happening in these departments of outlay directly connected with children before we can conclude. At the same time, it must be pointed out that by the end of the century the small middle-class family had become the accepted norm, and the only problem that remained was the morality of the methods to be used to keep it small. It is perhaps significant that the latest developments in the population controversy were eugenic in character, turning on the wisdom of allowing the working classes to breed more rapidly than the rest. Employers may have had an axe to grind here,[1] but most *writers* seem to have thought that it was better for the country as a whole that this should not be. No one appears, however, to have had the temerity to suggest that the middle classes should give up their smaller families and return to the mid-Victorian pattern. The final stage, therefore,

---

[1] They 'wish to have labour cheap; and, although they are often ready enough nowadays, even in England, to limit the size of their *own* families, they often object strongly that their poorer neighbours should imitate them in this,' wrote Charles Drysdale in *The Westminster Review*, May 1889, p. 571 (His italics.)

in the movement of opinion was the acceptance of family limitation as a concrete matter of fact, which had come to stay; and when the Bishops accepted the inevitable by admitting the 'safe' period, they gave the final sanction to what was already felt as the 'proper thing to do'.

CHAPTER XI

The Cost of Children

IN an earlier chapter dealing with household expenses[1] the cost of children was not considered separately but was counted in with the outlay for the family and servants taken together. That is to say, the domestic budgets given there were usually for a man, his wife, their children (the numbers sometimes unspecified) and the servants. Some attempt was made to estimate the board cost of the last group, but so far nothing has been said about the real expensiveness, or otherwise, of a number of children. The domestic handbook writers as a rule were not very eloquent on the subject and we have little to go upon from that source. Nevertheless there is a certain amount of evidence that for their meals at any rate the children were rarely a very costly item. John Ruskin, for example, recalled that he never had food of a dainty kind, neither at company dessert nor at other times.[2] This was in the 1830s when even reasonably wealthy middle-class parents accepted the teaching that children's diets should be wholesome and plain. According to Smiles they should not be given puff pastry or confectionery, but cabbage, turnips, cauliflowers and potatoes for the main midday meal, with perhaps some beer or plain water. For their other meals they might have some milk and a great deal of bread and water.[3] Tea or coffee, and of course wine, were prohibited altogether; so that the pattern followed would seem to

[1] Ch. 4, p. 48 *et seq.*
[2] J. Ruskin: *Praeterita: Outlines of Scenes and Thoughts perhaps worthy of Memory in my Past Life* (1885) Vol. I, Ch. I, Sec. 5.
[3] S. Smiles: *Physical Education; or, the Nurture and Management of Children* (1838), p. 53, and the medical references, pp. 59–60. Compare Ruskin's tea, viz. 'my cup of milk, and piece of bread and butter', *op. cit.*, Sec. 44.

have been very much the same as that for the servants, or if anything more simple and hence inexpensive.

Even in the 1870s the regimen does not appear to have become much more exciting.

'For breakfast we had a boiled egg each on Sundays, Tuesdays, and Thursdays, bread and milk on the other four (what a pity, we thought, that the seven days were not divided the other way round); followed by a slice of bread and butter. For dinner, roast meat and boiled potatoes; milk puddings in winter, and in summer a shape, accompanied by stewed fruit— nearly always prunes, apples, or rhubarb; for tea, two slices of bread and butter, one of bread and jam, and one bit of sponge cake; for supper, eight "animal" biscuits and one-third of a big cup of milk.'[1]

It should be emphasized that this was not the food of a poor family. Eleanor Acland's father was a prosperous mill-owner who could afford to employ a number of servants, take long holidays, and keep a carriage. There were, moreover, only three children. Yet the discipline was quite strict. Their milk, for example, was handed out in a single mug divided into three by thick purple stripes, and it was considered a very serious matter to drink below one's stripe.[2] It is no small wonder that 'Milly' was excited over special treats, the eggs for breakfast on a birthday—'even if it did not happen to be a "regular egg day" '—and the holiday trips with a travelling basket packed with unusual and delightful foods. The children too were often in trouble for robbing the raspberry-canes to supplement their strictly limited daily ration of ten raspberries each.[3] Tea with the servants in the servants' hall was regarded by them as a treat.[4] Indications of this nature suggest that the food of the

[1] E. Acland: *Good-bye for the Present: the Story of Two Childhoods, Milly, 1878–8, and Ellen, 1913–24* (1935). 'Milly' was Eleanor Acland herself (see G. M. Trevelyan 'Introduction', p. 8).

[2] *Ibid.*, p. 169.

[3] *Ibid.*, pp. 122, 124–5, and 165. Note that at Herne Hill where the garden was well stocked with fruit, Ruskin was forbidden to touch any. (J. Ruskin: *Praeterita* (1885), Sec. 59.)

[4] Acland, *op. cit.*, p. 101. O. Sitwell: *Left Hand, Right Hand—an Autobiography* (1945), Bk. 2, Ch. 1, p. 92. O. Sitwell: *Two Generations* (1940), G. C. Sitwell's reminiscences, p. 130.

nursery was not only plain but even sparse, part of the general attitude that children should not be 'mollycoddled' but put through a 'hardening process' of inuring them to certain minor privations of which plain fare and early rising and early bed-time were the main kinds.[1]

Expensive toys were, of course, quite out of the question, and very little was spent on the children other than for their food, clothing and education.[2] Dress was perhaps a more expensive item than food, but even here home dressmaking was the rule,[3] except perhaps for 'best' clothes.[4] Eleanor Acland indeed was rather emphatic about this aspect of the monotony of the daily round of her childhood when she wrote: 'It was the same with everything else. Milly's and Betty's frocks were cut to the same shape, year in, year out, whether they were made of gingham and muslin in summer, or serge and velvet in winter. I suppose Barley only knew how to make that one shape.'[5]

Underlying this, however, lies the suggestion that children's clothes *could* be made of expensive materials whatever the style, and Walsh hinted that the use of silks and satins in this connection was often the cause of financial disputes between the parents.[6] Some items of clothing, moreover, could not be produced at home: the school uniform, for example, which first became common in the sixties.[7] Hence we are left with the impression that dress could be quite an important item in the

[1] M. E. Perugini: *Victorian Days and Ways* (1946), Ch. 8, pp. 89–90, and *passim*.

[2] *Ibid.*, Ruskin, *op. cit.*, Secs. 13 and 14. He recalled that he had few toys and none at all at first. See also M. V. Hughes: *A London Family, 1870–1900* (1946). '. . . we had few toys, few magazines, few outside entertainments, and few means of getting about', p. 4. (The father was on the London Stock Exchange.)

[3] Cf. Walsh: £500 a year 'provides also for the keeping of a single horse or pony and carriage. If, however, the family is a large one, a young lady's maid must be kept for the purpose of making their dresses at home, and in that case a horse cannot be afforded.' Quoted on p. 75.

[4] M. Asquith: *The Autobiography of Margot Asquith* (1920). 'We had two bets dresses: one made in London, which we only wore on great occasions; the other made by my nurse, in which we went down to dessert' (Vol. 1, p. 21). Her father, Sir Charles Tennant was a City speculator who could afford *two* governesses at a time to cope with his twelve children.

[5] Acland, *op. cit.*, p. 113. Barley was the name of her nurse.

[6] J. H. Walsh: *A Manual of Domestic Economy* (1857), p. 341. (2nd ed., 1873, p. 369.)

[7] C. W. Cunnington: 'School Children's Dress in the Nineteenth Century' in *The Times Educational Supplement*, 16th February 1951, p. 126.

cost of children, although we have no very precise idea of what it actually amounted to. One writer reckoned children's clothes at £10–£15 out of an income of £300–£500 a year,[1] which compared with £80 which the father and mother spent on themselves, and £50 which was her allowance elsewhere for a child's keep.[2] The grown-up daughter of a professional man, however, would cost him £100 a year, living at home, while a son would need over and above his college requirements, £50 for clothes and £8 for extras.[3] Altogether the cost of a child was far from negligible, especially if it lived to adolescence, and it is not unlikely that this had some weight in helping to change the attitude towards family limitation as improvements in health and hygiene progressively lowered children's mortality rates in the second half of the century.

The most important item, however, in the upbringing of the child was the cost of fitting it for a future career. Before 1800 formal tuition had not been very necessary in this respect, but with the spread of professionalism into many of the new vocations brought into being by the Industrial Revolution, the specialized knowledge of an intellectual technique was called for, which could only be obtained at certain recognized institutions of training. The pattern followed was that of the older, learned, professions, and we shall obtain a fairly good idea of the expenses involved if we take some specimen careers for which the charges are known and estimate the sums parents would need to place their sons in these vocations. Thus, in order to become a barrister a young man had to show that he was a 'gentleman' which for most people meant that he had undergone the kind of training usually expected of a gentleman and was more or less intimate with the classics.[4] Indeed, in 1829, the Inner Temple adopted a regulation to this effect, subjecting all candidates for admission to an examination as to their proficiency in classical attainments and the general subjects of a liberal education.[5] Then, having been introduced by an existing member of one of the four Inns of Court, he was

---

[1] J. E. Panton: *From Kitchen to Garret* (7th ed., 1896), p. 192.
[2] J. E. Panton: *Nooks and Corners* (1889), p. 192.
[3] *Ibid.*, pp. 116 and 188.
[4] A. Polson: *Law and Lawyers* (1840), Vol. 1, Ch. 1, p. 5.
[5] 'The Discipline of the Bar' in *Meliora*, Vol. 5, 1863, p. 161.

required to pay some £40 in fees and a further deposit of £100 as a security of good faith. If, however, he was already a graduate of Oxford, Cambridge, London or Dublin, he was excused the deposit, which in any case was useful since it would more than pay the fees of his final admission, if called to the Bar.[1] At the same time, mere acceptance by one of the Inns of Court was not sufficient. The young man would be required to spend twelve terms there, that is, eating dinners on a set number of occasions, and, if he were really serious about making the law his life's work, he could only do it by serving a kind of apprenticeship with a practising barrister, the fee for which was 100 guineas per year.[2] This entailed merely going to the man's chambers for the first year to watch the business transacted. In the second and third year he would be given several tasks to do until he learned the business of special pleader or equity draftsman.[3] In all it was estimated that no one with less than £200 a year at his command could make anything of it.[4]

Moreover the successful young man called to the Bar could not expect to earn money immediately on becoming a barrister. It would be another four or five years before he could make a living at his chosen profession. There were exceptions to this generalization, but they were usually emphasized as exceptions. Thus William Lucas's brother Frank began well with sufficient business to bring him in, if paid, £250 worth of fees in his first year. This gave him a sense of his prospects far too optimistic for the real state of affairs, and in a few years he was feeling very discouraged.[5] The novelist-to-be, Samuel Warren, made twenty-four guineas a week in steady business when he began,[6] but he

[1] 'Report of the Select Committee on Legal Education', Appendix 2, p. 306 (*Parliamentary Papers*, 1846, Vol. 10).

[2] *Ibid.*, Answer to question 1265.

[3] 'Report of Her Majesty's Commissioners appointed to Inquire into the State, Discipline, Studies, and Revenues of the University and Colleges of Oxford. Minutes of evidence given by S. C. Denison.' (*Parliamentary Papers*, 1852, Vol. 22, p. 197.)

[4] F. Davenant: *What shall my son be? Hints to Parents on the choice of a profession or trade* (1870), p. 28.

[5] G. E. Bryant and G. P. Baker (eds.): *A Quaker Journal; being the Diary and Reminiscenses of William Lucas of Hitchin* (1934), p. 289, 24th December 1842. Compare this with p. 388, 26th March 1847.

[6] In 1837, see Mrs. Oliphant: *William Blackwood and his Sons* (1897), Vol. 2, p. 218.

records that although it was possible to make £300 a year, this
was unusual, and he caused his own Attorney-General to confess that it was eight years before he made enough to pay his
laundress.[1] We can accept, therefore, that *The Complete Book of
Trades* was not far wrong in putting the necessary capital for
this career at somewhere between £1,000 to £1,500 in 1842[2]—
a sum of money quite beyond the reach of most members of the
class we have been considering.

A career in the law, of course, was not confined to practice as
a barrister. A man could make a very comfortable income[3] as
an attorney, solicitor, procter, or one of the other branches of
the profession practising in the Courts of Law and Equity of
the United Kingdom and hence entitled to become a member
of the Law Society. The very highest incomes were beyond his
reach but on the other hand the profession was easier to enter.
Between 1821 and 1836, it is true, the examination system was
laid down requiring intending solicitors (the general term) to
pass a qualifying examination set by the Law Society[4] but the
fees were low.[5] Most intending solicitors became articled clerks
at the cost of £120 payable to the Government and then appren-
ticed themselves to a solicitor for a premium of £300 to £1,000[6]
—or £250 to £350 according to another source of information
which estimated the total capital needed as between £500 and
£1,000.[7] Alternatively they could study with a barrister, although this was not the custom. This would cost them 100
guineas a year.[8]

As opposed to the barristers, therefore, who were mostly
young men of 'that minor aristocracy which is interposed in
England, between the patrician gentry and the middle or

---

[1] S. Warren: *Ten Thousand a Year* (1841), Bk. 4, Ch. 4.
[2] *The Complete Book of Trades, or the Parents' Guide and Youths' Instructor* by several
hands (1842), p. 486. This was the minimum sum, needing careful managing.
[3] See Note K, p. 225.
[4] E. B. V. Christian: *A Short History of Solicitors* (1896), Chronological table.
[5] £25 or £30 according to Sir George Stephen (Report of the Select Committee
on Legal Education, question 2038) and also Mr. E. Payne (Answer to question
2629. *Parliamentary Papers*, 1846, Vol. 10).
[6] *Ibid.*, answer to question 2628.
[7] *The Complete Book of Trades* (1842). Payne reckoned it at £500 to £1,200.
[8] Report of the Select Committee on Legal Education, *op. cit.*, question
2629.

tradesman classes',[1] solicitors were recruited from the sons of tradesmen, shopkeepers, merchants and farmers,[2] and in most cases their own sons went on to become barristers.[3] This entailed the cultivation of a particular way of living, dressing and dining, the expenses of which tended to rise as the standards expected of 'gentlemen' rose, so that we find an authority at the end of the century putting the least possible cost of training a solicitor or barrister at £300 a year (50 per cent above our earlier estimates), although fees and barristers' 'apprenticeship' charges had not changed. This raised the capital required to at least £2,400,[4] and the cost of creating a solicitor would appear to have risen similarly.[5]

The medical profession too, was not easy to enter. By the Medical Act of 1858 the General Medical Council was given statutory powers to ensure that people unfit to practise medicine should not have their names recorded in the Medical Register and to delete from it the names of people unworthy to be there. In practice this worked out as a method of acceptance on a uniform basis of the licenses to practise issued by the medical schools and societies of the country, for although unregistered persons could still practise they suffered under certain legal disadvantages and it was quite obvious that only a medical man who had been through all the procedure of a medical education ending in registration by the General Medical Council could hope to do well in the profession.[6]

There were three branches, physicians, surgeons, and apothecaries, the last not coming under the jurisdiction of the Medical Act but under an earlier Act of 1815 which, if anything, was even more strict.[7] A physician was usually a graduate of one of the universities and a fellow or licentiate of the Royal College of Physicians. Indeed, if he wanted to practise in London he was obliged to have the diploma of the College and for this he had to be at least twenty-six years old, 'of unimpeachable moral

[1] A. Polson: *Law and Lawyers* (1840), Vol. 1, p. 146.
[2] Evidence of Sir George Stephen, *op. cit.*, answers to question 1963 *et seq.*
[3] Polson, *op. cit.*, p. 146.
[4] W. W. R. Ball: *The Student's Guide to the Bar* (7th ed., 1904), p. 61.
[5] H. Jones: *An Entrance Guide to Professions and Business* (1898), pp. 32–37.
[6] A. M. Carr-Saunders and P. A. Wilson: *The Professions* (1933), pp. 83–89.
[7] *Ibid.*, pp. 77–83.

character', and to have devoted himself for five years at least to the study of medicine.[1] There was a strict examination and the diploma cost £22. Entrance to the Royal College of Surgeons was similar.[2] In 1884 the two bodies licensed together.[3]

Obtaining the diploma, however, was only the first step. A man had also to find a practice, and this was fraught with dangers:

'To commence at once as a practitioner on his own account immediately after obtaining his diploma, is a bold step in any young man, and one that it would be madness to take, unless he have other resources. Let him take a private house in any situation, however public, fix a lamp of red and green glass over his door, make known to the world, by means of a brass plate, that his name is Mr. So and So, and that he is a surgeon, accoucheur, &c., and fix a bell handle on each side, writing "Surgery Bell" under one, and "Night Bell" under the other, and the probability is that twelve months will elapse before anybody will put his services in requisition.'[4]

Many began as assistants to existing practitioners on the small salary of £25–£30 plus board and lodging, and had great difficulty in becoming established on their own account. Indeed, without some alternative source of income it was well-nigh impossible, and the books and articles on careers hesitated to recommend the profession to anyone without sufficient capital to carry them over the first period. Thus *The Complete Book of Trades* reckoned that £2,000 was necessary from the time of matriculation to the point of setting up in practice and maintained that parents who could not afford this should send their boys 'to plough in other waters'.[5] In 1888, however, Rivington worked out the cost of a medical education, lasting five years, as £600 in the provinces and £670 in London,[6] which would

---

[1] J. C. Hudson: *The Parent's Handbook* (1842), p. 89.

[2] *Ibid.*, p. 89.

[3] Carr-Saunders and Wilson, *op. cit.*, p. 87.

[4] Hudson, *op. cit.*, pp. 99–101. For an excellent thumb-nail sketch of the difficulties of the first year or two of practice, see the first chapter of S. Warren: *Passages from the Diary of a Late Physician* (1831).

[5] *The Complete Book of Trades* (1842), p. 378.

[6] W. Rivington: *The Medical Profession of the United Kingdom* (1888), p. 694. See also Note L, p. 225.

suggest that the £2,000 of forty years earlier was perhaps meant to cover more than the mere instruction and subsistence of five years' training. Medicine was, for this reason, regarded as the most difficult of all professions in which to make a beginning and young medical students and graduates were recommended to attempt some form of journalism to help them on their way.[1]

The very best students were in one respect more fortunate since they were often offered posts in hospitals or could obtain them without much difficulty in the Army or Navy, or under Local Government Boards, but the salaries were not large,[2] and ambitious men without capital were not likely to feel their chances of high incomes enhanced by entering these fields.[3] On the other hand, men with capital could buy a practice outright or buy a partnership.[4] This was something of an uncertain proceeding and required a fair amount of business acumen. Nevertheless it was the procedure usually recommended to parents who are anxious to give their sons a start in life in the medical profession. By and large, therefore, £2,000 would have been needed at the middle of the century and it is clear that not many members of the middle-range income groups discussed earlier would have been able to spare this, even if they spread it over a period of ten years.

In the case of apothecaries, the remaining branch of the profession, apprenticeship for five years was necessary to a practising master, before a young man could apply for examination to the Apothecaries' Company. This required a premium of at least £50,[5] and might amount to £500.[6] The capital required, therefore, was put at somewhere between £250 and £500 to

[1] Hudson, *op. cit.*, p. 89.
[2] See Note M, p. 226.
[3] Richard Owen was one of the more successful of the nineteenth-century medical men who started his career as an apprentice to a barber surgeon. Without capital he reckoned it would take him at least ten years to pay his way, and he accepted a post eventually at a college hospital, at £200 a year. In 1833, when he was 29, he became Professor of Comparative Anatomy at St. Bartholomew's, on a salary of £500 a year. His subsequent career, although brilliant, was never opulent. See R. Owen: *The Life of Richard Owen* (1894), Vol. 1, pp. 41, 59–60, 62.
[4] Hudson, *op. cit.*, pp. 99–101, and F. Davenant: *What shall my son be?* (1870), p. 31.
[5] Hudson, *op. cit.*, p. 89.
[6] *The Complete Book of Trades* (1842), p. 6.

cover all the various fees and expenses arising in addition.[1] But, of course, the prizes to be obtained were not so alluring.

With the third of the ancient professions, the Church, the situation was not really very different. Although a degree was not absolutely essential, we are told that Bishops took notice of such academic attainments when candidates presented themselves for ordination,[2] and Oxford and Cambridge were the obvious first choices here.[3] Many of the university colleges, moreover, possessed livings which they could bestow on talented students and there were also scholarships and bursaries to help them over the difficult period of training, especially if they were themselves the sons of clergymen of the Church of England, orphans in particular having preference.

Livings were usually obtained by presentation, but it was not impossible to purchase them and a living of £300 a year, with an incumbent sixty years of age, might be obtained for less than £1,000.[4] On the other hand, prospects for those without influence or capital were not good, and starting salaries (curate's) were poor. Thus, the average salary for the three years ending in 1831 for curates was only £81, and for *all* incumbents £285 (or £244 if the curate's stipend was deducted from the incumbent's total).[5] Higher salaries than these, e.g. Bishops', averaged £6,000, could only be obtained by promotion and here the influence of family, school or college connections was important.[6] 'The state of church patronage', wrote Markby in 1867, 'is such that when a young man takes orders, he must make up his mind, unless he has a friend to give him a church or money to buy one for himself, to spend his life either in celibacy or else poverty so sordid as to forbid him and his family all the ornaments and many of the necessaries of life, including in very many cases even pure air and clean water.'[7]

[1] *Ibid.*, p. 487.

[2] Davenant, *op. cit.*, p. 13.

[3] Hudson, *op. cit.*, p. 3.

[4] *Ibid.*, pp. 11–15.

[5] Report of the Commissioners appointed to Inquire into the Ecclesiastical Revenues of England and Wales (*Parliamentary Papers*, 1835, Vol. 22, p. 40). See also Note N, p. 226.

[6] 'The Church as a Profession' in *The Cornhill Magazine*, June 1864, p. 750.

[7] T. Markby: 'University Extension' in *The Contemporary Review*, November 1867, p. 424.

An interesting fictional account of the comparison is to be found in Anthony Trollope's *Framley Parsonage*. On the one hand Josiah Crawley had no one to help him, so that he struggled on in grave poverty for ten years as a curate in a 'bleak, ugly, cold parish on the northern coast of Cornwall', where his stipend was no more than £70 a year. At the end of this time promotion looked as far away as ever, and would surely have remained so, had not his friend, Dr. Arabin chanced to have been made Dean of Barchester and as such have taken over the patronage of the incumbency of Hogglestock, which, when it became vacant, he bestowed on Crawley. This was worth only £130, but the Crawleys were now much better placed as there was a house attached. 'Poor Mrs. Crawley, when she heard of it, thought that their struggles of poverty were now well nigh over. What might not be done with a hundred and thirty pounds by people who had lived for years on seventy?'[1]

Mark Robarts, on the other hand, was the son of an Exeter physician, 'a gentleman possessed of no private means, but enjoying a lucrative practice, which had enabled him to maintain and educate a family with all the advantages which money can give in this country'. His experiences form a marked contrast to those of Crawley. Sent as a private pupil to the house of a clergyman friend of his father, he soon became friendly with his tutor's other pupil, the only son of Lady Lufton. His father immediately saw the opportunities latent in the situation and did not hesitate to send his son to Harrow when the young lord went there, and on to Oxford in due course. By this time Mark had become accepted at the Lufton home, Framley Court, and after he had taken his degree and spent eight or ten months travelling with his noble friend, he was ordained in accordance with the joint wishes of his father and Lady Lufton, who had met to discuss his future and decided that the Framley living should be his since there was no other member of the Lufton family to be provided for. The living was worth £900 and the existing incumbent was over seventy. For the present the young churchman was found a temporary curacy and when a year

[1] A. Trollope: *Framley Parsonage* (1861), Chs. 14 and 15.

later old Dr. Stopford died, Mark Robarts received the 'full fruition of his rich hopes'.[1]

Both Josiah Crawley and Mark Robarts married, but the poor living of the one compared with the rich living of the other amply illustrates the point of Markby's thesis.

The only other alternative for the poor man without influence was to take a post as chaplain in the Army or Navy at a starting salary of nearly £200. Here the prospects were not great but they were much more certain, and in the course of twenty-five years, a man could be earning £342 in the Navy and £523 17s. 6d. in the Army;[2] but, of course, a bishopric or any of the more lucrative posts was ruled out. In sum, although the minimum requirement for a career in the Church was a university degree, entailing the cost of education up to that standard, as with medicine and the law, a parent who wished to give his son a more certain start in life would have to consider some form of capital expenditure over and above the educational costs, unless he was sufficiently intimate with the owner of a living to obtain patronage without expense, or unless he was prepared to spend a far greater amount on the education than the mere qualification standard required, and send his son to one of the more expensive public schools in the hope that he might acquire the friendship of someone with power.

At the same time it must not be overlooked that a man who had obtained a degree at Oxford or Cambridge had a choice of possible occupation before him. He might, for example, be given a fellowship worth between £200 and £400 per annum, on condition of celibacy and ordination, a heritage of the monastic rule imposed during the Middle Ages. This carried, however, no further obligations except in a few cases and there the duties by and large were merely nominal.[3] Such fellowships, therefore, were valuable aids to young men anxious to build up

[1] *Ibid.*, Ch. 1.
[2] W. Dawson: 'The Church in the Navy' in *The Contemporary Review*, September 1869, p. 98.
[3] A. S. Wilkins: 'On University Endowments and the Higher Education of the Nation' in the *Transactions of the Manchester Statistical Society*, 16th November 1870, p. 4. There were between 500 and 600 fellowships at Oxford and Cambridge, of which at least 50 or 60 became vacant every year. J. Heywood: 'On Endowed Education and Oxford and Cambridge Fellowships.' Report of the 32nd meeting of the British Association, October 1862, *Notices and Abstracts of Meeting*, p. 154.

a career in one of the professions, and Sidgwick, in his attack on the system, explicitly mentioned how useful they were to barristers and doctors just starting out, as well as to beginners in journalism and magazine-writing.[1] For those, moreover, who decided to remain in residence at the college, there was always the possibility of promotion to Provost or some other post of the kind within the University, or after a few years as tutor, to go out as professor to some other place or as a schoolmaster or headmaster at one of the grammar or public schools. This in its turn might open up the way to a career in the Church for the headmastership of a great public school was often the stepping-stone to a bishopric.[2] The possession of an Oxford or Cambridge degree was thus of great value institutionally in terms of the future career, quite apart from the contacts a man made with people of influence through living in college with them for two or three years.[3]

Before going on to consider the expenses involved in providing a son with university education, however, a word or two on the subject of patronage in general will not be out of place. As we have seen, appointment and promotion in the church depended to a considerable extent upon the kinds of contact a young man made with people who possessed livings at their disposal or who were influential within the episcopalean hierarchy. Here the standing of his father or one of his uncles was very important, and without that family influence it was all the more necessary that he should be assisted to make the contact himself by sending him to a good public school and then on to either Oxford or Cambridge. But patronage was important not only in the Church. It played as great a part in the Civil Service and in the Royal Navy. In the case of the former, the right to bestow appointments belonged to the secretary for the time being of the particular department in which a vacancy happened to occur,[4] and the accepted practice was to use this privilege for providing

---

[1] H. Sidgwick: 'Idle Fellowships' in *The Contemporary Review*, April 1876, pp. 685–6.

[2] A. M. Carr-Saunders and P. A. Wilson: *The Professions* (1933), p. 250.

[3] For some indication of the advantages of an Oxford or Cambridge degree in this period, see N. Hans: 'Independent Schools and the Liberal Professions' in *The Year Book of Education, 1950*.

[4] Hudson, *op. cit.*, pp. 120–7. Davenant, *op. cit.*, p. 112.

'relations, friends, supporters, and dependants with a liveli-hood'.[1] Here again, the commencing salaries were low (less than £100) and often senior clerks, after many years of service, received no more than £350. Hence a university degree was by no means necessary, but a parent might be won over to pro-viding his son with a good education solely in order to obtain him influence. This might also be the case for those considering a career in the Navy where patronage was vested in the hands of the Lords Commissioners of the Admiralty, although, as here the pay and prospects were not very good, worse if anything than in the Church,[2] the incentive was probably not so strong.

The question therefore arises as to how far the abolition of patronage could have affected the middle-class family budget. It is usually held, for example, that the Northcote-Trevelyan reforms in the Civil Service, because they had replaced the old system of recruitment by one of competitive examination for almost every post by 1870, made necessary an adequate school-ing or university education for every candidate who aspired to the upper branches of the Service. Henceforward, a parent could no longer rely on influence alone to obtain a post for his son. He was obliged to provide him with the best education money could buy, if only for the reason that without it he would be defeated in the race by the sons of the new industrialists who could afford the school and university expenses but who earlier had been prevented from placing their sons in the Civil Service because they had not been sufficiently long enough established to obtain them posts by influence.[3] As opposed to this view must be made the point that patronage, although perhaps costless in itself, required money to create it or to keep it. That is to say, the privilege of providing relations or friends, supporters or dependants with appointments carried with it an understood obligation. These people were not to be recruited from any class in society regardless of their background. They should at least be 'gentlemen', able to talk and mix freely with 'gentle-men' and this meant that ideally they should have had the kind

[1] H. R. G. Greaves: *The Civil Service in the Changing State* (1947), p. 20.
[2] Hudson, *op. cit.*, p. 58–59.
[3] See, for example, G. G. Leybourne and K. White: *Education and the Birth-Rate* (1940), p. 32.

of classical education customarily provided for the sons of gentlemen, preferably at one of the public schools. It is not immediately obvious, therefore, that the abolition of patronage in the Civil Service had much effect on the budgets of those people who, up to 1870, had ordinarily obtained posts for their sons in some form of government service. Its real effect was to increase the educational outlay of those who until then had not aspired in that direction. It is not likely, for example, that Anthony Trollope's father would have been called upon seriously to increase the expenditure on his son's education because of the Northcote-Trevelyan reforms,[1] but people who until 1870 had considered the Civil Service *beyond* their reach might have been incited after that date into sending their sons to grammar school and university, not with the forlorn hope of their making contacts there, but with the more reasonable calculation that their ability would carry them through without influence provided that they were given adequate training. The Civil Service was expanding rapidly and was able to absorb sons of the new rich, but those could only make their way into its ranks if their parents were prepared to devote a part of their income to the costs of education.

This same argument may be made in the case of the abolition of Army Purchase. Under the Cardwell reforms of 1871 the system whereby most young candidates could only obtain a commission by purchasing one[2] and promotion by influence or by further purchase,[3] was swept away for a more truly professional organization in which the Army colleges, Sandhurst and Woolwich, were given an important role to play; but it does not appear that the social content of the officer class was changed one bit thereby.[4] We may hazard a guess therefore that the capital sum required for buying a commission was spent on

---

[1] Anthony Trollope was educated at Winchester and Harrow. It is, of course, possible that under a different system of recruitment from patronage he would never have been accepted into the Civil Service, but that is a different problem.

[2] Hudson, *op. cit.*, p. 20. '. . . The British army . . . is no place for the son of a poor man to enter as an officer.'

[3] M. L. Pechall: *Professions for Boys and How to Enter Them* (1898), p. 9.

[4] This was the view of General Walseley: 'The Army' in T. H. Ward (ed.) *The Reign of Queen Victoria: a Survey of Fifty Years of Progress* (1887), Vol. 1, p. 166 *et seq.*

obtaining an Army college education. Instead of paying £450–£1,260 for a commission, plus further sums amounting to as much as £7,800 for a man who aspired to the rank of Lieutenant-Colonel in the Foot Guards,[1] the parent could send his son to an expensive public school and on to one of the Army colleges for two or three years. This would cost him little more than £200 per annum[2] and he might even be in pocket over the change. At any rate, for those classes of people who were already accustomed to entering their sons into the well-established professions dealt with so far, the introduction of the competitive system of recruitment and its extension was not responsible for any serious increases in the cost of education—not, that is, for them as a class, although it may have involved certain additional outlays for some of them as individuals, just as it was no doubt the cause of certain savings for others. In so far, therefore, as we regard the 1870s as a turning-point in this matter, it is to the newly created members of the middle classes we must turn to see the changes becoming important. These people were now perhaps offered opportunities for their sons from which they were debarred before, and to see how far they were able to take them we must first estimate how much university and pre-university training cost.

This, however, is no easy task. Even at Oxford and Cambridge, about which we have a certain amount of definite information, there was no uniform system and different colleges had different rates of charge. Some witnesses before the Commissions held in the fifties, for example, gave one set of figures and others gave another. Nevertheless, taking all these variations into account, the Royal Commission on Oxford concluded that they believed a parent who, in addition to supplying his son with clothes and supporting him at home during the vacations, paid no more than £600 for him during his university course, had reason to congratulate himself.[3] There were people who managed it on less, one witness instancing a case of £300,[4] but

---

[1] Hudson, *op. cit.*, p. 22. See also Note O, p. 227.

[2] H. Jones: *An Entrance Guide to Professions and Business* (1898), pp. 5–7.

[2] Report of Her Majesty's Commissioners appointed to inquire into the State, Discipline, Studies and Revenues of the University and Colleges of Oxford (*Parliamentary Papers*, 1852, Vol. 22, p. 33).

[4] *Ibid.* Minutes of Evidence, p. 23.

the average would seem to have been rather more. Part of the problem, naturally, arose from the different kinds of needs of different individuals, but more important was the impact and influence of the customary norms. Thus a number of witnesses were eloquent on the subject of the 'evils of fashion', on 'vicious extravagance', and on 'squandering on superfluities'.[1] In sum, although the *necessary* expenses of university life at Oxford rarely amounted to more than £100 per year, the added expenses entailed by boating, riding, supper parties, wine, expensive dress and furniture, considered appropriate for the student's social position, raised the expenses, as one witness pointed out, beyond the means of the middle classes of society. The young men of large possessions set the pace and the others tried to live up to it.[2] Possibly the Royal Commission on Cambridge a year or so later was influenced by this argument. At any rate, it estimated differently for the two classes of people and reckoned the expenses of noblemen as ranging from £650 to £1,400 and fellow commoners as from £485 to £1,150. Here again the annual necessary expenses were much lower, between £61 and £90 per year, and the difference was made up by outlay caused through extravagant habits, acquired, it was claimed, at the public schools from which the students came.[3] At other places, such as Durham, where the nobility were not accustomed to go, the costs were apparently cheaper.[4]

Unfortunately, there is a serious lack of information for making comparisons over time. Later reports on the two major Universities do not mention costs except in general terms and the individual estimates that we have are not truly comparable. How far, for example, can we estimate what had happened over fifty years, from the £19 15s. 4d. spent by Lord Elton's grandfather at Balliol in the midsummer quarter of 1837, compared

[1] *Ibid.*, pp. 52, 69, 92, 110, 119–20, 143–4, and 152. For a specimen expenses sheet, see Note P, p. 227.

[2] Evidence of Professor J. A. Ogle, *ibid.*, p. 40.

[3] Report of Her Majesty's Commissioners appointed to inquire into the State, Discipline, Studies and Revenues of the University and Colleges of Cambridge (*Parliamentary Papers*, 1852–3, Vol. 44, p. 148). See also W. Emery: 'On the Past and Present Expenses and Social Conditions of University Education' (*Report of the British Association*, October 1862, pp. 193–4).

[4] J. W. Adamson: *English Education, 1789–1902* (1930), p. 172.

with the £43 10s. 8d. spent by his uncle at Oriel in 1885?[1]
Were these exceptional or average terms? Did the uncle, for
instance, include a rather heavier outlay on, say, dinners and
entertainments, which in the earlier case the grandfather had
cut down on that term? These things we do not know and without them we cannot assume that costs had more than doubled
over fifty years, as the specimen bills suggest. On the other hand,
quite apart from the extent of increases over time, it is clear
that university education was never very cheap—at least for
those who aspired to live in residence at Oxford or Cambridge
—and £200 a year there for three years may be taken as
the usual figure a parent could reckon to be expected to
find.

Board costs, of course, would tend to fluctuate with the prices
of provisions, but, as we have seen, from the 1870s onwards
retail prices tended on the whole to fall, and we should not
therefore consider it likely that basic charges for these things
rose at all. We have, indeed, some evidence to this effect. The
21st Volume (Tables) of the Schools Inquiry Commission[2] gave
detailed information on tuition fees and board charges of a large
number of endowed grammar and other secondary schools
throughout the country. Comparing this with the details given
in the second edition of the *Public Schools Year Book* (1891–2) we
obtain the following set of figures for a number of schools for
which the information given is comparable for the two different
years.

Composite fees, board and tuition

	1868							1892						
	£	s.	d.	£	s.	d.		£	s.	d.	£	s.	d.
Felsted	36	0	0					51	9	0–	61	9	0
Haileybury	45	0	0–	73	10	0		56	0	0–	100	0	0
Winchester	84	0	0–	98	9	0		112	0	0			

---

[1] Letter to *The Times*, 21st August 1951. His son's bill for midsummer 1951 was £78 17s. 3d.

[2] Report of the Schools Inquiry Commission (*Parliamentary Papers*, 1867–8, Vol. 28).

Tuition fees

	1868						1892					
Bedford Grammar	1	1	0				9	0	0–	12	0	0
Bradford Grammar	4	0	0				10	0	0			
Dulwich	6	0	0				22	0	0			
Repton	10	10	0				25	0	0			
Rugby	16	5	6				16	16	0			
Sherbourne	6	6	0–10	10	0		25	7	6			
Tonbridge	5	5	0–16	16	0		14	0	0–	27	0	0
Uppingham	6	7	6–12	0	0		40	0	0			
Westminster	17	7	0–26	5	0		30	0	0			

Board fees

	1868						1892					
Bedford Grammar	63	0	0–78	15	0		63	0	0–	66	5	0
Bradford Grammar		none						none				
Dulwich	33	0	0–45	0	0		63	0	0			
Repton	73	10	0				63	0	0			
Rugby	88	0	0				96	0	0			
Sherbourne	63	0	0				59	9	0			
Tonbridge	54	12	0–69	0	0		60	0	0–	66	0	0
Uppingham	69	4	0				70	0	0			
Westminster	35	0	0–94	0	0		65	0	0			
Marlborough	54	0	0	Clergy			50	0	0	Clergy		
	72	0	0	Lay			80	0	0	Lay		

Here the most noticeable thing is how little board charges really changed. Although a few large differences occurred, Dulwich, for example, raising its costs from £33–£45 to £63, most were small (Rugby increased by only £8) and some were actually lower in 1892 (Repton decreased by £9 10s.). On the the other hand, tuition fees almost doubled in every case. The real change in the cost of education over this period was thus a function of the higher charges made for actual instruction, so that the rise in the composite board and tuition fees at places like Haileybury and Winchester may be assumed to be the result mainly of this fact; and without evidence to the contrary, it is likely that the colleges at Oxford and Cambridge followed the pattern.

It must, however, be recorded that the figures on the above table referred only to the minimum basic charge. Thus, for

Felsted Grammar School the total cost, according to the table, was £36 in 1868; but elsewhere in the Reports of the Schools Inquiry Commission[1] as well as this figure, details were given of the lowest bill, average bill, and the highest bill paid at the school in 1864. These were £38 11s. 7d., £48 5s. 7d., and £70 11s. 1d. respectively. The cost of board and tuition, therefore, formed only a bare minimum. Other charges, books and stationery, washing, extra tuition, etc., could raise that by about a third again (average case) or even almost double it. Hence, although the mere doubling of tuition fees between 1868 and 1892 raised the cost of education by only 20 per cent, it is possible that changes in other costs were responsible for quite significant increases at the boarding schools, and, by inference, at the university colleges. Here we have a gap in our knowledge which makes it extremely difficult to estimate the effect on middle-class budgets of increases in the cost of education.

On the other hand, the development of the Public Boarding School system itself may be taken as an indication in general terms of how far the middle and upper classes were becoming more and more prepared to spend money on this form of education. At the beginning of the nineteenth century only seven schools in this country stood out as permanent institutions attended by the sons of the English ruling classes,[2] but with the coming of the Railway Age many new schools were founded on the lines laid down by Arnold at Rugby.[3] Thus in the 1840s fifteen new schools taking boarders appeared, in the 1850s six, and in the 1860s fourteen, making thirty-five new schools over thirty years. In addition during this period five existing schools were rebuilt in such a way as practically to constitute new schools and a number were re-established and reorganized on public-school lines.[4] It is important to emphasize that the expansion of this type of school was made in the forties and sixties, *before* the abolition of patronage on any scale in the Civil Service, whereas in the 1870s only six new schools of this type were

[1] *Ibid.*, Vol. 1, Appendix 3, pp. 34–35. See Note Q, p. 228.
[2] Winchester, Eton, Westminster, Harrow, Rugby, Charterhouse and Shrewsbury. See E. C. Mack: *Public Schools and British Opinion, 1780–1860* (1938), p. 73 *et seq.*
[3] *Ibid.*, p. 346 *et seq.*
[4] See Note R, p. 228.

opened, and in the 1880s only seven. Professor Tawney has emphasized the fact that three times as many public schools were founded between 1841 and 1870 as were founded throughout the whole century before.[1] He was inclined, however, to explain this development in terms of the rapid expansion of the railways making it possible for parents easily to send their sons to the new schools,[2] although this is rather to ignore another point made by him, that in the 1860s the greater part of the pupils covered by the several inquiry commissions were still day boys.[3] Notwithstanding the fact that the model set before them by the nine great public schools was in the main a boarding one, many of the new boarding schools provided facilities for day boys. However from our point of view what seems more significant is that the growth of the public school system coincided with the great expansion of wealth and growth in numbers of the middle classes, and it contracted somewhat as they found themselves faced with the problems raised by the Great Depression. Part of the pattern in the building up of standards in the 1860s, although the domestic handbooks were reticent about it, was a rise in the outlay on education, in itself not regarded as of great importance before.

At the same time, before 1870 it does not appear that there were more than a dozen preparatory schools of the type so necessary for the public school system as it later developed, whereas at the end of the century there were four hundred of them.[4] Hence we may regard the period after 1870 as the time when there was an expansion in the numbers of pre-public schools, set up to cater for the newly established public schools of a decade or so earlier. The pressure on parents to give their children a good chance in life, built up in the halcyon years of the 1850s and 1860s, entailed an even greater expense in the 1870s and 1880s to ensure that they really did get into the public schools provided for them. The point being made here is

[1] R. H. Tawney: 'The Problem of the Public Schools' in *The Political Quarterly*, April-June 1943, p. 124.
[2] *Ibid.* 'It is not an accident that the boarding-school boom followed closely on a railway boom.'
[3] *Ibid.*, n. 3 to p. 123.
[4] A. Rannie: 'The Preparatory School', Ch. 4 of J. D. Wilson (ed.): *The Schools of England* (1928), p. 65.

that it was in the 1850s and 1860s that the standard was laid down. Later developments made it more difficult to preserve the levels attained, and something had to go. A similar situation was also developing in the provision of education for girls, stemming from the employment of governesses in the home earlier,[1] but here the real expansion of the girls' public school system did not begin until the 1870s. Thus only ten schools were founded between 1840 and 1870, but thirty-six came into being between 1871 and 1880, thirty-four between 1881 and 1890, and thirteen between 1891 and 1900.[2] The extension of the system of public school education to the daughters of the middle classes, therefore, added a further burden to the middle-class household budget, at a period when the maintenance of the class differentials was already a strain on the incomes received.

The general conclusion to be drawn from these developments is that between 1840 and 1870 the middle classes had come to accept the idea of education for their children, especially for their sons, as an essential part of their pattern of life. What we still have to ask ourselves is how far this went. How many people, and what kinds of people, had come to consider the public school type of training as necessary for their boys? The answer to these questions cannot be given in very precise terms. All we can do is to pick out one or two hints here and there which may indicate certain broad generalizations.

Thus a reviewer in the *Edinburgh Review* in 1876 emphasized the particular interest which the upper middle class had in the provision of secondary education. 'Relieved from the enervating influences of luxury, on the one hand, and the depressing influences of poverty, on the other; conscious that its retention of the advantages which it enjoys is still dependent on the mental activity by which they were gained; and keenly alive to aesthetic and intellectual pleasures, the upper middle class seems the least likely of all to neglect its own educational concerns.'[3]

---

[1] A. C. Percival: *The English Miss, To-day and Yesterday* (1939), Chs. 8, 9, and 10. By the 1870s a 'good' education could be had for £16 per year. See also R. Strachey: *The Cause: a short history of the Women's Movement in Great Britain* (1928), Ch. 13.

[2] See Note S, p. 229.

[3] 'Secondary Education in Scotland' in *The Edinburgh Review*, April 1876, art. 8, p. 512.

What this amounts to is a lively interest on the part of professional men in the future careers of their boys. The fact that they had to *earn* their way made it imperative that they should be able to pass the necessary qualifying examinations.

In contrast the attitude of the farmers, who presumably were reasonably confident that there was always the land for their sons to rely on, was particularly noticeable. Thus Mr. C. H. Stanton, in his report on the counties of Devon and Somerset to the Schools Inquiry Commission, wrote:

'I was most struck in my inquiries with the general indifference of parents to the education of their sons. This especially was the case with the smaller farmers. The only spur which goaded them into a languid activity was the growing consciousness that their labourers were being better educated than their own sons.'[1] Nor did they hesitate to reduce the amount allotted to school fees when harvests were bad.[2]

Here indeed there is a most striking contrast. The professional men were anxious to keep up their sons' education and as the country moved into the Great Depression it is noteworthy that it was the professional men who first began to practise family limitation. On the other hand, the farmers, who lagged behind in the acceptance of this practice, preferred in poor times to reduce the amount spent on education.

At the same time it is clear that in the lower middle classes there was a drive for education, not it is true of the public-school type, but sufficient to produce candidates for commercial posts. Since the majority of young men who became clerks in government or other offices were regarded as coming from 'respectable' families,[3] there was a tendency among some parents to make, or keep, their sons 'respectable' by trying to push them into those occupations.

'Parents are eager to get their sons into houses of business where they may maintain the appearance, if not the standing,

[1] Report of the Schools Inquiry Commission, Vol. 7, General Reports by Assistant Commissioners, Pt. 4, p. 14 (*Parliamentary Papers*, 1867–8, Vol. 28).
[2] Royal Commission on Secondary Education. Report by H. T. Geirans on Devon (*Parliamentary Papers*, 1895, Vol. 48, p. 72 of Vol. 6).
[3] *Advice to Clerks and Hints to Employers* (1848), p. 6.

of gentlemen. The City is crowded with well-educated lads, who are doing men's work for boys' wages. . . . It is quite useless to argue with parents, and urge the propriety of sending boys to learn a trade; the idea of a lad returning from his work in the evening with dirty hands, and clad in fustian or corduroy, is quite shocking to the respectability of Peckham or Camberwell, and so the evil is perpetuated, and the prospect of the clerk becomes more gloomy from year to year.'[1]

Amongst such parents it is clear that the demand was for no more than a sound 'English' education for which four guineas a year was quite sufficient. There was nothing like the expense of the public-school system, and in any case the young man could leave school at fifteen or sixteen and begin to earn £70 or £80 immediately in a London office,[2] whereas the sons of the upper middle class were at least twenty-two or twenty-three before they could expect to receive some kind of income in one of the learned professions. Nevertheless it is quite clear that the real problem of expense arose from the fact that they were keeping their sons at school for a longer period than was necessary under a scheme of artisan apprenticeship. It was not the four guineas a year that the parents found embarrassing, but the cost involved in providing an adolescent with food and clothing when in an earlier generation he would have been helping to maintain himself. Although four guineas per annum is no more than 2 per cent of an income of £210 a year, few parents desired any other kind of education for their children.[3] It is likely therefore that the real deterrent came from the longer period of schooling required.

Four guineas per annum for education, moreover, was 2 per cent of an income of £210 for every child. With an average family size of six children, born over 10·5 years,[4] the total cost,

---

[1] Letter from J. J. to the *Daily News*, quoted by Davenant, *op. cit.*, p. 199. This work also quoted other similar letters.

[2] *Advice to Clerks, etc.*, p. 6.

[3] Schools Inquiry Commission, *op. cit.* Report, Vol. 1, p. 165–6. See also the evidence of the Headmaster of Repton Grammar School in Vol. 4, Pt. 3 minutes, pp. 439–40.

[4] Average figures from C. Ansell: *On the Rate of Mortality at Early Periods of Life, the Age at Marriage, the Number of Children to a Marriage, the Length of a Generation, and other Statistics of Families in the Upper and Professional Classes* (1874), pp. 52, 58–59.

O

reckoning eight years per child and assuming that all were educated in the same way, worked out at £202 spread over about eighteen years, or £11 4s. per year. This meant 5·3 per annum on £210, a total yearly expenditure of just under three times as much as the simple rate per annum per child suggests. Similarly the cost facing an upper middle class parent with three sons to be sent to public school, Oxford or Cambridge, and then into one of the professions, an average say of eight years per son at £200 per year, was £4,800 or £267 per annum for eighteen years. This raises the question of how far changes in children's mortality rates during the period were instrumental in placing extra burdens on the middle-class budget.

Unfortunately the only detailed study we have is that published by Ansell in 1871. He sent out questionnaires to clergymen, doctors, lawyers, and to a large number of noblemen and gentlemen. From their answers he was able to make a comparison with a similar study made by his father in 1830 on the children of the clergymen of the diocese of Canterbury, which showed that the mortality rates of this group had improved over the forty years.[1] The following simplified table shows the trend.

	Clergy	
Age of Child	1830 data	1871 data
0	100,000	100,000
1	91,667	92,618
5	83,852	88,572
10	81,852	86,681
15	79,536	84,798
20	76,743	81,734

If we take the experience of the clergy as typical of the middle-class group, for every twenty children born to them in the period ending in 1830, fifteen only lived to the age of twenty years, whereas sixteen lived to this age in the period ending in 1871. The increase in the cost of children from this source, therefore, may be reckoned at nearly 7 per cent for the class as a whole. This decline in mortality, moreover, continued in the next period, and indeed extended further down the social scale,

[1] *Ibid.*, Tables 2 (p. 71) and 5 (p. 77).

so that parents in the seventies and eighties were faced with the prospect of their children living longer at a time when preparatory school education was becoming more necessary and when the effort to preserve the social differential was being made increasingly difficult by economic change. 'The pride and satisfaction with which a father regards his first, and as yet only son, in the days of cockades, white frocks, and naked knees, are exchanged for anxiety and apprehension, when, some eighteen years afterwards, he sees himself surrounded by half a dozen full-grown and fast-growing candidates for frock coats, Wellington boots, walking-canes, watch guards, and cigars,' wrote Hudson in 1842.[1] How much greater must that anxiety and apprehension have become when, a generation later, advances in medicine and customary hygiene kept alive to adulthood young men and women whose uncles and aunts had died before adolescence?

The substance of this chapter, therefore, may be summarized as follows. Although in no single factor was the cost of children greatly advanced during the second half of the nineteenth century, taking them altogether the effect was quite marked. Standards of living rose in the sixties for adults, when a more frequent change of linen, wines at meals, and all the paraphernalia of gentility and conspicuous expenditure, became possible for a much larger proportion of the population. Children's fare was still relatively plain and cheap, but the fact that more of them now reached adulthood, at a period when more and longer schooling was becoming important, increased the household budget by a certainly not negligible amount. At the same time, alterations in the mode of entry to the older professions, first by tightening the qualifications for medicine and the law, and secondly by abolishing patronage in the Army and the Civil Service, made the way for aspiring candidates more institutionalized and formal, and hence easier to apprehend. A number of books appeared describing the opportunities for all who could afford the attempt, and although the sum of money required was still formidable, the greater incomes received in the sixties possibly gave birth to new ambitions, in the easy optimism that the days of progress were going to continue indefinitely. Parents

[1] Hudson, *op. cit.* Preface.

were prepared to send their sons to the public schools, as the growth of this system shows, and even for those whose incomes did not permit them to seek such dizzy heights, the lure of a white-collared occupation at a time when commerce was expanding more rapidly than industry, made outlay on tuition part of the customary way of life. Some form of education became recognized as a *sine qua non* for entrance to the 'gentlemanly' jobs, and these now seemed within the reach of all who were prepared to make the effort. At a period when incomes were expanding this could hardly have required much retrenchment in some other field of expenditure but when later the social differential became less easy to maintain, outlay deemed essential for the child's future could hardly be curtailed. Moreover a generation of men who had themselves been to the public school established in the forties, were now the parents of children whose schooling must be considered. Should the pattern be abandoned, or another child remain unborn? The answer was fairly clear. Long before, the middle-class ethos had been laid down, that it was immoral even to consider marriage while the income was too small to provide for everything that it involved. But postponment was only possible for the unmarried. What were the parents of children to do? It was possibly the consideration of these things which prepared the way for the change in the publicly expressed outlook on family limitation as achieved by contraception, between 1868 and 1877. The current view, so scathingly attacked by Matthew Arnold, that children were sent[1] gave place to the idea that it was not wrong to prevent them from coming—even by mechanical means—if their future chances, as members of the middle classes, were less bright than those of their parents had been.

[1] M. Arnold: *Culture and Anarchy* (1869), Ch. 6.

CHAPTER XII

The Standard of Living and the Fall in Fertility

OUR knowledge of the salient factors underlying the fall in fertility which has been so marked a feature of the demographic history of this country since the 1870s is extremely limited in many respects. Nevertheless, so far as we can tell, it does seem that the chief contributory influence has been the decision of an ever-growing number of parents deliberately to restrict the size of their families. To the contemporary mind this is regarded as a reasonable decision to make, since there can be little doubt that from the pecuniary point of view the smaller family has definite advantages over the larger. Yet at the time when the population controversy was raging, 130 years ago, considerations of cost were not acceptable as an argument in favour of limitation. Although Thomas Malthus and Francis Place both maintained, albeit in rather different ways, that a smaller number of children was the only solution to the problem of poverty, on the whole their opinions went unheeded, and more than forty years went by before the birth rate showed any sign of diminishing.

The reasoning employed by Malthus and his supporters was tolerably cogent. Because the reproductive instinct was very powerful in man, there was always a tendency for population to increase more rapidly than the supply of food. This did not mean that the outlook was absolutely hopeless, for the instinct could be kept in check to some extent by the exercise of moral restraint. If therefore the poorer sections of the community would postpone marriage until they could afford to maintain a family, fewer children would be born, the number of labourers would diminish, and the price of labour would rise. Wage workers would then be able to command a larger share of the necessities and comforts of life. Against the objection that the impulses of natural passion were too powerful for self-control to be effective for long, they opposed the example of the young men of the middle classes who did not burden themselves with the expenses of a wife and children until they were receiving an income large enough to cover the cost. The suggestion made by Francis Place that contraception might be used could thus be shown not only to be immoral but unnecessary. If the middle classes were able to restrain themselves in the interests of prudence, so might the working classes whose situation after all was not so very different.

The subsequent history of the controversy makes it plain that during the next forty years the case for contraception received scant consideration. The spotlight of attention had become focused on the marriage habits of the middle class. This had the effect of turning into a definitely moral obligation what had at first been put forward as no more than a good model for the improvident to copy. Prudence and postponement became inseparably linked in the middle-class mind, and the notion that no one ought to marry until he was reasonably certain of being able to provide his wife with as high a level of living as she was already enjoying under her parental roof, obtained categorical force in the middle-class world. Thus, from attempting to persuade the working classes to cure their poverty by self-restraint, the members of the middle classes found themselves applying the theme of control to their own way of life.

In the change of interest, however, an important feature of the argument was lost. The original Malthusian ground for the postponement of marriage had been based on the theory that population pressed upon the supply of food and that therefore there was a need to restrict the number of births in order to prevent destitution. But the middle classes were not faced with the problem of poverty. They were concerned with maintaining their relatively high standard of life. While for them prudence was combined with a definite understanding of the relationship between the level of living and the cost of a family, it did not go so far as to involve restricting family size. A number of children was normally expected to be the inevitable product of the first few years of married life; and if, as a result of their calculations of future possibilities, a young middle-class couple decided to wait a year or two before setting up house together, it was only because they had in mind the realization that the larger income the man would most probably be receiving at the future date would be more than adequate to cover their needs.

This calculation of life chances, so typical of the middle classes at this time, was directly related to the career structure of the older professions. At twenty-two or twenty-five years of age a middle-class lawyer or doctor could predict with a fair degree of accuracy what sums of money the men of his profession were likely to earn at various periods of their lives. Unlike the working man whose maximum was reached early on in adulthood, the middle-class man could anticipate a steady series of income increases in the future stretching out before him at least until middle age; and at the same time he need not expect to be susceptible on the income side to considerable fluctuations of an adverse kind due to the cycle of trade. Postponement of marriage, therefore, was judicious policy, for a higher income would almost certainly be his in the course of time. We do not know how far this was true of all the occupations into which the sons of the middle classes went, but it does seem that salaried appointments followed a pattern similar to that of the independent professions, and in a period of economic expansion like that of the 1850s and 1860s young business men and employers might well feel certain of an income growing steadily over time.

It is for this reason, among others, that the period before the 1870s was so very important. The numbers of people assessed in the middle-income ranges expanded more rapidly than the population as a whole, and, as we have seen, none of these were wage-earners. Proportionately more people, therefore, were not only able to afford to live in the middle-class manner, but they were also able to feel reasonably sure of the future. Indeed, there is some indication that their aspirations grew even more rapidly than their real opportunities. The current view that Victorian progress and prosperity were limitless, that things were going to continue growing better and better every year, bred an excessive optimism which would appear to have increased the sense of frustration of those whose incomes did not increase so quickly as they desired. At the same time the rise in real incomes made higher levels of living possible for the successful, whose expenditure on more expensive foods, on wines, on specialist servants, on carriages, on entertaining their friends, on travel, forced up the standards of aspiration in every sphere and made the upper middle-class way of life seem even more difficult of attainment to those whose incomes were not quite large enough. The correspondence and articles of this period, quoted in earlier chapters of this book, expressed the feeling of strain and tension developed by this highly competitive atmosphere.

Nevertheless, in spite of the urge to emulate the wealthy, it is reasonably clear that most members of the middle classes thought of their future families without serious qualms. Postponement of marriage was perhaps necessary for four or five years, until in fact the man was firmly entrenched in his career, but after that children might come at a fairly rapid rate and yet not be regarded as a financial embarrassment. The level of living could be preserved intact because the income would be rising sufficiently to cover the fresh commitments. The concept of the standard of living, therefore, while closely associated in the middle-class mind with the idea of marriage, did not require the additional notion of the control of births. Family limitation was not at this time part of the ethic of the middle-class way of life.

The change in outlook, indeed, as shown by the fall in family size, did not appear until the period was almost over, and it only really gained impetus in an economic situation of a rather different kind. Although the Great Depression was not in truth one in which the middle-class level of living was seriously threatened, most people who gained the ear of the public talked as though it were. As it happens it is likely that *real* middle-class incomes continued to rise since retail prices fell, but the business section of the community were not apparently aware that this was so. Their sense of security had been very seriously shaken and soon the easy optimism of an earlier age died away. For such people postponement of marriage would obviously cease to have appeal for there could be no point in waiting for a prosperity which they were now convinced might never come.

The Standard of Living and the Fall in Fertility

We cannot, of course, be sure that this was how most members of the middle-classes in this later period had begun to think, because we do not know to what degree the lack of confidence of business men permeated other fields. Doctors, it is true, protested that theirs was an overcrowded profession, but they had said this in the 1860s when a different state of affairs obtained. However, the fact that some occupations, such as the Civil Service, continued to provide a ladder of incomes up which a man of ability could mount, could have increased their desirability in the eyes of parents with smaller hopes in the future of their own vocations. The importance of education, already accepted by many in the prosperous years of the 1850s and 1860s might well have been enhanced during the lean years of the 1870s and 1880s, and the greater demand for specialized training through the mechanism of a rise in the prices charged for tuition, increased the expensiveness of placing a child in a chosen career and hence may have become a factor in the fall in family size.

This is in general form the conclusion to be drawn from the previous chapters of this book, and it is here that we are face to face with the crucial problem of the whole affair. Although the success of the neo-Malthusian movement after the Bradlaugh-Besant trials of 1877 demonstrated the extent to which the desire for a smaller family already prevailed, it is not immediately obvious why a rapid expansion in the level of living, followed by a sense of restriction, should *necessarily* have led to the acceptance of the idea of adopting birth-control by a generation which had rejected it earlier. It is clear that postponement of marriage could not be carried very far and that it could therefore have only a slight effect in limiting the number of children born, and it is also clear that improvements in the standards of health and hygiene were responsible for more and more children surviving up to and beyond adolescence; but even these things do not suffice to explain why it was that the members of the middle classes chose deliberately to limit the size of their families rather than to give up their aspirations for their existing children or their newly acquired taste for those material comforts which had become part of their standard of well-being.

Against these rather utilitarian considerations there must be set the age-old tradition that interference with the intentions of providence in the matter of births was morally wrong. Human life was still sacrosanct, and it has yet to be explained how it was that the appeal of the standard of living had now become stronger than the precedents of the past. Unless it can be shown that the failing hold of religion in this period was *directly* related to the changing real income structure and to the greater opportunities made available for the consumption and enjoyment of an ever-growing number of man's worldly goods, the argument that the rising standard of living was the *major* factor in the spread of family limitation, although strongly supported by a plausible array of evidence, must remain something of a *non sequitur.* There is no doubt at all that we can claim a place for the rising standard of living as one of the chief factors in the phenomenon and from a functionalist's point of view that is all that need be said. But to establish a correlation between two variables in science is to give no indication as to which is the cause of the other, and without attempting to do this we ignore the possibility that there might well have taken place in the mid-Victorian scene a more fundamental change of mind which was the really important factor responsible for them both.

This study began by distinguishing between two quite distinct notions often confused into a single concept of the standard of living, namely the actual level of well-being enjoyed, and the attitude of mind towards it; but nowhere so far has it been suggested that in the constitution of that attitude we should include the whole gamut of ideas men have about life. Throughout this work the standard of living has been conceived of in very definite material terms related to expenditure on household requirements, servants, travel, and the like, and it would be claiming too much now to make it include standards of a radically different type. It might well be the case, indeed, that the key to the whole problem lies in the development of science and the spread of the scientific attitude of mind, sweeping away traditional values at the same time as it made possible a greater production of wealth. This could conceivably be used to account for the changed attitude towards birth-control. Nevertheless it would be absurd to maintain that the scientific outlook itself was nothing more than the product of those aspirations which the middle classes possessed for the material comforts of life, or that the standards and norms of science were a simple product of the rising level of living.

Perhaps an example from the later developments of family limitation will help to make this clear. Although the organized medical profession remained hostile to mechanical contraception throughout the period under review, it nevertheless came more and more to accept the idea of spacing pregnancies on the grounds of conserving the mother's strength. That is to say, the growth of medical knowledge and a deeper understanding of the functioning of the body gave rise to new standards of hygiene for promoting health and preventing disease. These obviously played their part in the acceptance of the idea that it was not immoral to control family size in certain circumstances; yet it would be surely naïve to regard them as merely the product of the economic changes we have been considering as responsible for the rising standard of living. They are more plausibly explained in terms of the widening horizons of science.

Another example may be taken from one of the less-known aspects of our problem. As far as we can tell, at quite an early stage there existed a desire for relief from the burden of child-bearing among many middle-class mothers, but it remained linked with a fatalistic conception of life which considered the burden irremediable until the publicity of the Bradlaugh-Besant trials made widely known that means of control were available. We must not, however, misinterpret this. It was not mere ignorance that stood in the way. Some form of birth prevention had been practised since the early days of human society and knowledge of methods had existed right through history. Moreover in the 1820s Francis Place and his followers had circulated handbills giving detailed instructions. The simple fact of the matter was that at that time people were not prepared to exercise such a form of control.

At the same time it is important to realize that the development of science involved a growing awareness that the use of scientific methods gave men power over their material environment and that at no time was it ever consistently held that the exercise of this power was morally wrong. What was lacking at the time of Francis Place's activities was the conviction that humanity itself was really only part of nature, and with the spread of ideas of evolution, culminating in the Darwinism of the 1860s, the way was opened to the acceptance of the view that for human beings to control their power of reproduction, even by mechanical means, was not different in kind from any other application of science.

The fact that we cannot satisfactorily account for the spread of family limitation in terms of the rising standard of living, however, must not lead us to under-estimate the role of the concept in the fall of fertility. Because it is possible to sketch out an alternative set of explanations which have a certain appearance of plausibility, it must not be assumed that the whole story has been told. Indeed, the foregoing emphasis on the development of the scientific attitude needs itself to be challenged and supported by a detailed study of the relationship between the concept of science and the phenomenon of family size before it may be said that this conclusion is validly drawn. The processes of social change do not consist of simple chains of events. They are essentially processes of mass action in which a few individuals behave for a long time in an untraditional manner before a sufficient number of their fellows follow suit to make it apparent that the tradition has changed, and the motives underlying action present themselves as a complex web of interrelated opinions rather than as a single clear idea. The middle-class concept of the standard of living which has been discussed in these chapters had become too closely linked with the idea of marriage for it to have been only slightly effective in the spread of family limitation. It was indeed a major factor in the late nineteenth-century developments in family size. All that is being attempted now is to emphasize the implausibility of the view that it was *the* major factor in the change.

The argument may be looked at in the light of an example from the fifth chapter of this study. Although the movement of domestic servants out of the industry happened too late for it to have been a causal feature in the fall of fertility, it no doubt provided an extra motive for restricting the number of births. For a class of people who had become accustomed to thinking of the rearing of children in terms of domestic assistance for the

more unpleasant tasks, the greater difficulty of obtaining servant labour in the late 1880s and 1890s was a further barrier in
the way of a large family. We can well imagine a young couple,
unable perhaps to secure more than a single general servant,
deciding to postpone the second child, or even the first, until
such time as a nursemaid could be obtained, and this might
never occur; or again, and this in all probability is more likely to
have happened, knowing that servants were growing relatively
scarce a newly married pair might have been persuaded to
accept a smaller house in the suburbs which could be maintained with less domestic help, and this in itself would become
an added reason for keeping the family small. Once the notion
had become widely accepted that there was nothing immoral
about family limitation as such, there were many features of
household management, quite apart from considerations of
cost, which would operate to provide reasons why the number
of children should be kept low. In this way the concept of a
rising standard of living may be seen as acting as at least a
contributory influence in the spread of birth-control ideas.

This goes some way to explain why it was that the expenses
of child-rearing came to be so important. The cost of education
rose as the demand for it increased, and this acted as a pressure
to limit the number of births. It was, after all, not so expensive
to rear and educate three children instead of four, or two children instead of three. This in itself does not account for the
change in attitude towards education, although it makes plain
that as that attitude changed it set in motion forces which would
influence family size. It might, of course, be claimed that education became more highly valued as modifications in the economic and social structure made specialized tuition essential for
those who aspired to a certain kind of career. Nor is this all. The
reason why such careers had become more desirable was in part
pecuniary—the level of living made possible by the incomes
received in those careers—and in part less tangible, but involving nevertheless the notion of status, the standing of a man in
the eyes of his fellows, which to a great extent was measured by
the level of living he was able to maintain. Thus the rising
standard of living, together with fluctuations in incomes and
retail prices, formed a complicated web of interlocking influ-

ences which had the effect of raising the value of education in the minds of those with the middle-class outlook on life.

As against this view there must be held the fact that the great expansion in public school education for girls came in the 1870s and later, at a period when the middle classes might have been expected to retrench; and it could hardly be claimed that for them the concept of career had a clearly defined place. A more plausible explanation would certainly seem to lie in the movement for the emancipation of women, and as with the development of the scientific outlook, it has yet to be shown how the women's movement was linked up with the rising standard of life. For all that, however, it cannot be denied that the attitude towards the material comforts of modern existence and the growing expensiveness of children and adolescents contributed their share to the acceleration in the fall in family size. Although the full account of the spread of family limitation requires a detailed explanation of the waning of the traditional hostility to birth-control ideas, and although it has not been possible to show that this was derived from the rising standard of living, the role of the latter concept in the subsequent history of fertility trends cannot be ignored.

It is for this reason among others that there is value in taking the concept as a central theme for study. If historical sociology is to make progress it will do well to follow the pattern set by Max Weber in isolating certain variables for treatment over time. The social process involves such a welter of interacting features that the mind cannot cope with all the possible correlations existing at any one moment. By studying the relationship between just two distinct ideas the causal connection between them may become more readily understood and we may then extend the procedure to take in a wider range of factors. It does not matter if at any stage in this approach we find that an important feature remains unexplained. At least we shall know where next to turn.

It is, on the other hand, of extreme importance that we should cease to treat these historical matters in very general terms. To continue writing, as so many social historians have done, of the influence of the rising standard of living on the spread of family limitation without making a more detailed and intensive study of what precisely this involves, is to leave us with a vague generalization which sounds quite plausible merely because it is so general but which really tells us surprisingly little of the exact mechanism by which the influence made itself felt. In the interest of clarity it is necessary to categorize more fully those aspects of social life which have relevance to the theme; and if this should demonstrate, as we have found in the present study, that there is a weak link in the chain of reasoning which cannot be wholly supported by the facts, it is not to be regarded as a misfortune. Some of the alternative variables in the web of causal factors must now be followed through, such as the breakdown of the family as an economic unit, the growth of urban living, the decline in religious belief, or the emancipation of women. In this way we may yet be enabled to assign a relative weight to each of the suggested causes under review, and in the course of time be able to discern which of them, if any, has performed the most fundamental part in the fall in fertility. The present consideration of the relationship between the concept of the standard of living and the spread of family limitation should rightly be seen as merely the first approach to a complete study of the vital revolution of our age.

APPENDIX I

Domestic Economy

T HE following list of books contains all that have been
useful in attempting to establish the middle-class pattern
of expenditure as set out in this study. It does not contain
any of the works on domestic economy which were produced
during this period in America although presumably some of
them did help to create the customary pattern of living; nor
does it contain the many school books which appeared, especially after 1870, as these were mostly addressed to working-class
girls who might be expected to go into domestic service and
consequently do not contain anything about the broad pattern
we have been trying to establish. For the same reason it does
not contain books written by servants for servants. It does,
however, contain a few books addressed by the middle class to
the working class, e.g. *Sylvia's Family Management*, where
these seem to the writer to have some real bearing on the
problem.

(*Note*. Since so many of the British Museum Collection were
destroyed during the war it has been thought valuable to give
an indication of where these books are to be found. The abbre-
viations are to be read as follows:

B.M.   .. The Reading Room of the British Museum;
Bod.   .. The Bodleian Library, Oxford;
G.   .. The Goldsmith Library, London University;
L.S.E. .. The Library of the London School of Economics.)

I. M. Beeton: *The Book of Household Management*, 1861 (B.M.).
Editions of 1863 (Bod.), 1869 (Bod.), 1880 (Bod.), 1888
(Bod.), 1892 (B.M.), 1906 (B.M.). Later editions appeared
in 1923 and 1950.

Appendix I

The Book of Economy; or, How to Live Well in London on £100 per annum. Also how to live comfortably on £50 per annum, by a Gentleman. (8th ed., 1832), B.M.

Mrs. Caddy: *Household Organization,* 1877 (Bod.).

Cassell's Book of the Household: a Work of Reference on Domestic Economy, n.d. (B.M., 1890).

Economy for the Single and Married; or the Young Wife and Bachelor's Guide to Income and Expenditure on £50 per annum, £100 per annum, £150 per annum, £200 per annum, with estimates up to £500 per annum, comprising also a variety of useful and original information for the single, as well as all subjects relating to Domestic Comfort and Happiness, by One who 'Makes Ends Meet', n.d. (B.M. 1845).

'Espoir': *How to live on a Hundred a Year, Make a Good Appearance, and save money,* n.d., (B.M., 1874).

How to Keep House! or, comfort and elegance on £150 to £200 a year (6th ed.), 1832 (B.M.).

R. Murray (ed.): *Warne's Model Housekeeper; a Manual of Domestic Economy in all its Branches,* 1879 (Bod.). The University Library, Cambridge, has an 1873 edition of this work.

A New System of Practical Domestic Economy: founded on modern Discoveries, and the private communications of Persons of Experience. 3rd ed., 'Revised and Greatly Enlarged, to which are now first added, Estimates of Household Expenses, founded on economical principles, and adopted to families of every description', 1823 (L.S.E.). These estimates were also published separately.

J. E. Panton: *From Kitchen to Garret: Hints for Young Householders,* 1888. (7th ed., 1890, B.M.) (Another 1893 B.M.)

Nooks and Corners: being a companion volume to From Kitchen to Garret, 1889 (B.M.).

Homes of Taste. Economical Hints, 1890 (Bod.).

Leaves from a Housekeeper's Book, 1914 (B.M.). (This is really a new edition of *From Kitchen to Garret.*)

W. Parkes: *Domestic Duties; or, Instructions to Young Married Ladies, on the Management of their Households, and the Regulation of their Conduct in the Various Relations and Duties of Married Life,* 1825 (B.M.).

Appendix I

Mrs. Pedley: *Practical Housekeeping, or the Duties of a Home-Wife*, 1867 (Bod.).

R. K. Philp: *The Practical Housewife, forming a complete encyclopaedia of Domestic Economy*, 1855 (B.M.). Revised 1860 (B.M.).

H. Reeve: *Cookery and Housekeeping. A Manual of Domestic Economy for Large and Small Families*, 1882 (Bod.). The B.M. edition has a chapter of importance cut out.

H. Southgate: *Things a Lady Would Like to Know concerning Domestic Management and Expenditure*, 2nd ed., 1875 (B.M.).

Sylvia's Family Management. A Book of Thrift and Cottage Economy. A Practical Cyclopedia of Useful Knowledge, 1886 (Bod.).

J. H. Walsh: *A Manual of Domestic Economy: suited to families spending from £100 to £1,000 a Year*, 1857 (Bod.).

A Manual of Domestic Economy; suited to families spending from £150 to £1,500 a Year, new ed., 1873 (G), 1890 (Bod.).

Ward and Lock's Home Book: a Domestic Encyclopaedia, forming a Companion Volume to Mrs. Beeton's Book of Household Management, n.d. (B.M., 1880).

E. Warren: *How I managed my house on Two Hundred Pounds a Year*, 1865 (B.M.). An attack on this work appeared anonymously (Mrs. Beeton?) in the article 'Marriage' in the March issue of the *Englishwoman's Domestic Magazine*, 1865.

Comfort for Small Incomes, 1866 (Bod.).

A House and its Furnishings, 1869 (Bod.).

T. Webster (assisted by the late Mrs. Parkes): *An Encyclopaedia of Domestic Economy, comprising such subjects as are most immediately connected with housekeeping*, 1844 (Bod.). New ed., 1861 (Bod.).

W. H. Wigley: *Our Home Work: a manual of Domestic Economy*. 1876 (Bod.).

Workers at Home. A companion to Our Home Work, 1880 (Bod.).

APPENDIX II

A Middle-Class Housewife of the Early Seventies

THE October number of the 1871 issue of *The English-woman's Domestic Magazine* carried a letter from 'House-keeper', asking for advice from other lady readers on her problems of making an allowance of £4 10s. per week cover the expenses of four people. Among the replies which followed, that of a Mrs. S. in the November issue was so full of detail and gave such a fine description of the way in which she went about her housekeeping that, like the editor of the *E.D.M.*, I have thought it valuable to set it out in all its completeness below. It appears therefore as it appeared in Vol. XI, pp. 318–9 of the *English-woman's Domestic Magazine*, except that I have divided it up into paragraphs to make the reading easier.

'Mrs. S. thinks her experience may be of use to "House-keeper", with whom she is able to sympathize, having begun her married life seven years ago, with but little knowledge of the right way to manage. She had, however, one advantage, that of having early learned to handle and keep an accurate account of money.

Mrs. S. has a monthly allowance (of £26), out of which she has to provide wages, food, beer, and washing for a family of ten persons—herself and husband, two grown-up daughters, three young children, and three servants. The three children's clothes, occasional assistance from a dressmaker in the house, and a washerwoman in the house once a fortnight, are also paid from the above allowance.

The first thing Mrs. S. does, on receiving her money, is to lay aside what she knows will be required to pay wages, beer, and her butter account, which, as she procures it from a distance,

she settles once a month. Wages amount to £3 5s., beer to about
18s., butter varies from £1 to £1 12s. according to the price.
Total, on an average, from £5 10s. to £5 15s. This leaves
something over £20. She then lays aside what she thinks she
will require for food, etc., for each week in the month; in winter,
£3 10s.; in summer, from £4 to £4 5s. or even £4 10s.; washing,
fruit, and vegetables costing more in the summer, besides which,
visitors are more frequent.

What remains has to cover the expenses for children's clothes,
and every six months or so a quarter-chest of tea, about £3;
also coffee procured from abroad, household sundries, such as
dusters, brooms, etc., and all other occasional expenses which
she cannot fairly carry to her husband's account. Coals, gas,
furniture, repairs, stock of household linen when renewed, and
other extras are paid for by her husband, and she carefully
enters in a separate book the amount she has received from him
for such purposes each month.

Now as to details. Mrs. S. pays her tradesmen's books herself
every week, taking that opportunity of making any remark or
complaint she may find necessary. She enters in a memorandum
book (her inseparable companion) the sums paid, and copies
them into her account book afterwards, noting on it up to what
date the payment reached (an excellent check in cases of acci-
dental omission). She, of course, leaves the books at the shops,
to be made up again.

She keeps two account books, one for housekeeping proper,
and the other for dress, children's clothes, wages and sundries.
Besides this she has a third book, in which she draws up a summary of expenses for each month. This is divided into so many
columns ruled for £ s. d., and headed respectively: Butcher's
Meat—Pork and Bacon—Fish and Poultry—Eggs—Butter—
Milk—Bread—Fruit and vegetables—Wages—Dress—Sundries,
and so on. The whole expenditure for each month is entered
under each head, in one sum, and as the book is of a long shape,
like a drawing-book, and is ruled through the open page, *one
line* contains all. In twelve lines a complete summary for the
year may be seen, and by means of it Mrs. S. is always able to
know exactly in what direction her money has gone, as well as
to detect any undue increase of expense.

Appendix II

Mrs. S.' modes of living is as follows: Coffee and bread and butter for servants' breakfast; bread and milk, bread and butter, and weak tea for the children. For the upstairs breakfast, tea, toast, bread and butter, and one or two dishes, consisting of eggs, bacon, fish, mushrooms, meat-pie, or other similar things. The average cost of the meat dishes is about ninepence a day for four people. Dinner at one, for children and servants, meat and pudding, or fish and meat, often two vegetables—Mrs. S. thinking both pudding and vegetables as necessary for the servants as for herself. Late dinners for the rest of the family, fish or soup, plain joints (her husband disliking made dishes), always two vegetables, and puddings or pastry. Sometimes all three courses, sometimes only two, sometimes fruit instead of pudding; regular dessert only on Sunday or for company. On Sunday early dinner for all, hot but as simple as it can be made. Servants' supper at nine, and tea upstairs, with toast, bread and butter, and sometimes fruit. The servants have beer at dinner and supper, and an allowance of 3 lb. of cheese and 3 lb. of sugar in the fortnight. Mrs. S. will not give beer *money*. Her present servants drink coffee at tea as well as breakfast, and it is *occasionally* used after dinner and at breakfast if visitors are present. The consumption for the past six months has been 18 lb. Including the nursery, rather less than 1 lb. of tea is used upstairs per week, no other beverage being liked by the family. At dinner little beer is drunk upstairs, chiefly claret or light wines. A nine-gallon cask should last from sixteen to twenty days, under such circumstances, the servants' consumption being rather under half a gallon a day, reckoned liberally.

To keep house on the above scale, Mrs. S. finds cost her last year for butcher's meat £51 14s., being an average of £1 per week, or 2s. 3d. per head, reckoning the three children as one, and balancing visitors against the absence of one of the family for about nine months. When all are constantly at home the average is a little higher. Bread, including flour, about 7s. 6d. per week, or about two loaves for each person (half-quartern loaves) and 1¼ gallons of flour. The children consume a good deal. Vegetables and fruit average about 6s. per week; milk, about 4s. 6d. per week. Washing varies from 9s. to 10s. in the depth of winter to 16s. or 18s. in the height of summer. This is exclusive of the servants' washing, which is done at home by a charwoman once a fortnight, with the help of a machine and the cook. In the same wash are put the children's and other socks and stockings, house towels, dusters, and some other articles which can be mangled, not ironed; in all about six dozen in the fortnight. Taking an average week, the butcher's book, £1, baker 7s. 6d., milk 4s. 4d., washing 12s. 6d., grocer's book about 10s. (no butter, tea or coffee), charwoman and mangling 2s., greengrocer 6s., we reach a total of about £3, and 10s. is left for sundries, which is not too much, as they include such a variety of articles.

Add to the above, say 5 lb. butter per week (averaging on Mrs. S.'s plan about 1s. 3d. per lb., equal 6s. 3d.; 4s beer, and about 5s. for tea and coffee, and the whole does not quite amount to the extent of "Housekeeper's" allowance for six people. Some differences of price must, however, be taken into consideration. "Housekeeper" probably pays 1d. a pound dearer all round for meat than Mrs. S. in the country, where sirloin is 10½d. or 11d., rump-steak or veal cutlet 1s. 1d., and mutton 10d. or 10½d. for prime joints, Mrs. S. never buying any but the best meat. This might make 10s. difference in the month. Wages also are dearer in London.

Nevertheless, Mrs. S. is disposed to agree with the editor of the *Englishwoman's Domestic Magazine*, that the "little dinners" make a good hole in "Housekeeper's" allowance. Mrs. S. rarely has any company. When she does she reckons about 16s. per head as the expense for each person at table, including wine, always good; and she is persuaded this is ample. On these occasions her husband either sends in a handsome contribution to the fare, or Mrs. S. asks him at the next money settling to add something to her allowance, so that nothing is left to pay for with the following month's allowance. She occasionally has to do the same when two or three visitors are staying together in the house, but not when there is only one. She trusts then to good management to provide extras.

Mrs. S. never lets an account remain unpaid, all being as much as possible provided for beforehand; but neither will she ever defray a farthing of the household expenses from her dress money, and she advises "Housekeeper" to discontinue the practice. What she would recommend her to do is, as far as possible, to separate the extras provided for her dinner parties from her ordinary provisions, ascertain their amount, and if it is manifestly they which are causing her trouble, lay them before her husband, who, if sensible, will appreciate her carefulness and candour, and tell her whether he wishes her to retrench on this point, or whether he will add to her allowance enough to cover the deficiency. On no account let "Housekeeper" keep her difficulties to herself. Her husband's business is to support and help her; but on the other hand let her know clearly herself what she is going to talk about, and choose a favourable time for the conversation. Let her always *balance* her books, not simply write down as far as she can remember what she has spent. Men like accuracy.

If the dinners are not in fault, perhaps the mischief lies with "Housekeeper's" cook. Cooks differ greatly in their use (or waste) of materials, and in their power (or will) to send up a second time, in an appetising form, any remains of yesterday's dinner. Some *sell*, some *eat*, a great deal of what goes downstairs. Lard and dripping disappear, beer-barrels empty themselves, etc. If "Housekeeper" has any doubt of her cook, her best plan will be to change her when opportunity serves, and begin afresh with another. The finest of mistresses can do but little with a servant who has formed her own habits; but a new one, if really worth having, can be set at once in a good groove, and made to understand what is or is not tolerated.

The habit of knowing what quantities are consumed habitually of each article is a great help towards detecting excess. Mrs. S. always takes out from the tradesmen's books the exact quantities of sugar, lard, cheese, bacon, house-flannel, soda, soap, matches, wood, etc. used in the house, and without insisting on entirely uniformity (servants' *methods* differing as much as their mistresses'), she tries to check extravagance directly she perceives it, avoiding at the same time any closeness or stinginess, while endeavouring to practise economy, without which she could not make her allowance sufficient.

Mrs. S. highly applauds "Housekeeper's" resolution to make both ends meet, and although it certainly is not nearly so troublesome to have all one's accounts paid by cheque, she thinks, in the long run, an allowance more agreeable, if it is fairly sufficient. Unlimited cheques are all very well when money is also unlimited or very plentiful, but Mrs. S. has known more than one instance where, when adversity has overtaken the husband, or merely a temporary tightness of money occurred, the wife has hardly dared to ask or been able to get wherewith to pay the most necessary bills, although her husband, had he been obliged to give her a fixed sum, would have made at least an effort to provide it. Only let "Housekeeper" be frank with her husband on all occasions when she is short, for good reasons—for instance, extra expense at the birth of children, whose washing, and the milk needful for them, will cost little under £1 per month; or the taking of an extra servant, whose wages and keep must be counted at about £25 to £30 per annum.

Mrs. S. could say much more, but fears even this may prove tedious. She will, however, be happy to answer, as far as she can, any future questions if "Housekeeper" wishes to ask them. To butcher's meat should be added pork, bacon, fish, and poultry, about £18 in the year (more would be wanted with many visitors). Washing costs £31 7s. 6d.; milk, butter and eggs, £37 14s. 9½d.; oilman and grocer about £31. The oilman has a separate book, and *gas* is used, so that neither lamp nor candles are required. Mrs. S. has, of course, not given all the items of expense, but the above may be a guide.'

In spite of the advice of both Mrs. S. and the editor, 'Housekeeper' apparently took the easier way out. She dismissed the cook . . . 'but had a *dreadful* one to follow' (December 1871).

APPENDIX III

Books on Marriage at the end of the Century

THE following list of books cannot by any means pretend to be exhaustive. It consists merely of those used in the production of the later chapters of this work.

1882 *Hints on Matrimony by a Practical Man* (3rd ed.).

1882 J. Flower: *A Golden Guide to Matrimony: or Three Steps to the Altar, with six qualifications for wedded life: and all its secrets revealed.*

1882 E. Kingsbury: *Thoughts on Marriage.*

1885 *How to be happy though married, being a Handbook to Marriage, by a Graduate in the University of Matrimony.*

1887 *The Misuse of Marriage or Hymen Profaned. A voice.*

1888 H. C. Wright: *Marriage and Parentage; or, the Reproductive Element in Man, as a means to his elevation and happiness.*

1890 H. Jones: *Courtship and Marriage.*

1892 A. W. Thorold: *On Marriage.*

1892 W. Unsworth: *The Marriage-knot Wisely Tied.*

1893 A. S. Swan: *Courtship and Marriage, and the Gentle Art of Home-making.*

1894 R. ff. Blake: *The Greatest Temptation in the World to Man.*

1894 J. R. Miller: *Secrets of Happy Home Life.*

1895 W. W. Smyth: *A Baneful Popular Delusion on the Subject of Motherhood.*

1897: E. R. Chapman: *Marriage Questions in Modern Fiction, and other essays.*

1898 *Matrimony Made Easy, or How to Win a Lover.*

1898 'The Modern Marriage Market', a series of articles reprinted from *The Lady's Realm* for 1897 by Marie Corelli, Lady Jeune, Flora Annie Steel, and Susan, Countess of Malmesbury.

Notes

A. For the influence of Malthus see K. Smith: *The Malthusian Controversy* (1951) and D. V. Glass (ed.): *Introduction to Malthus* (1953). There is a biography of Farr in Greenwood: *The Medical Dictator and other Biographical Studies* (n.d.) and in W. Farr: *Vital Statistics* (1885). This last work, a collection of papers written by Farr during his period at the General Register Office from 1843 to 1880, clearly demonstrates his attempt to link together 'eating and drinking, marrying and giving in marriage'. The later statisticians referred to were W. Ogle ('On Marriage Rates and Marriage Ages, with special reference to the Growth of Population' in the *Journal of the Royal Statistical Society*, June 1890), R. H. Hooker ('Correlation of the Marriage-Rate with Trade' in the *Journal of the Royal Statistical Society*, September 1901), and G. U. Yule ('On the Changes in the Marriage-and-Birth-Rates in England and Wales during the Past Half Century; with an inquiry as to their probable cause' in the *Journal of the Royal Statistical Society*, March 1906). See also D. Thomas: *Social Aspects of the Business Cycle* (1925).

B. Catherine Grace Frances Gore (1799–1861) was the authoress of *The Manners of the Day, or Women as they are* (1830), *Mothers and Daughters: a tale of the year 1830* (1831), *Mrs. Armyntage, or Female Domination* (1836), and many other novels, stories, poems and plays. Thomas Henry Lister (1800–42) wrote *Granby* (1826), *Herbert Lacy* (1828), *Arlington* (1832), and other novels of a similar nature. Edward George Earle Lytton Bulwer, first Lord Lytton (1803–73), achieved some success with *Pelham, or the Adventures of a Gentleman* (1828), before turning to the historical novels most usually associated with his name. Benjamin Disraeli (1804–81), whose *Vivian Grey* (1826), *The Young Duke* (1830), and *Henrietta Temple* (1837), were his most notable contribution to the class of fashionable novels discussed in this paragraph, is also better known for a different kind of fiction. Susan Edmonstone Ferrar (1782–1854), has not been included because her novels *Marriage* (1818) and *Inheritance* (1824), while in the same tradition, were characteristic of the upper classes of Scottish society and we are dealing with England. For a more detailed list and bibliographies of minor fiction writers of this period, see F. W. Bateson (ed.): *The Cambridge Bibliography of English Literature* (1940), Vol. 3, Sections 3, iii, and v.

C. The reference to William Cowper is to his 'Pairing Time Anticipated', a poem on the woes of two finches who mated in the wrong season. It ended with the 'Instruction'

> *Misses! the tale that I relate*
> *This lesson seems to carry—*
> *Choose not alone a proper mate,*
> *But proper time to marry.*

These lines, modified to begin: 'Thus then "the tale that we relate" . . .' were made the burden of another book on the perils of early marriages ('one of the greatest foes to domestic happiness is poverty') by G. E. Sargent, entitled: *Domestic Happiness; Home Education; Politeness and Good Breeding* (1851) comprising a collection of articles republished from the *Domestic Economist*. Sargent held among other things that no man should marry before the age of twenty-five (p. 18).

Da. For the expansion of railway passenger travel see J. H. Clapham: *An Economic History of Modern England; the Early Railway Age, 1820-50* (2nd ed., 1930, Pt. 2, Ch. 9) and J. H. Clapham: *An Economic History of Modern England; Free Trade and Steel, 1850-86* (1932), Bk. 3, Ch. 5, and C. E. R. Sherrington: *A Hundred Years of Inland Transport, 1930–1933* (1934), Ch. 7.

Even as early as 1845 passenger fares contributed 64 per cent of the gross receipts and throughout the rest of the century they never fell below 40 per cent in spite of the great increase in the amount of goods traffic. The railway companies themselves deliberately set out to attract passengers, providing waiting and refreshment rooms before the 1850s (cf. D. Lardner: *Railway Economy* (1850), p. 147) and dining- and sleeping-cars in the 1870s and 1880s. In the 1880s too there was developed the

London suburban transport system (see H. J. Dyos: 'Workmen's Fares in South London, 1860–1914 in the *Journal of Transport History*, May 1953). The number of passengers (exclusive of season-ticket holders) had reached 336,500,000 per year by 1870. By 1880 it stood at 604,000,000.

This development pushed out the other forms of transport because it was both faster and cheaper. As early as 1844 the railways were competing successfully in terms of price with the stage-coach, as the following table from the Fifth Report of the Select Committee on Railways (1844) shows:

Manchester to London

	Coach (direct)			Railway (via Birmingham)		
	£	s.	d.	£	s.	d.
2 adults	3	0	0	2	10	0
3 children	2	5	0	1	17	6
Coachman and guard		7	0		—	
Food, etc.		10	0		7	6
	£6	2	0	£4	15	0

By this time too, thirty-seven miles an hour as an average speed for a journey was not uncommon and although forty years later (1883) this had only been pushed up to forty-two miles an hour, it was very much faster than horses were able to maintain. (See Clapham, *op. cit.*, Bk. 3, p. 180). The effect of this on holiday-making is well described in R. Manning-Sanders: *Seaside England* (1951) especially Chapter 9, 'Coaches and Trains'.

Db. The following table taken from Mulhall is of some interest:

Houses, Rental and Population of London

Year	Houses	Population	Rental	Rent per house			per inhabitant		
				£	s.	d.	£	s.	d.
1831	197,000	1,655,000	6,170,000	31	6	0	3	15	0
1841	256,000	1,948,000	9,150,000	35	10	0	4	14	0
1851	301,000	2,362,000	12,100,000	40	1	0	5	2	0
1861	369,000	2,804,000	16,200,000	43	0	0	5	15	0
1871	445,000	3,254,000	22,800,000	51	0	0	7	1	0
1881	541,000	3,955,000	35,060,000	64	12	0	8	15	0

(M. G. Mulhall: 'The Housing of the London Poor', Sec. 2, 'Ways and Means', in *The Contemporary Review*, February 1884, p. 233.)

Notes

E. The total number of people assessed under Schedule E for the three years up to and including the Census years 1851, 1861 and 1871 were as follows:

	£200–£999+	£1,000 and over
1849	17,860	1,521
1850	17,736	1,489
1851	17,626	1,418
Total	53,222	4,428
Mean	17,741	1,476
1859	22,342	1,525
1860	23,205	1,675
1861	23,292	1,669
Total	68,839	4,869
Mean	22,946	1,623
1869	31,559	2,061
1870	33,587	2,292
1871	34,924	2,268
Total	100,070	6,631
Mean	33,357	2,210

The total incomes received by these groups were:

	£200–£999+ £	£1,000 and over £
1849	5,902,849	2,792,235
1850	5,873,548	2,601,521
1851	5,896,094	2,473,567
Total	£17,672,491	£7,867,323
1859	7,841,364	2,927,535
1860	7,851,233	2,784,023
1861	7,822,172	2,767,839
Total	£23,574,769	£8,479,397
1869	10,491,089	3,560,240
1870	11,265,634	3,878,531
1871	11,877,168	3,765,489
Total	£33,633,891	£11,204,260

F. There are many works on Anthony Trollope ṛ excellent bibliographies, viz.:

Notes

M. L. Irwin: *Anthony Trollope: a Bibliography* (1926).

M. Sadleir: *Trollope: a Bibliography* (1928).

Of most use to this chapter have been

B. C. Brown: *Anthony Trollope* (1950).

T. H. S. Escott: *Anthony Trollope: his Work, Associates and Literary Originals* (1913).

W. G. and J. T. Gerould: *A Guide to Trollope* (1948).

M. Sadleir: *Trollope: a Commentary* (1927), 3rd ed. 1945.

L. P. and R. P. Stebbins: *The Trollopes: the Chronicle of a Writing Family* (1946).

A. Trollope: *An Autobiography* (1883).

G. A Return 'of the Names of the Heads of Departments and of the Staff Officers of the various Departments of the Post Office with a Statement of the Salaries, Emoluments, and Pensions or Annuities now received by each Individual, and also, a statement of Salaries, Emoluments, &c. received by the same Persons in 1849' dated 12th February 1861 (*Parliamentary Papers*, 1861, Volume 35) gives Trollope as a Surveyor, in 1861, receiving £700 plus 20s. per day travelling expenses for subsistence and the actual cost of conveyance. There were twelve other surveyors at this date with incomes ranging from £500–£800. Of these four had been surveyors in 1849 with salaries of between £300 and £400 plus 26s. per day for subsistence and a mileage allowance of 8d. a mile. A footnote reads: 'Owing to the reduced allowance for travelling expenses, the net income of a surveyor does not materially differ from its amount in 1849.' Six of the remaining surveyors were surveyor's clerks at the earlier date, earning between £115 and £150 (Trollope was down for £150) and travelling expenses of 15s. plus 6d. a mile.

H. Trollope's *Autobiography*, 1893, Chapter 20, gives the sums received by him for his books as follows:

		£	s.	d.
The Macdermots of Ballycloran	1847	48	6	9
The Kellys and the O'Kellys	1848	123	19	5
La Vendée	1850	20	0	0
The Warden	1855 }	727	11	3
Barchester Towers	1856 }			
The Three Clerks	1858	250	0	0

	£	s.	d.
Doctor Thorne 1858	400	0	0
The West Indies and the Spanish Main 1859	250	0	0
The Bertrams 1859	400	0	0
Castel Richmond 1860	600	0	0
Framley Parsonage 1861	1,000	0	0
Tales of All Countries—1st Ser. 1861			
Tales of All Countries—2nd Ser. 1863	1,830	0	0
Tales of All Countries—3rd Ser. 1870			
Orley Farm 1862	3,135	0	0
North America 1862	1,250	0	0
Rachel Ray 1863	1,645	0	0
The Small House at Allington 1864	3,000	0	0
Can You Forgive Her? 1864	3,525	0	0
Miss Mackenzie 1865	1,300	0	0
The Belton Estate 1866	1,757	0	0
The Claverings 1867	2,800	0	0
The Last Chronicle of Barset 1867	3,000	0	0
Nina Balatka 1867	450	0	0
Linda Tressel 1868	450	0	0
Phineas Finn 1869	3,200	0	0
He Knew He Was Right 1869	3,200	0	0
Brown, Jones, and Robinson 1870	600	0	0
The Vicar of Bullhampton 1870	2,500	0	0
An Editor's Tales 1870	378	0	0
Sir Harry Hotspur of Humblethwaite 1871	750	0	0
Ralph the Heir 1871	2,500	0	0
The Golden Lion of Granpère 1872	550	0	0
The Eustace Diamonds 1873	2,500	0	0
Australia and New Zealand 1873	1,300	0	0
Phineas Redux 1874	2,500	0	0
Harry Heathcote of Gangoil 1874	450	0	0
Lady Anna 1874	1,200	0	0
The Way We Live Now 1875	3,000	0	0
The Prime Minister 1876	2,500	0	0
The American Senator 1877	1,800	0	0
Is He Popenjoy? 1878	1,600	0	0
South Africa 1878	850	0	0
John Caldigate 1879	1,800	0	0
Sundries	7,800	0	0
	£68,939	17	5

The *Autobiography*, although not published until 1883, was written in 1878. Hence this list omits the following novels and

Notes

books: *An Eye for an Eye* (1879), *Cousin Henry* (1879), *Thackeray* (1879), *The Duke's Children* (1880), *Life of Cicero* (1880), *Ayala's Angel* (1881), *Doctor Wortle's School* (1881), *Frau Frohmann and other Stories* (1882), *Lord Palmerston* (1882), *The Fixed Period* (1882), *Kept in the Dark* (1882), *Marion Fay* (1882), *Mr. Scarborough's Family* (1883) as well as *Caesar* (Ancient Classics) (1870) which was given by Trollope to John Blackwood as a present.

I. The excess of births over deaths during this period was given by E. Levasseur: *La Population Française* (1889) as

Year	Births	Deaths	Difference
1850	954	761	192
1851	971	799	172
1852	964	810	154
1853	936	795	141
1854	923	992	—69
1855	902	937	—35
1856	952	837	115
1857	940	858	81
1858	969	874	95
1859	1017	979	38
1860	956	781	175
1861	1,005	866	139

All figures in thousands throughout. (Vol. 2, Table, pp. 8–9.) The deaths per thousand persons for 1841–50 were 23·3 and for 1851–60, 23·9. (*Ibid.*, p. 149.)

J. Bourgeois-Pichat: 'Evolution de la population française depuis le XVIIIe siècle' in *Population*, October–December 1951 (p. 653), also points out that the lowered fertility of the period 1851–55 was a direct result of the fall in the marriage rate at this same period. Thus for every 1,000 inhabitants the rates were:

1841–45	16·3
1846–50	15·6
1851–55	15·6
1856–60	16·2

J. The question of *The Priest in Absolution* was first raised in
the House of Lords by the Earl of Redesdale on 14th June 1877,
when the Archbishop of Canterbury replied. (*Hansard*, 1877,
Vol. 234, pp. 1742 *et seq.*) In the House of Commons it was raised
by Cowen on 21st June. He was followed by Forsyth who
likened the book to *The Fruits of Philosophy*, and asked why both
works had not been prosecuted. The Attorney-General in reply
said that it was 'no part of the duty of the Government to act as
censors of the public morals and to prosecute the publishers of
every book which in their judgement is objectionable'. *The
Priest in Absolution* had not been issued to the public. If it had,
it ought to be and would be liable to be open for prosecution
as obscene and disgusting literature. (Vol. 235, pp. 83–84.) A
further question was raised on 26th June (pp. 258–9) and on
3rd July Whalley moved a resolution condemning the book
but there were less than forty members present and the House
was counted out (p. 946). It was raised again in the House of
Lords on 6th July (pp. 883–4) and in the House of Commons
on 9th and 12th July (pp. 967 and 1174–5). On 24th July
Whalley again tried to get his resolution through but again the
House was counted out (p. 1795). His last attempt was made on
the 10th August when Previous Question was moved and for the
last time he was defeated. (Vol. 236, p. 748.)

K. The First Report of the Select Committee on Fees in
Courts of Law and Equity (*Parliamentary Papers*, 1847–8, Vol. 15)
gave a range of salaries received by Law Officers. Masters in
Chancery were paid £2,500 a year, their ten chief clerks £1,000,
and ten junior clerks £150. Masters in Lunacy received £2,000,
and their clerks £800, £350, £250, £150, £120, and £100. All
these posts were open to solicitors.

L. 'The cost of a medical education includes: (1) Hospital or
school fees. In London these range from about £100 to £140.
There are often extra fees to be paid at a school in addition to
the general or perpetual fee. (2) The cost of living for four or
five years—say £100 a year for this. (3) The cost of books,
instruments, microscope, stethoscope, thermometer, dissecting
dress, students' societies and clubs, possibly fees for private
tuition—say £25 to £30 for all these. (4) The cost of examinations and qualifications. If a student is referred to his studies at

an examination he has extra fees to pay and has to wait three
to six months before he can go up again. In England the double
qualification costs £36 15s. and the degrees of Bachelor of Medicine and Bachelor of Surgery of the London University £22.
. . . The total for five years will be over £700. . . . Then there is
£5 for registration by the Branch Registrar of the G.M.C. In
the provinces the cost is not much less. Four years: £600, i.e.
£100 for medical school and hospital, £100 a year living, and
£100 for diplomas, extras and journeys. Scholarships may help
a little but they cannot be depended upon.' W. Rivington: *The
Medical Profession of the United Kingdom* (1888), p. 694. This
work gave details of all the medical schools and scholarships.

M. Rivington (*op. cit.*, see Note L above) gave the following
details of medical salaries:

Medical Department to the Crown. Physician-in-Ordinary, £200;
Sergeant Surgeon, £280; Surgeon to the Household, £300;
Surgeon Apothecary to the Household at Windsor, £1,000;
Dentist to the Household, £70; Medical Inspector to Burial
Acts Office, £500; Medical Inspector to the Prison Department
of the Home Office, £900; Medical Inspector to the Local
Government Board, £600–£1,000; Medical Officer to the Local
Government Board, £1,300; his assistant, £1,000; Chief Medi-
cal Officer to the Post Office, £1,000; his second in command,
£489; third, £100; Chief Surgeon to the Metropolitan Police,
£600; Coroner, £600–£2,000; Registrar-General, £1,200;
Superintendent of Statistics, £900.

Hospital Appointments. Non-residents about £100 per annum.
Poor Law Infirmaries, £250–£500 according to length of service. Lunacy, £500–£650. Prison Medical Officer, £320–£450.

Army Medical Department. After twenty years' service a Surgeon
Major received £365, after twenty-five years £411, and after
thirty years £456. A Brigade Surgeon after twenty years received
£502, after thirty, £547. (Pp. 331–4.)

N. The Report of the Commissioners Appointed to Inquire
into the Ecclesiastical Revenues of England and Wales (*Parliamentary Papers*, 1835, Vol. 22, pp. 41–44) provided the following
abstract of incomes of incumbents and curates:

£	Cases
Under 50	297
50–	1,629
100–	1,602
150–	1,354
200–	1,979
300–	1,326
400–	830
500–	954
750–	323
1,000–	134
1,500–	32
2,000	18
	10,478

O. Hudson's *Parents Handbook* (1842) gave the following table of the regulation prices at which commissions were bought and sold in the Foot Guards.

	£		£
For the commission of an Ensign	1,200		
On promotion to the rank of a Lieutenant, a further	850	making	2,050
On promotion to the rank of Captain	2,750	,,	4,800
On promotion to the rank of a Major	3,500	,,	8,300
On promotion to the rank of Lieut.-Colonel	700	,,	9,000

This was the most expensive case. The commission of an Ensign of the Line cost £450, to the Life Guards £1,260. By private agreement higher prices were paid. (P. 22.)

P. Rev. J. D. Collis, M.A., headmaster of the Grammar School of King Edward VI, Bromsgrove, Worcestershire, matriculated in June 1834 and took his degree in October 1838. His expenses were as follows:

	£	s.	d.
College battels	237	5	0
University Fees (Matric. B.A., etc.)	32	4	0
College Servants	33	7	6
Private Tutor	33	10	0
Loss on Furniture of Rooms	21	5	0
Groceries	21	8	0
Wine, desserts, occ. expenses for dinners, etc.	38	12	6
Books	40	7	8
Letters, parcels, etc.	6	5	11

	£	s.	d.
Subscriptions, and private disbursements	22	13	6
Boating and amusements	10	17	0
Washing	18	19	6
Tailor	85	7	6
Boots, ete.	23	2	0
Various	29	19	6
Total cost of degree	655	4	7
Add travelling	69	18	0
	£725	2	7

'Report of Her Majesty's Commissioners appointed to Inquire into the State, Discipline, Studies, and Revenues of the University and Colleges of Oxford' (*Parliamentary Papers*, 1852, Vol. 22, Minutes of Evidence, p. 23).

Q. Appendix III of Vol. I of the Schools Inquiry Commission (*Parliamentary Papers*, 1867–8, Vol. XXVIII, pp. 34–35) provided the following minimum, mean, and maximum charges for five schools for 1864:

	Lowest Bill			Average Bill			Highest Bill		
	£	s.	d.	£	s.	d.	£	s.	d.
Haileybury College	57	17	5	77	0	2	97	11	10
Rossall School	42	16	11	50	1	5	53	8	2
Felsted Grammar School	38	11	7	48	5	7	70	11	1
Hurstpierpoint	35	0	2	37	10	1	45	4	11
Devon County School (1865)	23	11	$0\frac{1}{2}$	33	15	5	44	10	$0\frac{1}{2}$

R. The completely new schools founded between 1840 and 1890 were Cheltenham College (1841), Trinity College, Glenalmond (1841), Wellington School, Somerset (1841), Eltham College (1842), Mount St. Mary's College (1842), Marlborough College (1843), St. Columba's College (1843), Rossall School (1844), Brighton College (1845), Radley College (1847), Ratcliffe College (founded 1844, opened 1847), Taunton School (1847), Lancing College (1848), Llandovery College (1848), Hurstpierpoint College (1849), St. John's School (1851), Victoria College, Jersey (1852), Wellington College (1853), Mannamead School (1854), Ardingly (1870 but founded at St.

Saviour's in 1858), Bradfield College (1859), Birkenhead School (1860), Bloxham School (1860), Beaumont College, Old Windsor (1861), Clifton College (1862), Haileybury College (1862), Cranleigh School (1863), St. Edward's School (1863), Framlington College (1864), Malvern College (1862, opened 1865), Trent College (1866), Eastbourne College (1867), Bishop's Stortford College (1868), Denstone College (1868), Monkton Combe School (1868), Dover College (1871), Leys School (1875), Kelly College (founded 1867 but not opened until 1877), Plymouth College (1878), St. Lawrence College (1879), Truro School (1879), Wrekin College (1880), Culford School (1881), Wycliffe College (1882), Barnard Castle (1883), Ellesmere College (1884), Rydal College (1885), Dean Close School, Cheltenham (1886).

In addition the following were re-established, rebuilt or re-organized in some important way: Berkhamsted School (1841), Durham School (1842), St. Peter's School, York (1844), Ipswich School (1851), Christ College, Brecon (1853), St. Edmund's School, Canterbury (1855), Haverfordwest Grammar School (1856), Brentwood School (1857), Dulwich College (1857, rebuilt 1870), the Royal Masonic School (1865), King's College, Taunton (1867), Sir William Turner's School, Coatham (1868), Mill Hill School (1869), Abingdon (1870), Newcastle-under-Lyme High School (1872), King's School, Chester (1873), Sedbergh School (1874), Aldenham (1875), Exeter School (1876), Portsmouth Grammar School (1879), Wellingborough School (1881), Dorchester Grammar School (1882), Caterham School (1883), Bancroft's (1884).

(Taken from *The Public and Preparatory Schools' Year Book, 1947*.)

S. The Girls' Public Schools which came into being between 1840 and 1900 were: The Royal Naval School, Haslemere (1840), St. Elphin's, Warrington (1844), St. Michael's, Petworth (1844), Queen's College, London (1848), Loughborough High School (1850), St. Dunstan's Abbey, Plymouth (1850), North London Collegiate (1851), Cheltenham Ladies' College (founded 1853, opened 1854), Badminton School (1858), Howell's School (1859), Milton Mount College (1871), Guernsey Ladies' College (1872), St. Mary's, Gerard's Cross (1872),

Notting Hill High School (1873), Queen Anne's, Caversham (founded 1698, reconstituted 1873), St. Mary's, Colne (1873), St. Mary's, Wantage (1873), St. Mary and St. Anne, Abbots Bromley (1874), Croydon High School (1874), Bath High School (1875), Bradford Girls' Grammar School (1875), Buchan School, Isle of Man (1875), Dr. Williams's, Dolgelly (1875), Norwich High School (1875), Nottingham High School (1875), Oxford High School (1875), St. Martin's Endowed School, London (1875), Burlington School (founded 1699, reorganized 1876), Leeds Girls' (1876), Orme Girls' (1876), St. John's Wood (1876), Clifton (1877), Mary Datchelor (re-established 1877), Maynard School, Exeter (1877), Skellfield (1877), St. Leonard's (1877), Francis Holland, Regent's Park (1878), Ipswich (1878), Northampton (1878), Queen's, Chester (1878), Sheffield (1878), King's, Warwick (1879), Park School, Glasgow (1879), The Abbey (1880), Blackheath High (1880), Penrhos College (1880), City of London (1881), Francis Holland, Sloane Square (1881), Perse School, Cambridge (1881), James Allen's (1881), Portsmouth (1881), Redland, Bristol (1881), Alice Ottley (1883), Blackburn (1883), Bromley (1883), Bury (1884), Durham (1884), Leamington (1884), St. Swithun's (1884), Sunderland (1884), Sutton (1884), Kent College (1885), Newcastle-upon-Tyne (1885), Roedean (1885), St. Catherine's, Bramley (1885), Dame Alice Owen's (1886), Northgate Grammar, Ipswich (1886), Talbot Heath (1886), Abbey School, Reading (1887), Hulme Grammar, Oldham (1887), Steatham Hill and Clapham (1887), Sydenham (1887), Berkhamsted (1888), Guildford (1888), Kendal (1888), Merchant Taylors' (1888), Queen Elizabeth, Barnet (1888), Hitchin (1889), Hull (1890), Withington (1890), Monmouth (1891), Derby (1892), Lincoln Christ's Hospital (1893), Malvern (1893), Queenswood (1894), St. Bride's, Helensburgh (1895), Newport (1896), Wycombe Abbey (1896), St. Columba's, Kilmacolm (1897), St. Felix, Southwold (1897), St. Saviour's and St. Olave's (1899), Sherbourne (1899), Wentworth (1899).

(Taken from *The Girls' School Year Book (Public Schools), 1949.*

Subject Index

Index of Persons, Organizations, Sources, etc.

Index of Persons, Organizations, Sources, etc.

Carlile, R., 26

Carlyle, T., 33

Carr-Saunders, A. M. and Wilson, P. A., 176 n., 177 n., 182 n.

Cary, H. C., 38 n., 39 n.

Cassell's Book of the Household, 57, 58 n., 136 n., 137 n., 209

Census of England and Wales:
1811, 22; 1821, 22; 1851, 29 n., 83 n.; 1861, 83 n.; 1871, 83 n., 84 n.; 1881, 134; 1891, 136 n.; 1901, 134–5; 1911, 134–6
1911 *Fertility Report*, 4, 5 n.; 1951, 22 n., 83 n.

Chadwick, D., 105 n., 107 n.

Chambers's Journal, 52 n., 93 n.

Chapman, E. R., 160 n., 162 n., 217

Chapman, R. W., 34 n., 144 n.

Chrimes, brothers, 159

Christian, E. B. V., 175 n.

Christian World, 80, 161 n.

Christie, W. D., 149 n.

'Church as a Profession', 179 n.

Civil Service Inquiry Commission, 96 n., 106 n.

Clapham, J. H., 80 n., 219

Clark, C., 95 n.

Clough, A. H., 142 n.

Cobbe, F. P., 137 n.

Collet, Miss, 78–80

Colmore, G., 163 n., 165

Commissioners of Inland Revenue, 91–92, 103

Committee on the Bill to Regulate the Labour of Children, 24 n.

Complete Book of Trades, 175, 177, 178 n.

Condorcet, 16

Contemporary Review, 58 n., 66 n., 67 n., 179 n., 181 n., 182 n.

Corelli, M., 217

Cornhill Magazine, 46 n., 52 n., 58, 66, 100 n., 163 n., 165 n., 179 n.

'Cost of a Modern Belle', 98 n.

'Cost of Living', 58 n., 66 n.

Cowper, W., 36, 219

Cross, J. W., 128 n.

Cunnington, C. W., 99 n., 100, 172 n.

Daily Express, 58 n.

Daily News, 142 n., 152–3

Darimon, H., 141 n.

Darwin, C., 38, 114

Dawson, W., 181 n.

Davenant, F., 174 n., 178 n., 179 n., 182 n., 193 n.

Declining Birth-Rate (*see* National Birth-rate Commission)

Dialectical Society, 146–7, 155

'Discipline of the Bar', 173 n.

Disraeli, B., 32, 218–19

Domestic Account Book, 57 n.

'Domestic Economy', 53

'Domestic Servant Difficulty', 137 n.

'Domestic Work', 76 n.

Doubleday, T., 38–39

Dowell, S., 91 n., 93 n.

Drysdale, C. R., 146, 155 n., 157, 160 n., 168 n.

Drysdale, G., 37, 142, 146–7, 149–50

Dumont, A., 133 n.

Dyos, H. J., 58 n., 220

Earle, Mrs., 163 n.

Economic Review, 156 n.

Economist, 141

Economy for the Single and Married, 36, 62 n., 74 n., 209

Edinburgh Review, 20, 54 n., 191

Eliot, G., 54, 128 n.

Elderton, E. M., 159 n.

Elton, Lord, 186

Emery, W., 186 n.

Englishman, 151, 153

Englishwoman's Domestic Magazine, 53, 56, 68, 72, 78–79, 99 n.

Englishwoman's Review, 66, 166 n.

Ensor, R. C. K., 136 n.

'Espoir', 87, 209

'Ethics of Early and Frugal Marriages', 47 n.

Index of Persons, Organizations, Sources, etc.

Index of Persons, Organizations, Sources, etc.

Senior, N. W., 18, 21, 26–29, 33 n., 40
Shaftesbury, Lord, 82
Sidgwick, H., 182 n.
Sitwell, O., 171 n.
Smiles, S., 170
Smith, A., 16
Smith, G., 66 n.
Smith, J. S., 44–45
Smith, K., 17 n., 21 n., 218
Smyth, W. W., 217
Social Purity Alliance, 162
Sorokin, P., 38 n.
Southey, R., 19 n.
Southgate, H., 210
Spain, N., 99 n.
Spencer, H., 39, 40 n.
Spengler, J. J., 140 n.
Stamp, J. C., 103 n., 104, 105, 130–3
Stangeland, G. E., 25 n.
Stead, E. W., 160 n.
Stead, W. T., 160, 162
Stebbins, L. P. and R. P., 115 n.,
   119 n., 125 n., 167 n., 222
Steel, F. A., 217
Stopes, M., 23, 24 n., 149 n.
Strachey, R., 191 n.
Sumner, J. B., 20 n.
Sure Guide to Domestic Happiness, 35 n.
Swan, A. S., 136 n., 166 n., 217
Sylvia's Family Management, 160 n.,
   208, 210

Tait's Edinburgh Magazine, 47 n.,
   64 n.
Tawney, R. H., 190
Temple Bar, 48 n., 163 n.
Thackeray, W. M., 33
Thompson, W., 27 n.
Thornton, W. T., 40
Thorold, A. W., 161 n., 217
Thring, E., 145 n.
Thrupp, G. A., 91 n.
Times, 41, 43 n., 44–46, 80–81, 139–
   40, 142 n., 152–4
Tinsley's Magazine, 59 n.
Titmuss, R. and K., 12 n.

Tourists' Annual, 1868, 94 n.
Trall, R. T., 149 n., 150
*Transactions of the Manchester Statisti-
   cal Society*, 142–3, 164 n., 181 n.
Trollope, A., 90, 113–28, 161, 166–7,
   180–1, 184, 221–4
Trollope, F., 114
Truelove, E., 154
'Two Solutions', 149 n.

Unsworth, W., 217

Valuable Hints, 150
Victoria, 145

W., A., 49 n.
Wade, J., 30
Wallace, R., 16, 27, 32
Walseley, General, 184 n.
Walsh, J. H., 49–51, 54, 57, 59–61,
   63–65, 67, 71–76, 93, 100, 124,
   165–6, 172, 210
Ward and Lock's Home Book, 97 n., 210
Warren, E., 49, 77, 210
Warren, S., 91 n., 174, 175 n., 177 n.
Webb, S., 159 n.
Weber, M., 206
Webster, T., 75 n., 210
Westminster Review, 39 n., 136 n.,
   168 n.
Weyland, J., 27 n.
Whately, R., 18
Whatham, Rev., 160
Whitehead, A. N., 18
Wigley, W. H., 210
Wilkins, A. S., 181 n.
Wolfe, A. B., 16 n.
Wood, G. H., 63, 65, 81, 82 n., 107,
   111, 131–2, 134 n.
Woodham-Smith, C., 142 n.
'Word to Young Mistresses', 71 n.,
   137 n.
Wright, H. C., 217
'Why We Men do not Marry', 163 n.

Yates, E., 117 n.

240